"If Jack Reacher had a dog, he'd be Lou. If Jack Reacher were a dog, he'd be Lou." —Lee Child, *New York Times* bestselling author of the Jack Reacher series

"Anyone who has ever loved or lost a dog, or both, will be touched by this spellbinding story about two beings that crossed the human-dog divide and met on the other side."
—Stefan Bechtel, author of
Dogtown: Tales of Rescue, Rehabilitation, and Redemption

"There are so many accounts and testaments that verify beyond doubt that a dog is man's best friend. What makes this story special is that Lou, in terms of fate, was destined for a rough and unspectacular life. Lou and Steve found each other by sheer chance. Lou's life was richer for being Steve's dog, but the real twist of fate is how Steve's life and the lives of all those who knew Lou were enriched forever."
—Nuala Gardner, author of *A Friend Like Henry:*
The Remarkable True Story of an Autistic Boy and the Dog
That Unlocked His World

"Anyone who has ever loved with their heart wide open will want to come along for this ride. Unpredictable, heroic, and funny... just like Lou." —Monica Holloway, author of
Cowboy & Wills: A Love Story

"Steve Duno manages to inspire and touch the heart in a story about a hero dog that is, quite frankly, impossible to forget."
—Mandy Stadtmiller, *New York Post*

D0189928

Praise for *Last Dog on the Hill*

"This [book] will be greatly enjoyed by lovers of animal memoirs like John Grogan's *Marley & Me* and Vicki Myron's *Dewey* as well as other books exploring the human-canine connection. Equally humorous and serious, the book portrays the duo's heartwarming bond of love."   —*Library Journal*

"When making your pile of 'best dog stories ever,' make space for another one. This book is great! Lou is a real working dog, not just a pile of emotive fluff. His exploits and accomplishments are nothing short of heroic. You will cheer for this dog and the fullness of his life. The relationship between Steve Duno and Lou is remarkable. We all want to know a dog like Lou. Here's your chance. There is a tear or two, but they are tears of joy for lives well shared."   —Greg Kincaid, author of
A Dog Named Christmas

"There's nothing whispery or mysterious about the connection between Steve Duno and his remarkable Rottweiler mix, Lou. It's a full-voiced love story, a vigorous tale of rescue and mutual redemption, and an eloquent human-canine conversation that grows richer and deeper through the years. *Last Dog on the Hill* reminds us not only how much dogs can learn, but more importantly, how much they can teach us about the things that really matter—loyalty, honor, hard work, and plenty of sheer delight."   —Steven Winn, author of *Come Back, Como:
Winning the Heart of a Reluctant Dog*

"Everyone needs to experience a dog like Lou; and every dog needs a person like Steve Duno. *Last Dog on the Hill* is one of those rare animal memoirs that isn't sentimental, yet moves the reader to tears as easily as laughter."   —Susan Wilson, author of *One Good Dog*

LAST DOG ON THE HILL

The Extraordinary Life of Lou

Steve Duno

St. Martin's Griffin

New York

www.stmartins.com

Design by Kathryn Parise

The Library of Congress has cataloged the hardcover edition as follows:

Duno, Steve.
    Last dog on the hill : the extraordinary life of Lou / Steve Duno.—1st ed.
    p. cm.
    ISBN 978-0-312-60049-5
    1. Dogs—Anecdotes. 2. Dog owners—Anecdotes. 3. Human-animal
relationships—Anecdotes. 4. Dogs—Behavior. I. Title.
    SF426.2.D865 2010
    636.7092'9—dc22

                                                        2009047031

ISBN 978-0-312-56939-6 (trade paperback)

10 9 8 7 6 5 4 3 2

For WTC, for #93, for D.C.

"Let Enkidu go ahead of you;
for he knows the road to the Cedar Forest . . ."
—Tablet III
The Epic of Gilgamesh

LAST DOG
ON THE HILL

Introduction

Lou's last meal was a sirloin fed to him on the day of his passing. He couldn't walk anymore but he could still eat, that big-hearted dog, the steak flagging from his jaws like bloody treasure. The sanctity of food: eat through the pain—that's dog law.

During his sixteen years he battled coyotes and kidnapers, charmed babies and soothed the sick and elderly. He caught rapists, foiled robberies, graced the cover of a book, taught sign language to kids, and peed on knights in shining armor. Lou's intellect and abilities won me a life-changing job, which led to my sitting here now writing about *him*. He danced with wolves, herded sheep, charmed snakes and celebrities, won contests, climbed mountains, got kidnaped, and mastered a vocabulary bigger than that of some people I know. Lou redefined what it meant to be a great dog and a bona fide hero. Four years later I can still smell him, still hear his collar jingle, still see his movie-star mug looking up at me. Lou deserved that sirloin and a thousand more. I miss him more than I can say.

In my twenty years as a trainer and pet behaviorist, I have met thousands of dogs. Labs with country sweetness in their eyes, terriers with something to prove, Italian greyhounds with matchstick legs. Careful toys, thoughtful hounds, cowards, gastronomes, loudmouths, heroes, athletes, couch potatoes—I've known so many. But among them all, Lou had the most soul.

He'd come out of the woods, where, like the first dogs, he'd learned the real meaning of survival. I've often entertained the notion that Lou sometimes held a quiet disdain for all the "home grown" dogs he'd met, silly, self-absorbed pets who'd never known a day of hardship or self-reliance, and who'd never get the chance to show their true mettle. If he ever did, though, he'd been too polite to mention it.

I'd taken him from his family and his first home, and though I knew it had been the right thing to do, I can't help thinking sometimes that he'd missed them terribly, and that he'd let infatuation get the best of him, as it had of me.

But his loss was our gain, a thousandfold. Ask anyone who'd known him for more than twenty seconds and they'll tell you that they wanted to be with him, wanted his Garbo eyes on them. You imagined him of Narnian design, not some mangy mutt scooped up off a road in rural California.

Though known for my pet-care manuals, I rested my prescriptive pen to write this book, a book about an exceptional dog who touched so many lives, a real-life Rin Tin Tin. He was an extraordinary friend who allowed me to publish eighteen books and scores of Web and magazine articles. Lou, a dog who came so far and was good at so many things, who acted with aplomb, brilliance, and savoir faire. You saw his gears turning and understood that he was mulling things over, weighing, deciding. Lou was a thinker—the kind of dog that trainers love to work with. He could have been a movie star, a soldier, a coach, a judge—anything he'd wanted, if only he'd been born with fewer legs and more thumbs. But he went with what he had, and in so doing changed my life and the lives of many others. This is his story, and mine. It is the story of a real American hero.

1

Rotties, Roadkill, and the
Canine Cartel

Black topcoat hairs and tufts of downy undercoat lay in the corners of our home, in the periphery, like ghosts. The black hairs were odorless but his undercoat still held scent, and I'd lift some of him up to my nose and be back in the mountains with him, listening to coyotes or owls, or to mice nibbling on the tent fly. In death he had spoken to me in a way he knew I would best appreciate. His smell, still there in the carpet, side-stepped my brain and went straight for the heart, where the memories are.

The essential crime committed against all dog owners is born of the love we hold for them, which, like the love of a child, runs deep. No parent should have to bury a child, they say, but that is what we dog owners must do, not once but time after time, throughout our lives. While we remain unchangeable to their sweet eyes, they run from birth to the grave in an instant of our own measure. They burn like kindling, and though we know we can never replace one dog with another, we keep trying, in hopes of reviving hints of some great dog gone by. No; they are not children we bury. But dogs like Lou come close. They come very, very close.

Highway 101 sweeps north into the small Mendocino County town of Willits, California, gateway to redwood country, home to vineyards and fast rivers, and to the resting place of Seabiscuit, the great racehorse. And it is where I found Lou, the greatest dog I have ever known.

In 1986, teaching degree in hand, I packed my Civic and left the grit of Queens for the glitz of Los Angeles. Upon arriving, I renewed an old fascination with dogs, one I'd first nurtured in childhood. Living in a one-bedroom New York tenement with my parents and brother, I'd asked for a dog but had gotten only a pale blue parakeet named Chipper, a bitter bird who'd bend apart the bars of his cage and escape, to strafe our heads and scream his discontent.

In Los Angeles I read scores of books about breeding, training manuals, and pet magazines until I fancied myself a bookish "authority." I thought I was ready for a dog of my choosing. Then chance changed the course of my life, and the lives of so many others.

My girlfriend Nancy and I took a few December days off, packed the car, and drove up Highway 101 toward Northern California. The entire West Coast had fine weather; we took our time, often detouring over to the coast in places to enjoy the scenery.

North of Ukiah, in Mendocino County, the highway snaked through the countryside. Halfway through a long, right sweeper, we spotted furry shapes porpoising up a steep grassy hill, toward the tree line above.

"Puppies!" said Nancy. We pulled over onto the wide shoulder and got out.

On the crest of the hill a half-dozen dogs scampered for the cover of trees; midsized, dark-coated mutts with shepherd looks, tongues flagging, teeth bright in the sun.

"Five, six months old," I said, suddenly aware of a much larger creature lying by the shoulder ahead, half hidden in the grass. An enormous Rottweiler, he basked in the sun like a Dakota buffalo, his black-and-tan coat dusted with dirt. And in his mouth rested the tawny snout of a limp, road-killed deer.

"Don't go near him," I said, the deer's snout crunching like a carrot stick in his jaws.

"Not a chance," Nancy said, more interested in the puppies, who had a lithe, black, shepherd mix with them, perhaps their mother.

The Rottweiler gnawed away thoughtfully and watched us.

Following their skittish mother up into the tree line, the pups were nearly out of sight. I gave a quick whistle just to see what would happen; all but one scampered off. But the last dog on the hill stopped, gazed down at the road, then made a mad downhill dash toward us, as if recognizing someone.

Black and tan, it looked more like a diminutive Rottweiler than did the others. Like a Looney Tunes character, the quick little mutt skidded to a stop right in front of us, dropped into a perfect soldier-sit, then stared up at me like I was Simon Cowell. It was Lou.

Those lucky enough to meet Lou were struck by his soulful

eyes, riveting good looks and brotherly charm. People simply couldn't get enough of him. But the dog sitting politely in front of me that day was anything but debonair. At most six months old, he had an infected tear on his throat, and ticks peppering his face and body. The bloated bugs hung like Christmas ornaments, even from the corners of his eyes and mouth and inside his ears and nose.

"He's infested," I said. "And look at that gash."

"Look at his eyes," Nancy said, grinning. "He's gorgeous."

Lou looked up at me and let out an interrogative, *"Rower?"*

"That gash is infected. And who knows anything about him."

"But *look* at him," she repeated. "Look at those eyes."

I felt Lou's warm breath on my hand. The sound of his dad crunching deer snout punctuated the swish of cars passing by.

I petted him. He looked at me like I was Mother Teresa. Fleas popped off his head like seltzer bubbles and ricocheted off the palm of my hand.

As I stood there wondering what to do, a pug-nosed Freightliner pulling a load of timber hit its air brakes and snorted to a stop across the road, onto the shoulder. Out popped a gritty little guy in Levi's and a dirty white T-shirt. He shuffled across 101 as if wearing leg irons.

"The biggun yours?" he asked, pointing to the Rottweiler with a shaky cigarette, looking like he'd been up for a week.

"Biggun?" I asked.

"The biggun chawin' on doe face," he said, bouncing on the balls of his feet.

The deer's snout secure in his mouth, the Rottweiler eyed the little trucker. The big dog was thoughtful and calm, a first clue, perhaps, to what his son would become. I remember thinking at the time that this dog could kill us all without much fanfare, then go back to his venison sashimi. He didn't, of course; he simply took the measure of the trucker for a moment, then kept chewing.

"He's part of a pack of strays that just ran up the slope," I said.

"Bitchin' truck dog."

"I don't know," I said, picturing the jumpy little guy sideways in the big dog's mouth.

"I think I'll take him."

"Oh I wouldn't," said Nancy.

"I got a way with dogs."

Before the trucker could commit suicide by Rottweiler, a park-ranger pickup pulled over and a boyish-faced fellow got out, plugged on his ranger hat, and came over.

"Howdy, folks," he said, eyes on the Rottweiler and doe.

"Gonna shoot him?" asked the trucker.

The Rottie dropped the doe and shook drool from his rubbery black lips.

"No. If he'd downed this deer on his own, we'd have to deal with him, but this was roadkill from last night. I saw it at sunrise on the side of the road."

"*Rower,*" said Lou.

"You'd kill a dog if it hunted down a deer?" I asked.

"Stray dogs that hunt deer get euthanized." He seemed too nice of a guy to shoot a dog.

"Who owns him?" asked the trucker, scuffling his cowboy boots in the dirt, moving closer to the Rottie.

"This big boy and the shepherd bitch up the hill are guard dogs from a marijuana grow over on the other side of this ridge. This time of year there's not much to protect, so they just wander about, looking for food."

"Marijuana grow?" asked Nancy.

"Yeah," he said. "Patches of pot grow all through here, mostly on national forest land. Big cash crop. Not much else to do around these parts."

Lou scratched himself, then looked up at me sweetly, calm but impatient, as if he'd made up his mind about us and expected the same.

"I'm guessing this one and the pups up on the hill are his," said the ranger. "Dad and Junior here seem sociable, but the rest are wild. A local rescue group tried to catch them last week, but they're too cagey."

"I like that biggun," said the trucker, rubbing his furrowed neck and snickering like a kid.

"I'd think twice about him," said the ranger. "There's a reason why he hasn't spooked yet."

"What about him?" I asked, petting Lou on his head, the fleas flying.

"Tame, isn't he? I bet he'd go with you. Lean and cut up, though. Might have gotten caught up on some barbed wire."

"Nothing that can't be fixed," said Nancy, already deep in Lou's camp.

"We're four hundred miles from home," I said. "He needs a vet and he's infested."

I had imagined it this way: find a caring breeder, choose the perfect, healthy pup, frame the pedigree, and live happily ever after. I hadn't planned on making a snap decision beside the road with giant dogs and dead deer and caffeinated truckers and ganja fields and boyish rangers and sweet gypsy eyes looking up at me, wondering when we'd be going home.

"If you don't want him, I'll take him," said the trucker, laughing oddly, as if he'd decided to slow-roast Lou at the next rest area.

Nancy giggled. She knew what pushed my buttons.

The big Rottie let go a thick stream of pee onto the asphalt, then stretched his back legs out one at a time. I wondered if Lou would get that big.

"There's a vet in Willits as you come into town," said the ranger. He had a slow, bearish quality. I imagined him quietly tending to his own secreted pot patch. "It's Sunday morning, though; you might have to wake him up."

The Rottie grabbed his meal by the neck and dragged her up the hill into a grove of pines, cords of muscle flexing beneath his shiny black coat. Lou watched his father go.

"Dang."

"He would have killed you," I said.

"You want the youngun or not?"

"You said you wanted a dog," said Nancy, poking me. "Trust me, this is the dog."

I felt like I was on the phone with a telemarketer, about to buy a time-share in the Bronx. "Let's clear out the back of the car," I said, surrendering. "We can put down the tent tarp."

"Yes!" she said, jumping up and down. "Let's go find the vet."

"He's on the right side of the road as you come into town," said the ranger. "Big sign by the side of the road—Willits Animal Hospital, or something like that."

The trucker stomped out his cigarette and walked over to Lou. "Good little feller," he said softly, waving off a flea and caressing Lou's ears. For an instant he seemed almost normal, almost somber. "Make sure you feed him chicken livers!" he blurted, back to his old self. Then he checked the traffic and shuffled back across the highway to his idling semi.

I've thought about that trucker a lot over the years. We'd both been searching for a friend; he wanted a copilot, and I wanted an Old Yeller who'd fight the wild hogs and make me laugh— someone I could count on, like a truck dog, like a sentinel. The trucker would keep looking, but, thanks to Nancy, my search was over.

Providence, timing, pure luck—whatever one chooses to call it—graced me for the first time in my life, in the form of a flea-ridden Mendocino mutt. His dignified father, wiser and more kindhearted than I'd realized at the time, watched from the pines as I lifted his mangy son and placed him into my hatchback, fleas leaping off him like shooting stars. I'd found my Old Yeller.

Fleas suck. Our car became a traveling flea circus, a condition that would last until we got back to Los Angeles, where I'd unleash an aerosol bug bomb inside the confines of my Civic, killing the vermin, shorting out the interior lights, and leaving the car with a cancerous stench for the next year or so. I learned a lot about fleas on that trip—how alien, how invulnerable, how prolific and incredibly annoying and evil. And how it helps to have fingernails long enough to slice the armored bastards in half.

Lou got comfy in the back of the car among the now-infested camping gear and clothes. He gave Nancy a lick, then gazed out at the scenery passing by, the outdoor kindergarten he'd never see again.

"He likes your socks," said Nancy.

I looked at Lou in the mirror. He had his nose deep into one of my wool hiking socks.

"Cheese connoisseur," I said.

Lou was inquisitive but oddly calm for a stray. He'd be that way always: serene, involved, intense. From eating garbage and dodging cars in the wild to living in an inner-city apartment and eyeing derelicts shimmying down drainpipes, Lou would take it all in stride. In the wild he'd learned to think, adapt, and get by, like a wolf. It would remain one of the keys to his success later on.

A tall, gray-haired man in a bathrobe opened the door. He wiped his mouth with a napkin and sized us up, the scent of coffee wafting out of the old house. Using a bungee cord for a leash, I let Lou stretch out toward the big man, who gave him a pet and me a look.

"Found him down the road, I'd guess," he said.

"About three miles south."

"I'm Dr. Smith. Bring him into the exam room. I'll be right back."

He came back wearing a white lab coat, a stethoscope draped around his neck. Lou walked around the room, scenting out whatever pets had been in there recently.

"Get a weight on him, then put him up on the table," he said, pointing to the scale in the corner. He was considerate but all business, and probably wanted to get back to his coffee.

He wouldn't be the last Dr. Smith in Lou's life. A year later, Lou would befriend Jonathan Harris, the actor who played Dr. Smith on the television show *Lost in Space*. I would leave Lou tethered outside my health club while I played racquetball, and Harris would fawn all over Lou, by then fully grown and Hollywood handsome.

"Thirty-four pounds even," I said, lifting him off the scale and placing him atop the slippery steel examination table. Lou tap-danced around as I kept him steady.

"He's about six months old," he said, looking into Lou's mouth, his teeth white as cream. "Some sort of string in here."

"He ate a sock," I said.

"A park ranger said his parents were guard dogs on a marijuana grow," Nancy said, proud of Lou's criminal pedigree.

Dr. Smith listened to Lou's heart and lungs. "Bigger than logging around here. He's got a slight heart murmur."

"Is that bad?" asked Nancy, picking at a tick that had burrowed into Lou's ear.

"The marijuana?"

"No—the murmur."

"Most dogs with murmurs live normal lives. He's crawling with ticks and fleas, though, and this wound is infected."

He squeezed yellowish pus from the gash, then wiped it clean with gauze.

"Gross," I said, looking at Nancy, who smiled. Pus always pleased her.

He irrigated the wound with Betadine solution, then administered a local anesthetic to numb Lou up for suturing. He worked like a watchmaker, examining the wound, removing dead skin, and cleaning it up a bit. Lou wiggled but didn't seem to mind; his tail wagged as I fed him tears of string cheese, which he took gently.

Lou had a "soft" mouth, like a Lab: he always took treats tenderly. It made him great with kids and helped him learn to pick objects up off the floor without damaging them. I once taught him to fetch a chicken egg as a prelude to my training service dogs, whose mouths had to be soft enough to pick up dropped eyeglasses or medication bottles, or retrieve food from a cupboard or refrigerator. Practicing these things on Lou helped me prepare for the real thing. Of course, I always let him eat the egg afterward.

"Before I suture him up, he needs a flea-and-tick bath," said Dr. Smith. "No sense in letting vermin get into the wound before I close him up."

"Can we help?" I asked, watching him pack the wound with what looked like petroleum jelly. Lou let out a soft *"rower,"* his way of asking, "Is this necessary?"

"Take him over to the tub and run the water. I'll bring you the shampoo. Don't get the wound too wet."

The water ran dark with so much flea dirt and dying fleas that it nearly clogged the drain. Lou wasn't at all fond of water, a trait that would stay with him his whole life.

"This is gross," Nancy said, rinsing dead fleas off her hands and dodging one of Lou's many shake-offs, the flea-infested water and foam fanning out in every direction.

"Pus is okay, but this is gross?" I said, ducking another shake-off. Most of the ticks would have to be pulled off one by one later, a chore that would take weeks.

While we washed Lou, Dr. Smith disappeared, probably to tell his wife about us. He came back while we were drying Lou off.

"Looks like a different dog. Needs two meals a day for a while, though," he said, touching Lou's ribs. "At least twelve pounds light for a Rott/shepherd mix his age."

"You think that's what he is?" I asked, placing Lou back onto the table.

"Oh yes. Let's get him on his side."

Dr. Smith cleared off the petroleum jelly, then sutured him quickly, the pattern like stitches on a baseball. Lou had a "whale eye" look, a sideways, white-eyed glare dogs get when searching for trust and confidence. For the first time in my life, I felt responsible for a dog.

"Good boy, Lou," I said.

"Lou?" Dr. Smith asked, fitting a length of rubber tubing into the bottom of the wound.

"He looks like a Lou to me."

"I suppose he does," he said, almost smiling. "I'm sewing a drain into the wound to prevent closure and let the drainage escape. Otherwise the buildup will cause the sutures to break down from pressure."

"So he'll have a tube sticking out of his neck?" asked Nancy.

"Your vet will remove it in a week or so."

"Our vet?" I said to Nancy. "Do we even know a vet?"

"There's one near your apartment."

"How do you know that?"

"It's right down the street. Mar Vista Animal Hospital."

"You'll have to watch the drain and make sure he doesn't tear it out or clog it up with dirt," Dr. Smith said, finishing up. "I don't think he'll need a cone, though."

"Cone?"

"An Elizabethan collar. Looks like a lampshade. Prevents him from chewing on the wound. But he can't get his mouth onto this part of his body."

"That's a relief," I said, imagining how fast Lou might get a lampshade off his head.

"Now let's get some of these ticks off."

He must have plucked fifty ticks off Lou. They were everywhere—in his ears, in the corners of his eyes—even in his nostrils and on his anus. He pulled the bloated bastards off, then dropped them into a small cup of alcohol. Lou whimpered and gave me the whale eye again. The cup nearly half filled, the alcohol turned pink from Lou's stolen blood.

"They carry Rocky Mountain spotted fever, Lyme disease, ehrlichiosis, typhus—they're villains. I'll remove as many as I can but you'll have to keep looking. I'll give you some alcohol and a pair of tweezers."

"Thanks." For a Grumpy Gus he was an awfully good guy.

"I'll vaccinate and de-worm him and give you meds to take with you. I'll put him on antibiotics, too. And you'll need to keep an eye on that lame leg."

"Lame leg?"

"He's favoring his left front leg."

"Really?"

"Yes."

"Okay," I said, as he pulled a fat tick out from between Lou's toes. "It's okay, buddy."

"Has he defecated yet?"

"Not yet."

"Keep an eye out for worms and such. With strays you never know what'll come out of them. It'll be entertaining, I'll wager."

He led us into his front office, where he gave us a cheap leash and collar, alcohol, and tweezers. The collar was big enough to fit loosely below the sutured wound, so as not to irritate it.

"Don't put a regular collar on him until that wound heals up, probably three weeks. Get a vet to take out the sutures and drain in about a week or so."

"Thank you so much," said Nancy.

"What do we owe?" I asked, taking out my credit card.

"Have you got cash?"

We checked our wallets. "Not enough for all this," I said.

"Twenty dollars," he said.

"Twenty?" I asked, laughing.

"Look, I've been trying to help a local rescue group catch this dog's pack for a while now. You've helped do that. And, truth is, this guy would have been dead in a month."

"We don't know what to say," said Nancy. Lou sniffed at her pants leg, then yodeled. He'd had enough medical attention and wanted to go.

I handed the doctor a twenty. "Thanks. You're a lifesaver."

"So are you. I just hope you're up to the task. Now get going so I can read my paper."

"Right," I said, leading Lou to the door. Not used to being on the end of a rope, he balked a bit, but then he relented once he realized that we were all going in the same direction.

"Hey—" Dr. Smith added, seeing us out, "he'll be a darned good dog. Just be patient."

"I *told* you," said Nancy, grabbing my shirtsleeve. Lou sniffed the cool morning air and watched traffic drive by.

"Twenty bucks," I said, wondering what he'd meant by "up to the task."

We turned south and began the drive home. We'd all become

reinfested with fleas, as they had taken up residence in the Civic. Lou would poop out squirrel bones, pebbles, sock string, aluminum foil, and a Bazooka Bubble Gum wrapper on the trip home, and temporarily vanish into the woods on an overnight stop near Sequoia National Park, only to reappear with what looked like slug guts on his lips. I didn't know it at the time, but the biggest decision of my life had been made, and life would never be quite the same again, for Lou or for me.

2

Sweet Lou, the One-Dog
Wrecking Crew

Lou grew up eating squirrels, garbage, and gum, jumping fences, and watching the hemp wars unfold. Life in a West Los Angeles apartment just couldn't compare. Where was the DEA? The roadkill?

He could not grasp two-dimensional living. Instead, he jumped catlike up onto tabletops, televisions, kitchen counters, and car roofs. He preferred a loftier point of view.

I rented a sunny one-bedroom apartment near Culver City, a blue-collar neighborhood safe by day but unsavory at night. The odd pop of gunfire in the distance no longer kept me up at night, and Lou didn't seem to mind, either.

A taquería three blocks away, on the corner of Sepulveda and Washington made the best Mission-style burrito in town, so Lou and I began walking down there for lunch every day. Members of the Mexican gang the Culver City Boyz frequented the place; having Lou with me was both a comfort and an attraction. The younger members called Lou "Guapo," and on more than one occasion offered cash or drugs in exchange for my handsome pooch. I politely declined the offers but let them feed him chips or the occasional cheese enchilada, his favorite Mexican food. Lou became my free pass through gangsta land.

The first week back, we began jogging the Ballona Creek bike path, a seven-mile concrete trail from Culver City west to Marina del Rey, where it connected to the coastal bike path. I thought the workout would help Lou sleep, something he hadn't yet gotten the hang of "in captivity." Living like Kipling's Mowgli for the first six months of your life will do that to you.

The bike path ran by the infamous Mar Vista Gardens housing project, a gang haven where the Crips and the Culver City Boyz kept a brittle truce. Less than a mile from my apartment, the city-run project was not the place to loiter; even local postal carriers sometimes refused to deliver mail there. Riders and joggers on the path got mugged in broad daylight, losing wallets, bikes, and sometimes their lives to teen hoods in search of easy prey. I called Ballona Creek "the gauntlet of reality," because for many middle-class Angelenos, the experience often morphed from exercise into fleeing for one's life.

One sunny Saturday, Lou and I stepped onto the path near Slauson Avenue. Scores of bikers and joggers were out having a good time. I was teaching Lou to jog nicely beside me and was focused on him and not paying attention to people around me.

Near Inglewood Boulevard, three Mexican kids with a rusty shopping cart sprang out from some bushes along the path. Intending to use the cart as a battering ram, they were unmistakably practiced at knocking bikers or joggers down and robbing them. But this time it was me and my good-looking young dog.

Lou slowed to a walk and stared the kids down. For a moment I thought he was about to give them hell, and I would've let him. Then Lou's tail slowly began to wag.

"Hey, Guapo!" one called out, running up to Lou, turning back into a kid again. He'd fed Lou an enchilada and a bag of chips for lunch the day before.

My small second-floor apartment had a big picture window and a nice view of West Los Angeles. Lou lay beneath the table in the warm sun and stared out the window at people and traffic passing by, and at pigeons roosting atop the tarred roof of a nearby transmission-repair shop. He wanted to dine on them, I'm sure, but never made a big scene over it.

The apartment manager gave me the bad news a few weeks after I had brought Lou home. He was an African American named John, a burly, good-hearted old guy with a disabled wife to care for. He and I often sat on the balcony outside his apartment, drinking beer and talking sports; he'd toss unshelled peanuts and Cheez-Its to Lou and tell me about the hunting dogs he'd owned back in Mississippi. John was the first one to teach Lou to "catch."

"He's a good dog but the landlord says he gotta go."

"What?"

"That's what he said."

"But the French lady downstairs has two cats."

"They never leave the apartment. And, anyway, she's French."

"What?"

"Listen, son, Lou's a real good dog. I told the landlord that, but he don't want to hear nothing about it."

"But I like it here."

"We like you here. Rent check on time every month. But you know, the landlord's kind of a jackass. Said if he let your dog stay, then pretty soon everybody's gonna want a dog."

"Lou doesn't even bark." It was true: Lou was one of the quietest dogs I've ever known. I had to teach him to bark on command just to get him to speak up. He'd say *"rower"* or yodel some and let out the occasional *"chug"* when worried, but barked only when it was called for. Another holdover from his covert life as a Mendocino drug enforcer.

"We never hear him."

"Maybe if the landlord came over and met Lou."

"He's in Rancho Cucamonga. Never comes over here."

'Then how does he even know?"

"Gardener."

"But Lou likes him, too."

"Can't help you, son. But I'll help you find a place."

I liked it there. It was cheap, small, and clean. I had immunity from the Culver City Boyz, and Lou got free enchiladas and a pigeon show every day.

"I'll get us some beers," he said.

John went inside. I heard him speak to his wife, who was in the early stages of Alzheimer's. She sat on the sofa most of the day in the dark, watching soaps, but brightened up whenever I brought Lou into their apartment. He'd cozy up to her like they'd known each other for ten years. He had the Rottweiler habit of leaning into you and placing a paw gently atop your foot; she would smile and caress his head and talk to him in full sentences about how handsome he was or what she'd be cooking that night. It was one of Lou's great gifts right from the start: he cut through her fog, if only for a few minutes each day.

John tossed me a beer. I popped it and poured a taste into Lou's bowl. He loved beer.

"She gonna miss him," he said, looking at me, nodding.

"I'll bring him around."

"He clears her right up. Like turning on a switch. Lasts awhile, too, after he goes."

"We'll come over when the Dodgers and Mets play."

"There you go."

Lou nudged me for more beer but got a peanut from John instead, tossed up high. Lou eyed it like DiMaggio, caught it, and crunched it down. "Good catch, Lou," I said.

"Damn landlord," John said, touching his can to mine.

I answered an ad for a duplex with a garage and yard on Castle Heights Avenue, two miles away. The ad had said "small pet okay." I convinced myself that *small* was a relative term, and that there were plenty of pet-worthy animals in the world larger than Lou. Great Danes, Appaloosas, alpacas, boa constrictors— plenty bigger than my Lou boy, who had put on more than twelve pounds since we'd found him.

The Zagalias had moved to Palm Desert after he'd gotten mugged a block from their home of forty years. They'd held on to their beloved little West L.A. house, though, renting it out carefully to people they could trust. They made the drive into Los Angeles every weekend just so he could tend to the fruit trees they'd planted over the decades—Italian plum, fig, lemon, and pear. They'd get here at dawn and he'd garden while she sat and knitted.

I had to convince them that Lou would be an asset, a protector of the place they loved, and that their sweet home would not be torn up by a feral mutt with insomnia and a penchant for leaping up onto kitchen counters. But I'd need to convince myself first.

The house, near the corner of Castle Heights and National, looked like a Rockwell replica. Before I could knock, a sinewy old man in overalls, brandishing garden clippers like a pistol, walked over to me from the backyard.

"You Steve?" he asked, sweat dripping down his tanned face.

"Mr. Zagalia?"

"Lou."

"Nice to meet you, Lou." *You're kidding,* I thought.

"That your dog in the car?"

Nothing got by this guy. "He is, and believe it or not, his name is Lou."

"Must be a fine dog. Let's go say hello."

So much for easing into my dog pitch.

Lou's nose prints adorned the back window. He began his happy little marching-in-place routine, his social stamp of approval.

Lou Zagalia grinned like a kid and put his clippers into his pocket as I opened the hatchback. The old guy actually rubbed his palms together.

"Lou, meet Lou."

"Hey there, young fella!" he said, briskly rubbing Lou's ears and head with the confidence of a man who'd owned a dozen dogs in his life. Lou luxuriated in the attention and let out a happy *rower!*

"He likes everybody," I said.

"Had a dog like him a while back," he said, pointing to the small Dog Crossing sign still stuck into the manicured front lawn. "Shepherd mix; smart as a whip."

"Lou's smart, too. Is he too big?"

"For what?"

"Your ad said, 'small pet okay.' "

"I've seen bigger," he said, winking at me. "Just have to sell the wife."

I let Lou out of the car and walked him on leash into the backyard, where Mrs. Zagalia sat knitting in the sun. Wrapped in a navy blanket and a crimson head scarf, she looked like the queen mother.

Lou whined and pulled to get to her. Another senior citizen to seduce.

"He looks just like Duke," she said, scratching him behind the ears. "Same big eyes."

Yes, yes, he's just like Duke . . . he is Duke reincarnated, I thought. *You need Duke redux to live here in this cozy little house, to channel his memory, to guard the fruit. Be a good boy, Lou,* I thought as he flashed her his Mother Teresa look, then lightly touched his foot to hers. *Oh, you're good, boy.*

Mrs. Zagalia's ball of blue yarn rolled off her lap and onto the patio. Lou picked it up and deposited it softly back into her lap. *Holy crap.*

"Let's go take a look at the house," said Mr. Zagalia.

Atta boy, Lou.

The house smelled like old magazines, good spaghetti sauce, and stale carpet. I liked it. Lou and Gemma Zagalia had raised kids here; I'd raise a dog.

I signed a year lease and paid a hefty security deposit in case Lou decided to trash the place. It was two hundred more a month than my last place, but it had a yard, a garage, and all the fruit I could eat.

Lou wasn't as impressed. From the start, I could tell that he missed the old apartment: he paced and searched out every corner as if he'd lost something. At first I couldn't figure out what was bugging him. He'd taken to the old apartment so well; why wouldn't the new place suit him, too?

I figured it out the second morning, after he'd kept me up all night pacing and whining. Walking into the kitchen to make tea, I found him sitting atop the kitchen table gazing out the window, a glazed look in his eyes. Over the years I'd come to recognize this as his "remembering" look—somber and suggestive of his lost family and the hills of his birth. Lou would randomly go off into this trancelike state, like a Sufi searching for inspiration. It was cool but a little unnerving to watch a dog do it.

In the old apartment he'd lie beneath the table and look out the picture window down at traffic, people, and pigeons below— you saw miles of West L.A. from up there. Palms replaced the redwoods, gray pines, and madrone trees of his puppyhood. The view had pleased him. Now he was in a ground-floor home with new smells and no view.

He missed the enchiladas, the peanuts on the balcony, and the dodgy jogs beside Ballona Creek. I'd learned my first lesson as a dog trainer: stray dogs bond like iron not only to the people who rescue them but to the places they first call home, even second-story shoe boxes in the hood.

The doggy demolition began slowly. Clothes, hairbrushes, dishes, pens, wristwatch, toothbrush (yes, he'd reached it somehow)—anything I came in contact with became an object to chew, maul, consume. Toys, dog chews, or rawhides were scoffed at while he was alone; it had to be something of *mine*.

He ate two remote controls, binoculars, a cherished baseball from high school, two belts, a computer mouse and keyboard, Ray-Ban sunglasses, and too many shoes to count. Even the shifter knob and window cranks in my Civic fell victim to Lou's teeth. Anything I handled eventually became dog food.

Food, cookie, eat, treat, and *dinner* became holy words in Lou's lexicon. Meals were sacred rituals; imagine—no fights, no hunting, no angry humans chasing you away from garbage cans or chicken coops. Lou's lifelong Dickensian love of food proved to be one of the tools I'd use to access his ability to learn so much in so short a time.

I tried to pick up his food bowl one evening while he was still licking it clean. He snarled, as he'd probably done a hundred times to other dogs over a scrap of rat guts or a pizza crust. I was his pack now, and damned if I was going to remove this magical meal portal before every atom of kibble had been surgically removed from it.

Not yet knowing the proper way to deal with such conflict, I grabbed him by the scruff and gave him a stern what-for. I got lucky: Lou was sweet and young and hopelessly in love with me, his savior. He never complained again over my touching his bowl, or anything else, for that matter. Had I used this doggish method on some of the future Rottweilers and shepherds I'd eventually train, I might have ended up singing falsetto in a boy's choir.

House-training was an adventure unto itself. Lou was used to pooping and peeing wherever and whenever he felt like it, even if that meant on a drowsy old woman's leg at the park (she never knew and I didn't tell her). Like other increasing behavior problems, it hadn't been an issue at the old apartment: he'd never had an "accident" there. But at the new house he peed on houseplants, pooped neatly behind the sofa, and puked on the bathroom rug. Luckily, unless laced with Bic pens or lens caps, the puke usually got re-eaten. The fouler deposits he'd leave for me.

Lou's gaffes happened almost exclusively at night. I'd taken to closing him out of the bedroom because of his insomnia; I bought him a big cushy dog bed to lie on in a warm corner of the living room, beneath a long table I used as a workstation. The next morning, I found its foam entrails scattered across the home like confetti, and its faux-sheepskin cover was arranged neatly atop the kitchen table, as if he'd been sleeping up there.

One morning around three o'clock I snuck out to find him crunching down on yet another TV remote control, which I'd hidden atop a bookcase *six feet* off the floor. The sound reminded me of his dad's deer-snout snacking.

Despite the carnage, Lou was clear and sentient and thought-ful when with me. There was no mania, no running around like a ferret with a hotfoot, no acting out. He simply missed the hills and didn't want to be alone. At times he appeared almost morti-fied at the silly things he'd do, like a sleepwalker awakened in the middle of Penn Station. If a dog could look sheepish, he did.

Before bedtime, we'd sit in the middle of the living room in the dark and face each other like brothers in a stare-off contest. We'd stare until someone blinked, laughed, chortled, or licked the other, then play a game I called "mad dog," in which Lou was a rabid killer and I a frightened city slicker lost in the woods. Lou would do his happy growl and shove his muzzle into my gut, then break off and frolic around the room like a bucking bronc. Then he'd come back and be "mad dog" again and I'd try to escape to the bedroom but fail, only to be eviscerated yet again. We'd stop and I'd hug him and give him cookies, then ask him not to destroy anything that night. Some nights he listened, but usually something got altered in some irreparable way.

Then came the day of reckoning.

I'd wanted a beer. That was my crime. It would take me all of five minutes to run across the street to the 7-Eleven to get it. Five minutes.

"I'm going to leave you alone in the house for *five* minutes," I said to him, handing over a Kong toy stuffed to the gills with cream cheese. "Can you watch the place for me and not go postal?"

He took the Kong and lay on the carpet. Holding it in his paws, he got to work on it. "Good boy, Lou. I'll be back in a flash."

I'd been building up his tolerance to being alone in the house, a bit at a time. Quick trips out the door to the garage and back—no damage. Outside to shut off the sprinkler—nothing destroyed. Out to the car to get a book—all's well. He'd be waiting at the screen door with his train-conductor look when I'd get back, but overall the strategy seemed to be working. I thought that a quick run across the street for a beer was now in his wheelhouse.

To be safe, I decided to corral Lou in the carpeted hallway that connected my bedroom to the living room, with the doors to the living room and bedroom shut. I'd leave his Kong and a few other toys in there with him, and the stereo on in the living room to give the illusion of company.

"Honestly, Lou, be a *good* boy," I said, looking into his soulful eyes. "I mean it." Then I closed the hallway door, slipped out of the house, and ran like a criminal for the 7-Eleven.

Coming back down the drive, all seemed well. No floods, fires, or cops. I expected him to greet me, Kong in mouth.

Lou sat calmly in the middle of the living room, blood dripping from his nose. About two hundred square feet of wall-to-wall carpeting and padding covering the living room and office area had been ripped up and rolled—*rolled,* mind you—neatly to the side, exposing the dull, dusty hardwood floors beneath. The splintered door to the hallway leaned haphazardly against a wall six feet away, as if The Hulk had blasted through it. The torn-out doorjamb lay in pieces a few feet off. Inside the hallway, a long strip of molding had been ripped up and chewed to pulp, and a perfect, foot-wide hole had been punched into the Sheetrock near the bathroom, as if he'd stuck his head through it, looking for me.

The kitchen was an even more remarkable scene. The window he'd taken to gazing through from atop the table had been shattered *outward* down to the walkway below the windowsill—a *five-foot* drop from inside the home to the concrete below. Evidently, after removing the door and carpeting, Lou had decided to leap *through* the pane-glass window to the walkway below, cutting only his nose in the process. Then he had somehow leaped *back* into the kitchen from outside, a standing vertical jump of more than five feet. It was a miracle that his only injury was a cut nose.

I'd been gone five minutes. I sat down and drank the beer.

3

Fixing Lou

T hat's what credit cards are for," said Chet.

"It's too much."

"I can't just replace the section he ripped out. It's wall-to-wall all the way into the office area. If you want it to look the way it was, the whole thing has to be replaced."

"Twenty-seven hundred dollars is a *lot* of money."

"You want me to match it to what they had, right? It's like when a kid draws on the wall—you have to repaint the whole wall."

"A can of paint costs ten bucks."

"My price includes installation and a lifetime stain warranty."

Lou sniffed at Chet's leg and gave him his Mother Teresa look.

"Stain warranty?"

"Yeah. Of course, it doesn't cover pet stains."

"Of course not."

"You sure *this* dog did all that damage?" he asked, immersed in Lou's gaze. "He seems so . . . sensible."

"In five minutes."

"So sweet," he said, stroking Lou's head and ears. "Hell, he did a better job of carpet removal than my guys could have. I should hire him."

I put it on the credit card, along with the cost of fixing the window, doorjamb, and Sheetrock, plus the cost of hanging a new door and painting the entire hallway. What else was I going to do? And it all had to be done before Lou and Gemma showed up that weekend to garden and knit.

I had to purge Lou's demons before he maxed out my credit cards and put me out on the street, which in Los Angeles could be problematic. Of course having him with me would ensure immunity and free enchiladas from the Culver City Boyz, but that was a paltry list of perks. Fixing him would be a better solution. So I called Dean.

An old friend from New Jersey, Dean owned corgis, a smart, active herding breed that could get into trouble without proper training early on. Lou wasn't a corgi by any means, but he was a clever troublemaker. If anyone could help, Dean could.

"Just buy a crate, dumbshit."

"I've thought about it."

"So?"

"I thought putting him in a box might drive him nuts."

"He's driving *you* nuts, isn't he? And besides, dogs like crates. They're like private little dog bungalows. Nice and cozy," he said.

"Just feed him in it, every day. And read a book on crate training, for chrissakes."

It seemed too good to be true, but I was willing to try anything, including stuffing Lou into an escape-proof box at night.

"If he's in a crate when I'm gone, he won't be able to guard the house."

"The dog just cost you four thousand bucks. You don't have that much stuff *to* steal."

"Good point."

"Get a crate, beef brain. Look, it's easy: feed him in the crate, and make him sleep in it. Put him in there whenever you leave him in the house alone. For the next six months he is either with you or in the crate. End of story."

"What else?"

"Take a class or a private training session. Hide everything you don't want him to destroy. Keep the shade pulled down on the kitchen window. And whenever he can go somewhere with you, take him. Make sure you get the plastic airline-type crate and not the wire one. Wire ones suck."

"That's it?"

"That's it. Goodbye."

He hung up. That was Dean.

The training books said that dogs were denning animals and liked small spaces. A crate would help with house-training, too, because it utilized the dog's instinct not to soil its sleeping area. "No one wants to sleep in shit, huh, Lou?" I said, picking up my car keys. He cocked his head, chortled, then disappeared down the hallway, reappearing a moment later with my toothbrush in his mouth. "Let's get to the pet store, Lou."

The sales kid pulled a crate down off the shelf. It didn't look big enough, so I wedged my upper body into it to check it out. Lou followed me in.

I could see the sales kid's legs through the crate's wire window. Lou licked my face. We were crammed inside a plastic box.

"Pretty sturdy, huh?" he said, kicking the crate as if it was shod with brand-new Goodyears.

"Cozy. What do think, Lou?" I blew air into his nose to try to get him to bark. He sneezed and looked at me: *Please do not do that again.*

"That's the large size. I could put you into an extra-large if you plan on spending time in there together."

"This is good," I said, tangled up with Lou. He snuggled into me, wondering what kind of game this was. It was kind of fun in there, like kids playing fortress in a refrigerator box.

"I'll take it."

I read *How to Be Your Dog's Best Friend,* by the Monks of New Skete, in two nights. The brothers bred and trained German shepherds at an Upstate New York monastery and, from what I heard, made a fine Trappist ale as well.

Lou was part shepherd. As I read through the book I could see him clearly on every page. He was smart and adaptable, and intense in his ability to read emotions and purpose. And he was insatiably sniffy, curious, and loyal—more shepherd traits.

Bred to be an all-around superdog, German shepherds are highly intelligent and adaptable, with perhaps more innate abilities than any other breed. They can herd, track, guard, and hunt, and are unflinchingly loyal to their families. Though sociable, they have the smarts to know when something is fishy and will act accordingly. It's no accident that police and military forces use shepherds almost exclusively. Lou was my feral decathlete.

But he was also his daddy's son. Like shepherds, Rottweilers are smart and protective, but they are stronger and more territorial. Lou never weighed more than seventy-two pounds, but all seventy-two were solid muscle. When he leaned into you, you could feel the steel in his body. Lou was like a Lab on steroids, with special-forces training.

The monks' book was an eye-opener. I learned about destructive behavior in young dogs, and how Lou's form of it reflected his insecurity about being left alone at night. He'd lived twenty-four hours a day with a pack of thieving scoundrels before coming into my life; I'd become the sole substitute for all that doggish company, and I couldn't quite match up yet.

I put Lou's new crate beside my workstation table, in the same spot where his shredded dog bed had been. Grabbing a handful of treats, I climbed in, legs flagging out the open door. Lou squeezed in, too, and lay down with me, happy to play the sardine game again. I fed him treats and massaged him and told him about how different things were going to be, how he'd sleep and eat in the crate, and that his days of carnage were over. He chortled and slimed my neck, then tapped me on the head a few times with a paw, as if checking for ripeness.

The first "dog trainer" I called showed up an hour late in a primer-gray Ford pickup with three enraged pit bulls in the canopied back, desperate to break out and devour something. A better advertisement a dog trainer could not have.

A muscle-bound bald man in a striped T-shirt and jeans stepped out of the truck, which had URI's OBEDIENCE TRAINING stenciled onto the door in red paint. A winged pit bull tattooed on his neck had a bloody goat in its mouth, an arrow-tipped tail, and devil's horns.

"So this is the little one who eats you out of house and home!" he said with a strong Russian accent. He smelled of tomato soup and dog urine.

"This is Lou all right."

"Uri Primakov," he said, shaking my hand so hard that the ring on my finger left a welt in the skin for a day. "We go inside and see what's what."

I had a premonition that Lou and I were about to be slain by a serial killer. I closed the screen door but left the front door open just in case. *Can't fault a sociopathic ex-Stalinist for embracing capitalism,* I thought, wondering if his pit bulls would play a pivotal role in the murders.

"Good place. Smells like new rug. And a nice little dog crate in the corner over here," he said, opening the crate's wire door with his boot.

Uri cased the house. Lou planted his nose onto the big Russian's pants leg and memorized the smell of pit bull. A few years later, stronger and more seasoned, he'd sample it again firsthand.

Uri pulled a leather leash out of his back pocket and clipped it to Lou's flat collar. "His obedience is good?" he asked, walking Lou around the room.

"Not bad. Doesn't stay or lie down yet. The destruction is the biggest problem, though," I said.

Lou shot me a *Why, Judas?* look. Except for Nancy, no one else had ever held his leash before.

"It is about control and attitude, my friend. You must teach them who is boss *right away*. This is what the wolves do," he said, sauntering around the room like Khrushchev. "A powerful wolf will tear another wolf to pieces just for looking at him the wrong way!"

"Really?"

"Of course! I know this personally. I live in Siberia many years."

I pictured him wearing a grizzly robe, booger icicles hanging from his nose, a haunch of boar meat in his hands.

"You must be strong; otherwise it is chaos, all chaos. You do not want to be your dog's girlfriend, do you?"

Uri yanked Lou around the room like a tarpon. Lou let out a plaintive yodel, then, facing Uri, slammed on his brakes and neatly slipped his head out of his collar. Uri grabbed for him, but Lou vaulted gracefully over his beefy arms, then launched himself *through* the closed screen door.

"Holy mackerel," he said.

"He's not your average dog."

Lou sat atop the canopy of Uri's truck, licking his paws like a puma. The pit bulls slammed their thick skulls up into the canopy roof, over and over, Lou bouncing with each smash. Uri ran around the truck with his hands on his head as the aluminum canopy buckled skyward.

"It cannot take such punishment!" he said.

"*House*, Lou," I said, opening the screen door. Lou leaped off the canopy and onto the Ford's hood, then down onto the concrete, his tail wagging, as three slobbering pit-bull faces mashed into the glass of the windshield like frat boys stuffed into a phone booth. Lou sauntered into the house and walked into his crate, which we called his "house." I closed the crate door in case Uri decided to release his orcs, but when I went back out, he'd already started up his Ford. I watched him go, devil dogs snapping at one another, the truck's canopy bowed up like a bowler hat.

"Trainers like that should be locked up," she said, sitting cross-legged on the carpet, feeding Lou turkey. He sat beside her, hypnotized by the gratuitous meat. Chandra (she said it meant "goddess") had been training dogs for several years and was a proponent of the "positive only" school of dog training. She was the biggest woman I had ever seen. At least six-six, 250 pounds.

Sci-fi big, XYY big, carny big. Lou couldn't take his eyes off her.

"You shouldn't use stressful methods on your dog. Think about how they train orcas; you *can't* discipline them—it's just feeding them fish at the right time."

"Want some tea?" I asked, imagining that if anyone could discipline an orca, she could.

"Do you have chai?"

"I don't know what that is."

"It's a spiced Indian tea. Very good."

Lou's nose and mouth shone with turkey grease. Drunk on meat, he was smiling and joyful. I hadn't recalled anything in the training books about treating destructive behavior with massive doses of tryptophan.

"I'll have to try it," I said. "I've only got Lipton."

"No, thanks."

"You were talking about orcas."

"Yes. Only positive methods work on them. You can't punish them at all."

"Isn't that because they're killer whales?"

"Doesn't matter. Now, with Lou here, you have a great little dog who is confused over what is expected of him. In the forest he probably chewed on everything—sticks, pinecones, rocks—whatever he wanted. Nothing was off-limits. But now he's in a house with all of these . . . possessions," she said, waving a mammoth, dismissive hand at my stuff.

"So how do I get him to stop eating my stuff?"

"First, stop thinking of it as 'your stuff.' He owns them, too."

"He does?"

"Of course. Dogs are natural communists."

A Uri connection.

"They are?"

"Of course. Think of wolves, who share everything." Another

Uri connection. Communists and pagans were tag-teaming me and my dog.

"So if I stop thinking of it as my stuff, that'll stop him from eating it?"

"Lou will sense you letting go of your possessive nature, which will in turn cause him to value the things less and lose interest. Combine that with some distraction training and the behavior will be extinguished."

"How do I distract him?"

"I've been doing that for the last twenty minutes."

"Just feed him turkey meat?"

"Or whatever else he likes. Then replace the bad behavior with a good behavior. Encourage him to chew on a plastic bone or a rope toy."

"The only plastic he'll chew on is the TV remote."

"You have to encourage him."

Lou thought the toys and chews I'd bought him were dimwitted diversions. I could see that in his eyes when I'd pretend to chew on one, then surrender it to him at great sacrifice. He'd give me a condescending glance, as if to say, *Do I look like a Lab, dork?* Even at seven months he had more refined tastes than that.

Chandra must have gone through a pound of turkey before slowly standing. "See how attentive he is?" she said, luring Lou into a sit beside her. She loomed like an NBA center at a preschool. "You don't ever need a leash if you have turkey handy."

Chandra. Wiccan turkey trainer. I wondered if Wiccans were vegans, what with all the rituals and cold cuts and all. Someone this big had to eat meat.

"So I should buy turkey meat and have it with me always."

"Yes."

"But at night he can sleep in the crate."

"Oh god no. Crates are punitive. Remember the orcas."

"Right. Can't crate an orca."

"Lou should sleep with you, just like wolves do, remember?"

Evidently anything could be justified by pointing to something wolves did or didn't do. Murder, incest, public nudity, tyranny—add a liberal dose of turkey and it was all good.

"In the bed?"

"All my dogs sleep with me."

"How many?"

"Six rescue greyhounds."

Holy shit. "All in the bed?"

"Argent, Arwen, and Blade, always. Lilith and Mysteria take turns, and Saffron prefers the sofa."

Oh that Saffron. The specter of Chandra and her pagan pooches lazing atop a fetid, stained comforter made me queasy.

"Okay then," I said, reaching up to shake her hand. I felt like the doomed scientist in "To Serve Man," that old *Twilight Zone* episode with the giant, human-eating aliens. Chandra's greasy fingers engulfed mine. Lou chortled, then hopped up onto the kitchen table to stare out the new window at the neighbor's kids.

"You should encourage his athleticism, too," she said.

"Thanks, Chandra. I'll call you."

"Bye, Lou."

I handed her a check for forty bucks, then watched as she ducked her head on the way out. "And you should get this screen door fixed."

Dog training isn't exactly the most regulated of professions. Close to psychic or home stager in compulsory credentialing. Get out of jail, print up a business card, and, voilà, you're an authority. Ex-Soviet grifters, giant Wiccans, obsessive-compulsives, xenophobes, shut-ins—I've seen some crazies over the years.

I like to imagine that Uri and Chandra met one day at a trainers' convention, insane asylum, or county jail, fell in love, and moved to Vegas to run a pit-bull Ponzi scheme. But they did do me a great favor that week: they scared me off outside help and convinced me to go it alone with Lou, which in retrospect probably helped make him into the most extraordinary dog I've ever known.

I listened to Dean, used the crate, read books, and took Lou with me wherever I went. We became inseparable, and learned on the fly by trial and error. I could get away with making a few mistakes with him, because he was, well . . . *Lou.* The crate kept the Zagalias' hallowed home in one piece and let Lou and me get a decent night's sleep. The fix was in.

We went to the beach often. It was the perfect place to let Lou run and mingle, without my having to worry about him wandering off. Really—where could he go? Catalina? The Pacific on one side and Santa Monica on the other, with people, dogs, sand, and bikes in between.

We had a ball. I worked on perfecting his recall nearly every day. And Chandra, God bless her pagan heart, was right—Lou would walk on water for a rip of turkey. No matter how far off he ran or how much fun he had with some other dog, if I blew my whistle he'd come running for his Wiccan turkey fix.

One cool, clear Saturday morning Nancy and I took Lou to the beach. A handful of dog walkers and joggers were out. Lou kicked up rooster tails of sand and herded gulls into the surf. He drank of the ocean but once, a week before, and had paid for it with a marathon vomit session later on. This time he sniffed it and, remembering, shook his head.

A shepherd pup came running down the beach, right for Lou. Though younger, he was nearly as large, with tall, pricked ears and pearly white teeth. Black and blond, he looked beautiful against the bright sand.

Lou crouched down into play posture. Then, just as the pup

was about to pounce, Lou leaped straight up in the air, like an arctic fox flushing out voles hidden in the snow. Vaulting *over* the pup, he turned in midair and landed behind his confused playmate.

"He's got some moves," I said to Nancy, as the two dogs sprinted down the beach past two surfers exiting the water.

"He's the Wildman of Willits," she said.

I blew the turkey whistle. Like magic, Lou skidded to a stop and came back at a sprint, the shepherd pup no match for Lou's speed.

"Holy crap, he's *fast*," I said, digging for a tear of turkey meat.

"Scary fast," said Nancy, sidestepping Lou as he flew by us, a cloud of sand peppering our clothes.

Fast he was, especially when young. The only races Lou ever lost while in his prime were to sight hounds, in a speed league all their own. But no other dog, be it a Border collie, Vizsla, Doberman, Dalmatian, or husky, ever outran him. At an empty beach parking lot near Redondo Beach, I once paced him with my car at nearly thirty-five miles per hour, for over a quarter mile. That's *fast*.

Lou circled back and sat in front of me, motionless, waiting for his reward, which I promptly gave him. The shepherd pup pulled up, breathing hard, wondering what all the fuss was about.

"Your dog is flippin' fast," said the pup's owner, running up. Both Lou and the pup greeted the young man, who clipped his leash onto his dog. "What breed is he?"

"Rott/shepherd," I said.

"He's feral," said Nancy proudly. She loved that.

"You mean wild?"

"Fresh out of the woods a month ago."

"But he's so friendly," he said, his pup straining to get to Lou, who kept poking the pup in the nose as if to play tag.

The shepherd barked in frustration. "You can let him go," I said.

He unclipped his leash and both dogs shot down the beach. Lou toyed with the pup—slowing, whirling around, vaulting over him, and then rising up on his hind legs to box. For the first time, we got to see just how agile and quick Lou was. He moved like a martial artist avoiding a drunkard.

"You should get him into an agility class," the young man said. "He's like a circus performer."

Two years later I would teach an agility class, and Lou would set an unofficial record for completing the course in the fastest time of any dog, regardless of size.

He took to the crate without much fuss. We had a nice routine going. We slept peacefully. The Zagalia home was saved.

Lou and I became brothers. He went to work with me. We played the staring contest and "mad dog," ran on the beach, and learned each other's timing, body language, and intent. We explored subtlety, inflection, and tone. We could tell what the other was thinking from a look, a pose, or an utterance. Often I'd catch him watching me, not in the way a dog does when he wants something but in a more studied way, as if he needed to know if the sacrifice he'd made had been worth it.

I loved him, but not in the way a parent does a child. It wasn't that saccharine, surrogate affection many dog owners fashion, that overbonded, embarrassing, schmaltzy spoilage that ruins dogs. I felt more like a big dog-brother, and that it was my job to teach him the ropes.

I felt tasked by him. I was the novice violin player who

accidentally finds a dusty Stradivarius in a pawn shop. Lou was my Enkidu, my link to the wild, and I loved him that way, loved him for how he tested me and himself, and for how he kept getting better and better each day. I envied him for how he won hearts, and in the way he'd stare off into the ether, grieving for his family the way an immigrant would who had come too far to ever go back.

4

Loading-dock Dog

Lou sat by the bed, staring at me.

"What?" I asked. I'd let him out an hour before, then had lain down for a midday nap. "You don't need to go out, and it's not dinnertime, so don't bug me."

He kept staring. Lou was beautiful to behold, but sometimes when he locked on to you it seemed as if he was about to sever your carotid.

"I'm not getting up," I said. The clock read 3:45 P.M.

He looked into the open closet, looked back at me, then glanced into the closet again.

"What?" I repeated.

He ran out of the room, then came back to the same spot.

"Rower."

"You're not going to have diarrhea again, are you?"

Then the jingling began. My groggy head couldn't decipher jingling. I had no bells, tambourines, or cymbals. Lou's collar IDs made a different sound. The neighborhood ice-cream trucks didn't jingle—they broadcast tipsy, off-key music to lure kids out of their homes. No—jingling was a new sound.

Lou peered into the closet again. I did, too, and saw it—empty metal coat hangers clinking into one another, making happy music, like Buddhist prayer bells.

My framed print of Clara Bow jumped off the wall. Lou nearly caught her in his mouth. We were having our first earthquake together and he'd known it a good minute before I had.

The room jerked around like a subway car. Lou left the room, came back in with a ball, left again, returned with a sofa pillow, and then again with a frying pan.

I surfed around the room. Lou jumped onto the bed and chortled. He was having fun.

I had read once how Greek historians reported on rats, snakes, and weasels abandoning the Greek city of Helice in droves before a major earthquake leveled the place. I thought it must have been quite a sight, so I staggered over to the window and looked out but saw no mass exodus of vermin.

As quickly as it had begun, the coat hangers ended their Buddhist benedictions. I wandered through the now-motionless house, wondering what to do, while Lou inspected the flotsam that had leaped to the floor during the temblor, a 5.2, big enough to impress me but hardly noticeable to seasoned Angelinos.

"Welcome to Tinseltown, Lou." He licked my face, then picked my Mets cap up off the living-room carpet and brought it over. "Thanks." Then he disappeared and came back with his leash. "Why not."

. . .

We explored the new neighborhood together. Lou had learned to walk by my side rather than surge out ahead. It took only a few days of some unpredictable about-faces and turns on my part; he realized that paying attention to what I was doing made walking more fun for both of us. Most dogs who learn an informal heel position acquiesce to it only after weeks of struggle, but Lou seemed to favor it; he liked walking with me.

Dogs and owners flew by us like drunken Iditarod entrants. Like mimes in a tempest, the owners could barely stand, and were clueless as to where their dogs would drag them that morning. *Who's walking whom?* I wondered.

When one of these runaway freight trains happened by us, the dog often jumped all over Lou, who enjoyed the camaraderie and attention. But whenever a dog became confrontational, a different side of Lou came out: instead of using his strength and speed to defend himself, he'd switch over to a more focused, diplomatic mindset. He'd study the other dog's moves, then react stealthily, like Jackie Chan ducking the ham-fisted punches of a hapless villain until, exhausted, the attacker gives up.

Looking back on it, I'm sure this instinctive rope-a-dope skill of his was, as were many of his behaviors, born of his early life in the woods: growing up wild had taught him a wolfish diplomacy that he now applied to these "store bought" city dogs. Lou leaped, boxed, spun, rolled, laughed—whatever was needed to frustrate the other dog into giving up and calming down.

I'd drop my leash and let Lou go it alone, while the other owner held on for dear life. Through it all, Lou usually kept a Cheshire grin plastered on his face. I didn't know it at the time, but this "tactful" side of him would soon be used by me (and him) to start saving hundreds of dogs from the grim reaper.

Lou was still a pup, filled with curiosity and a hunger for affection. He couldn't yet comprehend that not every stranger or dog he met would find him absolutely adorable and engaging. He'd eventually come up with a strategy for dealing with the more brutish holdouts, but for now he wore his youthful enthusiasm well.

We clearly had a crush on each other. He would literally jump through fire for me (and did on one occasion). And I had fallen for a damn *dog*. The Lassie and Timmy sentiment I'd internalized as a tenement kid—I finally owned it, and, frankly, it felt awkward to a guy in his thirties. What I couldn't have known yet was how Lou would eventually equal that fictional collie's standing.

For most of my career, I've derided owners for elevating their dogs to cult status. A dog shouldn't be the center of attention but rather just another member of the family, with unique rules and responsibilities to attend to. Treat them like rock stars and they'll trash your world every time.

For Lou and me, the rapport was different. He knew exactly who he was, very quickly. After getting past his "break-in" period, he'd developed an air of sentience and self-restraint that freed me up and let me grow as a trainer. I could soon focus on the positives, learn just how far a dog could go. I could challenge him and be confident in his responses. In Lou's mind, he wasn't the center of my attention; I was the center of his, and that made all the difference in the world.

Mornings we often walked down to a small park at about the time local kids headed off for school. I planned it that way, to make sure he'd have regular contact with kids. I'd even given some of the neighborhood youngsters bags of dog treats to keep in their book bags, to offer to Lou whenever we happened by.

It became a favorite ceremony for Lou and the kids: tail and tongue wagging, smiles, kids bragging about how the handsome black-and-tan dog with human eyes would listen to them, new kids shy and scared and giggly about it all, Lou reveling in the attention, chortling, rubbing catlike into the kids and sniffing at them like they were long-lost littermates.

Lou had gained twenty pounds in two months. He now sported a miniature version of his father's ripped physique—shoulders, thighs, withers, and rear sculpted and strong. His forearms were cut like the body builders' we'd see at the Rose Café, a Venice institution down the block from Gold's Gym. Sometimes we went there during the day and sat outside in the sun; I'd work on fiction while Lou, tethered to the fence near the back entrance, got loved on by everyone.

Celebrity patrons lavished attention on him, impressed by his countenance and good looks. Intimidating Gold's Gym hulks who were so muscle-bound they could barely bend over would fawn over him like little kids. Lou had gone from feral squirrel-eater to L.A. schmoozer in two months.

But he worked hard, too. Both of us infatuated with training, we learned fast. He'd mastered all the basic behaviors and clearly wanted more.

One day on a walk down our street, I looked at the leash, loose and looped down, and realized that at that moment, it was redundant. So I lay it over Lou's back and just kept walking and talking to him, and lightly touching the top of his head. He looked up and smiled. Lou was heeling off-leash, just like that. I felt like a dad letting go of the seat back of his kid's Sting-Ray bike for his first triumphant two-wheeled ride.

I'd slow down, he'd slow down. I'd speed up, he'd speed up. I'd stop and he would, too, then he'd sit. I'd praise him but not make a big deal out of it; I wanted him to think it was normal. But inside I was busting with pride, in him and myself.

I threw in turns and unpredictable movements. I'd speed up to a run and he'd stay right there with me. I'd stop short and he would, too, then he'd back up a pace or two to stay even with me. I hadn't taught him that—he'd just started doing it.

Through all my capricious attempts to surprise him, he'd keep up, and look at me with that Cheshire grin he'd get when he knew he was perfecting something. It was a game to him. He'd shoot me his big browns, grin, and think, *Got it, bro—let's move on.*

While I trained the greatest dog I have ever known, right down the road, Earl Woods trained the greatest golfer the world has ever known—his son Tiger Woods. Blessed with God-given talent, Tiger, only fourteen at the time, was but a few years away from beginning his storied professional career. So I stole a trick from Earl's playbook and used it on my prodigy.

Tiger had to learn to focus his talent under pressure and perform, no matter what unexpected commotions occurred. To train Tiger to do this, Earl used distraction training, a technique often used in sports and military instruction, as well as in animal training. While Tiger readied for a swing, Earl would jingle his pocket change, throw golf balls or tees at Tiger, cough, yell—whatever it took to throw Tiger off. Gradually his son learned to excel under any circumstances, and to focus no matter what the disruption.

It meant nothing if Lou would obey me only in a quiet room or yard, or on a calm street corner; he had to perform under any and all conditions, no matter what. He had too much potential not to be put to the real test.

Near the corner of Lincoln and Venice Boulevards was an industrial park with a busy loading dock for semis, and some green space for employees to use during lunch breaks. A narrow strip of sod separated the busy one-way roads that serviced the loading dock, allowing a regular amount of traffic in and out.

Trucks from all over the country dropped off or picked up what appeared to be machine parts and other types of manufactured goods. It was loud, busy, and unpredictable—the perfect place to put Lou to the test. If Earl Woods could train a prodigy, so could I.

And so, Tuesdays and Thursdays, before my afternoon academic tutoring sessions, became our time to work on Lou's off-leash behavior at the industrial park. I'd walk him around first, let him flirt with employees and truckers on their lunch break, and get him used to the level of activity.

To Lou it was a doggy Disneyland. He never shied from chaos: to him, where there was a racket, there was fun.

We worked hard on perfecting his sit/stays and down/stays, until I could get him to hold position for extended periods of time. He'd gotten it well enough around the house and on the street; now, wanting to up the pressure, we visited the loading dock. I walked him over to the ten-foot-wide strip of sod sandwiched between the busy one-way roads, put him into a sit, and told him to stay, using a hand signal and a verbal command. Then I unclipped his leash and walked away.

Sitting at a table across the entry road, fifty feet from Lou, I sipped Snapple and watched. He sat like an effigy, head moving slightly to eye the semis snorting by ten feet away. No leash, Peterbilts, Freightliners, and Macks lugging thirty-ton loads right by him, Lou sitting there like a member of the queen's guard.

A man walked over from an office building and sat down to eat his lunch. We nodded to each other. As he unwrapped the plastic wrap from his sandwich, he caught sight of Lou.

"You see that?" he said, pointing to Lou with his sandwich.

"He's directing traffic," I said, finishing my iced tea.

"Really? You mean for the trucking company?"

"Yeah. They're using dogs now," I said.

"He's not even moving. My dog would be crapping."

"What do you have?"

"A Dalmatian."

"They like horses."

"That's what they say," he said. Lou looked up at a trucker who'd stopped to say something to him. I couldn't hear, but it looked like Lou *rowered* up at him.

"And they can have hearing problems."

"Right again. You know a lot about dogs?"

"I read a lot about them when I was a kid."

"Gotta love them."

"Oh, I do," I said.

I tossed out the bottle and walked to Lou, who wagged his tail and did his happy, marching-in-place routine. But he didn't break, even when an outgoing semi blew his air horn and gave Lou the thumbs-up.

"Good stay, Lou!" I said over the din. I gave him a hug and a cookie and said, "Okay," the release word. He slimed my face and chortled, then did a spinny jig. "Good spin!" I said, knowing that if I named and reinforced an appealing, spontaneous behavior often enough, I'd eventually be able to reproduce it on command. I made a mental note of his penchant for joyous rotation, then clipped on his leash and led him over to the Dalmatian owner to confess to my peccadillo.

John had taught Lou to catch peanuts and Cheez-Its. It would take a feisty Taiwanese woman to teach him "Shake," in one drama-laden afternoon.

Nancy's parents lived in La Crescenta, a town north of Los Angeles near the southern boundaries of the Angeles National Forest. The most unforgettable thing about the area were the feral peacocks that randomly roosted atop area homes and cars. Though stunning, these iridescent, turkey-size birds were hated by local residents for their ungodly nighttime mating screams, and their dog-sized turds left everywhere.

No one knew exactly when or how these natives of India had established themselves in the Los Angeles foothills. Most felt that they were pains in the ass. In addition to the screaming and pooping, the omnivorous birds ravaged vegetation and decimated small native fauna.

The psychopathic fowl shrieked at Lou and me from atop poop-encrusted roofs and cars as we'd walk the neighborhood. Being the consummate acrobat, Lou had to be kept on-leash, to prevent the inevitable massacre. He despised peacocks, and I did not blame him one bit.

"You go; I take care of Louie," Nancy's mom said. Nancy and I needed some "no dog" time, and her mom was more than willing to dog-sit for the afternoon.

"Are you sure?" I asked. So far I'd been the only one to take care of Lou; I wasn't sure how he would react. He could jump a fence, bust through a door or window—Lou was an expert escape artist, and if loosed onto La Crescenta, the peacock death toll could reach historic proportions.

"I like Louie. You go. I cook for him, maybe teach him something."

I wasn't sure if Mrs. Banks had ever owned a dog, but she surely liked Lou. She was also the first one to use the diminutive "Louie," which eventually became the name everyone used to refer to him. Oddly, though I'd use it, too, I always addressed him directly as "Lou."

Mr. and Mrs. Banks had met in the 1960s, while he was stationed in Taiwan. She'd fallen for the quiet American mechanic, and he for the pretty, outgoing Taiwanese woman who, though barely able to speak English, made up for it with personality and pluck. They balanced: he was introspective and meticulous and she, friendly and resolute. They'd had a son and a daughter.

I owed their daughter for standing strong like her mom and persuading me to take that flea-bitten mongrel with us on that day in Willits.

I imagined the damage Lou could do to the tidy Banks home. The ornate, expensive Chinese furnishings that filled the house would be chewed to dust. But they had a high fence around the property, and Mrs. Banks seemed more than up to the task of watching Lou.

We left Lou with Nancy's mom in the neighborhood of shrieking peacocks and spent the day together exploring Old Pasadena, the historic heart of the town. We had fun in the spring sunshine, window shopping and having lunch at an outdoor café on Fair Oaks Avenue. Not wanting to push the privilege that Mrs. Banks had afforded us, we headed back after a few hours, curious to see how they'd gotten along.

We found Mrs. Banks trotting down the middle of the street a block from their home.

"Uh-oh," said Nancy.

"Oh yeah—he's gone," I said, rolling down my window.

She came over. "I put him in the yard to potty. He jump the fence. He go right over."

"When?" I asked, my heart dropping. In a millisecond, my brain calculated how far he could have gone, his likeliest route, his motivations, the best- and worst-case scenarios, the prevailing winds, the closest parks—every possible incentive within a five-mile radius.

"Two, three minute ago," she said, her eyes wet. It was the first time I'd seen her get emotional.

"I think I know where he's headed," I said to Mrs. Banks. Even Lou couldn't go very far in a few minutes. "Stay here in case he comes back."

Two blocks upwind, we spotted his sleek shape patrolling the property of a split-level home, its requisite rooftop peacock screeching out his apocalyptic mating cry. I exhaled and watched him search for a way up to the roof, to silence the wretched creature. We watched him try to work it out: he mounted the home's stoop, jogged over to the tool shed, sniffed the air, leaped up onto a garbage can, reached a tentative paw out to a windowsill, craned his neck up, and woofed. He wanted that stinking bird. I sighed, knowing that he'd come over the moment I called him.

"He's hunting," I said to Nancy as she rubbed my neck. I felt the blood rush settle.

"The neighborhood should hire him."

"The 'birdinator.'"

Lou stared up at the peacock, its extravagant tail fanned open. "Lou!" I called through the open window. He turned his head, saw the car, smiled, and came running. I opened the door and let him jump into the backseat. "Get in, Bozo."

He beat his tail against the insides of the Civic and acted like a kid on the last day of school. Back at the Bankses' home, Nancy's mom paced in the front yard, arms crossed.

"Bad dog!" she said as Lou trotted over to her. She wagged a finger in his face, which he sniffed, then licked. She stroked his head. "You scare me!"

"He was chasing peacocks down the street," Nancy explained. "Sorry, Ma."

"Wait—I show you what he learn," she said, wiping her eyes with a sleeve. She pulled something edible out of her pocket and showed it to Lou, who immediately sat and stared intently at her. "Okay, Louie—shake, shake," she said while reaching down and tapping on the back of his right wrist. Lou's paw shot up into the air. "Good shake, Louie!" she said, giving him the treat.

"Wow!" I said. "How long did that take?"

"Two, three minute. He use his feet a lot anyway," she said.

Lou kept raising his paw even after she'd run out of whatever mystery treat she'd been feeding him. She grinned and kept shaking the offered paw and scolding him for running off. He worked her, alternating paws now, yodeling, and sniffing at her pockets for more of the dumpling filler or whatever it was. When he shot her the Mother Teresa look, she reached down to hug him.

Mrs. Banks and I added fencing to the low spot where Lou had vaulted out to freedom. I knew he could probably still get out, but didn't tell her that. In fact, he wouldn't ever try it again. The scent of Chinese dumplings and spicy chicken and marinated beef and oyster noodles with fish sauce wafting through the home was just too delicious for Lou: his peacock safari would take a second seat to his fondness for Chinese cooking, and his affection for Nancy's mom.

We took our last walk before bed. The street was quiet. I could smell my neighbor's nightshade, its blue flowers sweet-smelling and pretty. Lou sniffed at them, then moved on, falling back into position beside me, his leash unclipped and around my neck.

Our night walks were off-leash now; just the two of us walking, listening to the hum of tires on the freeway and the occasional bark of a backyard dog wanting in.

At a street corner, Lou stepped into a deep patch of ivy, the pole for a street sign planted squarely in its center. It'd become his favorite spot to explore since he'd eyed a rat scurry into it a few nights past. Disappointed that no vermin hid in there this night, he peed on the signpost, then pooped for good measure. Though I usually did pick up after him, I let these night deposits lie, partly for the difficulty of fishing them out, but mostly because I knew that the rats were attracted to the feces. I wanted Lou to have a bit of adventure in his life, and the occasional rodent gave that to him.

He scratched out his back legs one at a time in the ivy, to

mark the rat-rich terrain. Another holdover from his Tarzan days. Lou had a penchant for marking trees, hydrants, dogs, ivy—whatever I let him get away with. In the woods, he and his puppy pack had probably held pissing contests for days on end; I guessed that the smell of rats and a thousand dogs in that ivy brought back old memories.

I sat on the curb. He settled in close beside me. Lou was the right height now for me to drape an arm around, so I did. We listened to crickets in the park. I felt the rhythm of his breathing and the warmth of his body. He sniffed at my neck. I'd dodged a bullet that day. I would have lost him if not for a peacock, upwind.

5

Serpents, Stars, and
Stick-ups

He wore his domesticity well. But now Lou would lead me up into the wilds of Southern California, into a world he'd been born into. Different from the Mendocino hills for sure, but hills nonetheless—fenceless, no doors or pavement. His world of grasses, trees, creeks, and dust, of game trails, chittering raccoons and coyotes crooning down to the city below. A thousand fragrant animal stories crisscrossing the hills, leading Lou to secret stashes and sleeping places and hidden babies and dung and hunger and old campfires and death and birth.

We ran the paths like dog and dog, up into the dry hills, for the bond, and for me to relearn what, as a hiker, I thought I'd known so well. This time I'd be guided by the senses of a connoisseur, a wild dog with a passion born of real living, like a river salmon with flesh pinked not by pellets of color-added fish chow but by swimming a thousand miles past hungry bear, whale, and seal, right to the end. I saw Lou in his element, and it was awesome.

We ranged the hills and forests often. Nancy came on the weekends, but, unlike my tutoring work, her insurance job kept her desk-bound during the week. The sparse weekday crowds made exploring with Lou easy and fun; at least once a week we ranged the backcountry within easy driving distance of the city.

Will Rogers and Topanga State Parks waited close-by; we'd go for hikes, then jump back into the car and be back in time to make my tutoring sessions in West L.A., Beverly Hills, Bel-Air, or wherever I was scheduled. If I didn't have time to drop Lou off at home, he'd just come with me and either stay in the car or, if invited, accompany me into the student's house. By this point his obedience was sharp enough to guarantee that if I put him into a down/stay beside me at a table or desk, he'd stay put no matter what (except for the occasional cat or pet ferret).

Sometimes we'd venture farther, into the Mount Wilson area of the Angeles National Forest, the Malibu Creek or Point Mugu State Parks, or even the San Bernardino National Forest near Big Bear and Lake Arrowhead. Weekend trips to Kings Canyon and Sequoia National Parks, Joshua Tree, and even Yosemite happened, too. Though by law Lou had to be on-leash in any national park, he often found himself untethered or on a retractable long lead. Chalk that one up to a scofflaw owner made even more brazen by a savvy trail dog.

One sunny morning we drove up to the Topanga trailhead of the Backbone Trail, a serpentine patchwork of fire roads, game paths, and old wooden bridges twisting through the Santa Monica Mountains from Will Rogers State Park in the east to Point

Mugu State Park in the west. Today, a prohibition on dogs is in effect for the Backbone, but back in 1990 no such ban existed, and we took advantage of it.

The ridgeline trail ranged from oak woodlands and coastal prairie grasses to dense chaparral above, with creeks and valleys, pungent sage, scrub oak and yucca, and mountain whitethorn so thick a jackrabbit couldn't get through it.

I have a fondness for plants and animals with the resolve to endure drought, fire, cold, and heat—a tenacity that all things denied resolutely adopt. They share a special breed of beauty, an elegant sparseness with a stamina to be respected, like the flavor of a fine wine born of tortured vines.

Spring wildflowers, birds, and busy insects abounded. Once far enough down the trail, I'd unclip Lou's leash and let him wander. He'd sniff out scat, bless scrub oaks with his territorial perfume, nibble at sun-drenched sage, and leap up after purple-capped Costa's hummingbirds—he ran with joy and an authenticity that most dogs could not imagine.

Lou was old school—like a seasoned farm dog who hunted, herded, and slept in the sun, the kind of dog whose owners felt cheered by his company but never silly or sentimental about it. Lou had the tenor of a working dog, with a sovereign thought process and an insatiable interest in how things worked. Whether performing tricks for a group of school kids or guiding me through an abandoned silver mine, Lou approached things with the heart of a craftsman. Even in his first year of life, he was accountable, and he dug it.

In the woods, Lou ranged like a military scout but stayed within shouting distance, his independence checked by our intense connection. Every minute he would stop, double back, and lock eyes on me to make sure I was still in the loop, still okay. Lou's freedom-loving spirit balanced nicely with his doting, and the nagging idea that I might just vanish into the hills.

I wanted to harness this "push-pull" personality of his in some way, to hone training and performance. So I began playing hide-and-seek with him out there in the hills, to make his recall or "come" command as dependable as possible, and to develop his tracking abilities. Not the human version of this age-old kids' game; I mean serious, long-range *dog* hide-and-seek, as if my life depended on it. I wanted to take his abilities to the next level.

Once he was totally absorbed in the tracking of some creature, I'd slip down a side trail and crawl into a bush or cave, atop a boulder, or up a tree. I'd get as far away as possible, preferably downwind and off-trail. Within moments I'd hear him charge back down the trail, *rowering* and yodeling out what I took to be my name in dog.

He always found me. Hiding from Lou was, after all, like dodging raindrops. The point wasn't to stump him but to tax him. This recall/tracking experiment differed in that I wasn't actually calling him to me but *hiding;* he was, in effect, orchestrating his own recall command.

Each time I hid deeper in, trying to stump him. Eventually I had to put Lou into a stay position just to be able to get far enough away, as he'd caught on to my shenanigans and wouldn't let me wander off at all anymore. The "stay" usually afforded me a three- or four-minute head start to find a hiding place before he'd say "hell with this" and take off after me. I'd throw him off-scent by placing used tissues up trees or under rocks, or by wedging sandwich wrappers deep into bushes. I felt like Cool Hand Luke trying to stay a step ahead of the sheriff's bloodhounds.

He always found me. He'd *rower* and prance about proudly when he did, and rightly so. I was proud, too, for I'd created a foolproof system for ensuring that he'd never again wander off of his own accord, no matter what the distraction.

After Lou mastered the sit/stay and down/stay commands, I taught him the "wait" command. Unlike "stay," "wait" required a dog only to respect a boundary line or area for a short period of time. A dog could learn to wait at a door, gate, or entrance to a room, on a rug or dog bed, or even in a crate or dog house, until called off.

The basic wait command took Lou a day to learn. I started by teaching him to wait at the entrance to the house before going in or out. Then I taught him "go to your rug," a handy command that anchors a pooch and gets him out of the way when necessary. Once Lou learned to go over to his fleece rug (using treats, praise, leash guidance, and body posture), I'd tell him to wait and have him hold it for longer and longer periods of time, until it became second nature. I could eventually send him to the rug from any spot in the home.

I began working a start-stop version of "wait" in fields, parking lots, and at local parks. I'd have him sit, then tell him to wait, using the verbal command and hand sign, a simple, open vertical palm, the same as for "stay" (except that "stay" utilizes a sideways palm). Then I'd walk thirty yards off, face him, wait a few seconds, then yell out, "Come here!" Once he'd closed half the distance (which for him happened in a second or two), I'd put both hands up in the air and boom out, "Wait!" Eventually, Lou would slide to a stop and wait there until commanded otherwise.

I increased my distance from him, allowing me to bark out the wait command multiple times for each run. He'd travel ten yards, and then wait, five yards and then wait, twenty yards and then wait—getting closer and closer. Soon I was able to start and stop him like kids playing "red light, green light," eventually dropping the verbal command and using just the "touchdown" hand signal. I didn't know it at the time, but this indulgent little "wait" game I'd taught him would in due course save his life up there on the Backbone Trail.

. . .

Atop a knobby ridge east of Sandstone Peak, I looked down at the Pacific stretching out before us, the Channel Islands visible to the northwest and Catalina barely in view farther south. A gentle, warming breeze spread the savory scents of sage, manzanita, and greasewood, quick sprouters that defied the power of summer fire, ever waiting to ravage these hills.

Scouting the ridge top, Lou kicked up dust from the trail, then played tag with a bumblebee. I put his bowl down and splashed some water into it. "Water!" I called out.

He came over, lapped it up, and then, grinning, dripped water onto my lap. I slapped his dusty butt, played a quick game of tag with him, then dropped down to play "mad dog" in the cool, coppery dirt.

Lou caught scent of something and tracked it over to the next knobby ridge, fifty yards off. I leaned back on a rock to rest while he meandered, sticking his nose into bushes and under rocks.

A red-tailed hawk circled above, perhaps looking for the same thing Lou was. *His eyes against Lou's nose,* I mused, checking on his progress. I could tell he'd caught sight or scent of something by his change in speed and intent; he began to move more passionately, so I casually walked over.

Lou advanced toward a sunny patch of dirt at a turn in the trail. In the middle of the patch lay a twisted, sun-bleached stick, perhaps an improvised walking aid abandoned by another hiker. Lou seemed mystified enough by it to stop and sniff the air.

Then the stick moved.

I boomed out, "Wait!" as loud as I could. He shot me a quizzical look, as if asking, "Since when do sticks move?"

I threw my hands up into the touchdown position. He stopped cold in his tracks, then looked back longingly at the rattlesnake, which hadn't yet made up its mind what to do.

It lay there in the morning sun, warming its sluggish, cold-blooded body. Despite Lou's being four feet away from its business end, it hadn't yet begun to rattle.

Lou's absence of fear suggested that he hadn't crossed paths with any rattlesnakes in his first six months alfresco. Knowing that my shrill retort would but briefly stop him from giving the wiggly stick a good long sniff, I had to act fast. I was not going to lose this dog to a mindless reptile.

"Lou Boy!" I yelled out, the snake on the move, its rattle now clattering like a Cuban maraca. I clapped and teasingly backed down the trail, tempting Lou into a game of "catch me if you can."

He wagged his tail. I could tell from his body posture that catching me had become a more enticing option than an examination of the slithering creature now positioned between us. *Be smart, Lou, be smart,* I thought, clapping and woo-hooing it back down the trail.

The snake coiled to strike. Lou yodeled and reared like a stallion. Then, instead going around the damn viper, he merrily vaulted *over* it, clearing the killer by three feet. The snake made a halfhearted attempt at him, and though it didn't come close, my heart dropped into my shorts when I saw the upward strike.

Lou ran me down in short order. I caught him up in my arms and hugged him, hard. He chortled and licked my neck. He always appreciated a good hug; he'd let you wrap your arms around him and squeeze. You'd feel the life in him, and his fondness for you.

He raised a front leg and slung it up onto my shoulder, completing the embrace. I held on to him for a while. "Showboater," I whispered into his ear.

"Rower."

"Yes," I agreed. *"Rower."*

He peed on a greasewood bush, then grabbed up a thin, fallen limb of oak. "Good stick," I said, waving him over. He had a penchant for chewing on sticks, another holdover from the good old days when puppy toys grew on trees. "Just make sure to check them for movement first."

I leaned back against an oak and pulled out a granola bar. He lay beside me, chewing on the branch. "Here," I said, offering him a sticky pull of the bar. He dropped the limb and caught the offering in one smart flick of his jaws, then got back to working the stick, peeling bark off in strips, then thoughtfully gnawing on the wood.

The branch was too long for him to hold comfortably in his paws. "Give," I said, taking the limb, snapping it, then handing back half. "Better, right?"

He chortled, then got back to whittling. I peeled the bark off my half and gave the stick a nibble. Lou looked surprised, as if I'd discovered some hidden Masonic secret. "Tastes like crap," I said, spitting, the bitter wood like overbrewed green tea.

I pulled out my pocket knife and whittled on my half. He cozied up and we rested there for a time, each whittling on his own stick, thinking about snakes, and each other.

Phyllis from the tutoring agency called. "Have I got a client for you."

"Who now?"

"This one's a VIP."

"Sheik or politician?"

"Celeb."

"That's nothing new," I said.

"This one is."

As I cleared the security gate and drove up the winding cobblestone drive, I glanced at Lou in the rearview mirror. "You'd better be on your best behavior, young man," I said, tossing a cookie back at him. He snapped it out of the air and licked his lips. "Good catch. You'll have to stay in the car for this one, at least for now."

Lou eyed the beautiful Bel-Air mansion, his nose prints plastered all over the window. I maneuvered slowly around the circular drive, parked on its far side, and got out. I was nervous. "Stay here, and be nice and *quiet*."

Left of its entrance lay a perfectly manicured putting green, subtly sloped, with small, flagged pins poking out of two cups. A debonair African American gentleman wearing a crimson smoking jacket stood there holding a putter, golf balls at his feet.

He stroked a ball. I watched it plunk sweetly into the closest hole. Then he came over, the putter held lightly in his hand. "May I help you?"

"Hello, sir. I'm Steve Duno, Anika's new tutor."

"Hello, son," he said graciously, his eyes unblinking, like an eagle's. "You need to speak to my wife, Joanna, about that. Go right in."

"Thank you, sir."

"You are most welcome."

I couldn't shake the feeling that in those few seconds he'd taken my measure. The kid in me wanted to ask a thousand questions—"Would you like to meet my dog?" or, "So, Mr. Poitier, what's your handicap?" Star-struck idiocies to be sure, but this was *Virgil Tibbs,* for chrissakes.

He had many people like me on his periphery, whom he appreciated and showed great kindness to. But we would remain parked in his orbit, like the moon, never closer. He was insulated by his fame and it was palpable, and deserved. But walking into Sidney Poitier's house twice a week was, to say the least, an extraordinary event in my life.

Lou thought it all quite normal. While I tutored Anika inside, he'd laze in the car and watch Mr. Poitier practice his putting.

On warm days I'd tether him to a sprinkler head, and he'd just stay there, chortle a bit, and quietly rate Mr. Poitier's technique.

None of the Poitiers seemed to mind Lou's presence. But most of the time he just stayed in the car or on the cobbled drive, waiting, watching the country's most revered actor stroke golf balls.

As far as I knew, the two icons never did say hello. It was almost as if Lou did not exist for him. Distraction training, maybe. Perhaps they'd shared quiet moments together while I worked inside; I'll have to ask Mr. Poitier if I ever again get the chance. But, looking back, the idea of the world's best dog patiently watching the world's greatest actor practice his putting is a memory worth having.

I'd found Lou in December, when he was about six months old. That put his birth at around June 1989. I assigned June 6 to be his officially celebrated birthday: D-Day, or, perhaps more precisely, Decision Day, the day I'd stuffed his sorry, flea-bitten butt into the back of my car.

Fast approaching his first birthday, Lou grew into his heredity fast. Almost fully grown, he was strong, sleek, and as handsome as any dog I'd ever seen. The reaction most people had to him reflected my feelings about Mr. Poitier: charm and awe. Many felt drawn to yet intimidated by Lou, like moths to a pretty flame.

Those who'd never owned a dog were the funniest to watch with him. I'd have Lou tethered out on the back patio of the Rose Café, near the back entrance; people coming in would suddenly be face-to-face with his presence and the force of personality. They'd warily pat him on the head, and he'd march in place and wag his tail and *rower,* then grin his big grin, and that was it. Sold.

When he really liked someone, he'd breathe in and out like a parked locomotive, slow and cavernous, an acoustic Darth Vader sound that big dogs often make. He'd lean into them, lay a paw atop theirs, gaze up and give his Mother Teresa, and they were his.

Lou grasped early on that greeting patrons in this way guaranteed him a steady supply of leftover croissants, scones, and sandwich crusts. Some of these same canine converts would come in months later with a new puppy in tow, inspired to ownership by the sociable black-and-tan dog with Garbo eyes.

But not everyone at the Rose Café had good intentions. After tethering him to his normal spot one sunny day, I went inside to get some soup. Coming back out, I put down my bowl, grabbed my bread, and took it over to Lou, who appreciated a nice butter-slathered slice of rye.

He was gone.

I looked around. Sometimes a customer who knew Lou would walk him out to pee. No dog in sight. "Lou!" I called out, running out to the parking lot. He was nowhere to be seen.

"Some guys take him," the busboy said, pointing south down Second toward Gold's.

"What guys?"

"Couple guys. They look like bums."

It's one thing if your dog jumps a fence to hunt peacocks but another thing entirely when somebody steals him in broad daylight. You'd expect a New York native to have more sense, but it just never occurred to me that anyone would *take* him. I ran down Second in a panic, ready to knock someone's block off.

I didn't have far to go. Like a scene from a Tom Mix film, there was Lou, happily trotting back up the street, his two dog-napers hot on his trail, trying to step on the leash. I ran toward them at a full sprint, ready to kick some ass.

Up to now, Lou must have thought it all a game. But when he saw me running full tilt and screaming like a crazed Celt, something clicked in his head. He smelled my rage and realized at that moment that the pack was in trouble. And wow, was I in for a surprise.

I picked up the end of the leash, then turned to face the two scuzzballs, taller and heavier than I (what else is new). But I was fuming mad and ready.

"Gimme that dog!" the bigger one slurred, his stench like summer Dumpster. They both had orange "street" tans and sounded half tanked.

Before my eyes, another Lou emerged. He wheeled, took a braced stance in front of me, and snarled like a creature from the third circle of hell. It began down deep, swelled with passion, then exploded out of him in a frothing, head-shaking detonation of sound and fury. It scared the piss out of them and me. Who the hell was this?

Lou snarled and strained at the leash. He wanted to dismember them, render them. He looked like the bronze bull on Wall Street. Lou's jaws snapped out, the sound like axes biting into wood. I couldn't hold on much longer and suddenly realized that he would *kill* these two.

Lou and I advanced on the idiots. He stood up on his hind legs, growled, snapped, and jabbed out with his front paws.

"Hit the road or I let him go!"

I didn't need to repeat myself. As the leash began to slip from my hands, they ran off like Monty Python characters and disappeared down Sunset Avenue, past Gold's.

A crowd of muscled men in front of the Gold's Gym parking lot applauded. I hugged Lou, who was breathing hard and still worked up. "Good boy," I said, choking up a little. "You did good."

Back at the Rose Café, another crowd waited outside the parking-lot entrance. They were all fond of Lou and he sensed it. He smiled and licked at them and understood now how some people were good and others bad, and that the best dogs could tell the difference, the best dogs could figure it out.

He'd protected me and shown what he was capable of, that he had the courage and the judgment. I don't think I'd ever felt as safe or loved in my entire life.

I liked my tutoring job. I actually focused less on teaching and more on getting kids organized; they needed to see that with the right groundwork, the panic and failure born of poor preparation just melted away. Basically, my mantra was "don't study longer—study smarter."

The first thing I had kids do was clean up their rooms. Parents loved that. I even made them organize their desks, do their laundry, and make out lists of daily chores. Most of these kids didn't even *do* chores, which in my humble opinion contributed to the overall problem. The kids appreciated me, too, not only as their academic secret weapon but because when they actually did achieve something, I was there to validate it to their parents.

When I tutored, I often had to search out the right motivation to get a kid interested; be it sports, food, games, or even pets, there was always something to light a fire under even the most recalcitrant kid's butt. That's just what I did with Lou, and what I do now with the dogs I train. I never shared this child/dog analogy with parents, but they'd see it in action whenever I brought Lou into their homes to use as a prop or learning tool.

A tutor who came equipped with his own dog genius—it was invaluable. I'd plant Lou in a sit position in the middle of the living room, then have him perform a bevy of tricks and behaviors, responding just to hand signals. The kids thought I was Gandalf. Parents began asking me to train not only their kids but their dogs as well.

I began working with a middle-school student in Santa Monica, to help him with basic study skills and organization. Smart and good-hearted, he had "clutter head" and needed me to come in and line up his ducks.

I smelled the Pacific from the car. So did Lou; he pointed his nose west and sampled the salty onshore breeze.

In this beautiful, airy home close to Ocean Avenue, Noah's room looked like a monkey convention had just checked out. "Get a rake," I kidded him, picking a T-shirt up off the carpet and tossing it at Lou. It caught on his tail and flagged around as he inspected the room, sniffing and licking at things.

"You're making me clean my room?" he asked, freeing the shirt from Lou's tail. Noah was a dog lover; you could see it in the easy way he related to Lou.

"And make your bed and do your laundry."

"Seriously?"

"Yep."

"Can I do homework instead?"

"That's the spirit. Let's do both."

We cleaned and organized while Lou savored a bone I'd stuffed with string cheese. In fifteen minutes we could see the floor and the surface of Noah's desk.

"Good job. I'll be here Tuesdays and Thursdays at four. Your first assignment is to make sure the room is clean before I come."

"Will you bring Lou again?"

"Once in a while. You know he's in school, too, sort of."

"Like obedience school?"

"Yeah, except that it's just me teaching him."

"So you teach kids and dogs."

"Apparently."

"Which do you like teaching more?"

I was afraid he'd ask me that. Truth was, though I had more

experience teaching kids, I preferred working with Lou. Kids were tangles of motivations and emotions that needed unraveling before they could learn anything. But Lou *wanted* to learn. He learned even when I wasn't teaching him. Like when he figured out how to open doors, drawers, cupboards, and even windows (instead of jumping through them). Or when he began to help pick Mr. Zagalia's Italian plums right off the tree in our back-yard, or when he'd drag the garden hose over to me when he wanted a drink. He was an easy student.

"I like teaching Lou because he's smart, and because he learns so fast. Teaching him is easy. But I like teaching kids, too. It's just a little harder."

"He's such a cool dog."

"He sure is. Now let's work on your chores list, then get your daily planner set up."

I was waiting in the kitchen for Noah to get home from school when a lithe young woman in a T-shirt and sweats came in and began to make tea. She looked no older than twenty-five and was tall, with a bashful, beautiful smile and ruffled blond hair down in her eyes.

"I'm Steve, Noah's tutor," I said.

"I'm his aunt Daryl. He really likes you."

"Except when I make him clean his room."

She laughed and dipped her tea bag into the water. "Every-body appreciates you helping out with his classes. He passes ev-erything now."

"I always try to put myself out of business," I said, suddenly realizing who I was talking to.

"You know, I think my sister Page could use your help, too. She's going back to college and is having trouble filling out her admissions form."

"Be glad to help. By the way, I'm a big fan. Sorry if I didn't recognize you at first."

"Oh, I don't mind."

Daryl Hannah makes tea ten feet away from me and I don't recognize her until she speaks.

Noah filled me in later. "Aunt Daryl is my mother's stepsister. She lives down the street with Jackson Browne. She and Page come over all the time."

"I thought she was the babysitter," I confessed. Lou was on his back, paddling at the air with his front paws.

"She doesn't wear makeup unless she's going out," he said, kneeling beside Lou, playing patty-cake with him.

"Rower."

"What does *rower* mean?"

"It's his way of saying, 'This is fun.' "

"Does he ever bark?"

"Only if I ask him to, or when absolutely necessary."

"Like if he has to pee?"

"No—more like if something bad is happening."

"Like what?"

I told him the story about the kidnapers at the Rose Café. He stopped rubbing Lou's belly and pointed to him.

"This dog?"

"Can you believe it?"

"That is *so cool!*"

He'd never fail a class again.

I stopped at a Culver City 7-Eleven for a cup of coffee before my first afternoon tutoring session. Parked in the far-right parking space, I sipped coffee and pored over prep notes for my new student. Lou sat in the back of the Civic; I tried to bring him along whenever I had a new kid to win over.

I'd popped open both back vent windows for Lou and had my driver's-side window cracked. Customers came and went; I didn't pay much attention.

Lou stuck his nose out the window and sniffed the air. When he took an interest in something, the volume and speed of his inhalations would ramp up for a few seconds to build up scent in his nasal cavity. Then he'd stop abruptly, like a sleep-apnea patient. The pause let him savor the scent, in the way an oenophile swishes wine around in his mouth, then stops to let it bathe the taste buds.

His breathing ramped up. I focused on my notes. Lou let the odors settle in his nasal cavity to tell their story.

Humans cannot smell bad intent. Lou could.

A low rumble, like the detonations of a distant Harley. For a moment, I could not identify it as dog generated. But as it intensified, it became plain that Lou was the source.

I turned to look back at him. Lou stared intently out the window, his happy face gone, transformed into a Cujo snarl, lips pulled back to show bright, curved fangs.

The aggression he'd shown with the dognapers had been overt and dramatic, but this was more primitive, as if he'd sensed a seminal threat, something extraordinary. I felt transported back in time to some imminent primordial battle.

Three passengers in an old blue Pontiac convertible parked beside us argued in Spanish. Though I understood some, I couldn't make out what the row was about. Lou believed that something bad was about to happen, so I abandoned my notes and paid attention to the three young Latinos, two thin men and a short, heavy woman.

The thin guy in the front passenger seat opened the Pontiac's long, heavy door. I watched to ensure that he didn't dent my car.

He turned his back on me and slammed the door shut. The

grip and hammer of a large-caliber, chromed revolver protruded from the waistband of his jeans.

"Damn."

Lou's rolling snarl ratcheted up. The guy pulled the gun from his waistband. It was a big gun. He took a step toward the front door, then shot me a look that cooled my blood.

"Hup," I said to Lou. He jumped up into the front passenger seat.

The guy's eyes trailed off as he and the other two walked into the 7-Eleven.

How had Lou known? I've asked myself that many times. Though dogs can often be race bigots, he certainly had no issues with Latinos, who regularly fed him enchiladas and chips at the taquería. Had he smelled their nerves? What did an armed robber smell like? Perhaps he'd recalled a similar odor from puppy-hood, when some irate property owner had taken a shot at him and his garbage-eating pack.

I don't know why or how he knew. But had he not snarled out his warning, I probably would have sat there with my nose buried in my notes, oblivious to the whole scene.

I could have sat there and minded my own business, or driven away. But I didn't like the idea of a minimum-wage clerk getting his head blown off for a hundred bucks. And I'd always had a flair for the self-righteous, and evidently so did Lou.

This was 1990, before cell phones, so dialing 911 meant walking over to a bank of pay phones just to the right of the entrance. A quick dial and a fast caveat to the operator—twenty seconds tops, I thought.

"Come on, Lou."

We went out the passenger door. I held Lou by his collar. His snarls telegraphed from his throat to the collar and into my hand.

He had no intention of walking nicely. This time he pulled,

hard. Something inside him, something new, rose to the occasion. He wanted to get into that store. He had a job to do.

"Easy, Lou," I said, holding him with my left, grabbing the receiver with my right and setting it onto my shoulder. If I'd let go of him right then, he'd have rocketed through the air to the door.

"Nine one one. What kind of emergency are you reporting?"

"Three armed Latinos just walked into the 7-Eleven on Washington Boulevard., a few blocks north of Sepulveda."

"Where are you, sir?"

"At a pay phone outside the store."

"Is that at Huron and Washington?"

"I think so."

"Can you see them right now?"

"No, they're in the store. I saw one gun."

"Please stay on the line, sir. Units are on their way."

"They'll probably be out in a few seconds."

"Can you describe them, sir?"

"Three Latinos under twenty-five, two skinny males and a heavy female. White T-shirts, I think. The guy in the front passenger seat had a large-caliber revolver stuck into the waistband of his jeans. Chromed, maybe a .357."

"What type of vehicle are they driving?"

"Old blue Pontiac convertible, maybe a LeMans."

"Can you read the plate number?"

"No. I think it's up on the dash."

She kept me on the line, asking questions, doing her job. Lou pulled my arm taut, growling and barking.

"Quiet."

"Sir?"

"Not you. I have my dog with me. He's the one that alerted me to them in the first place."

"Is the dog under control, sir?"

"Yes," I said. I hadn't thought about that. What would the cops do upon seeing Lou seething and frothing on the end of my dislocated arm? "He is under control."

"Are the individuals still in the store, sir?"

They came out. The guy who'd looked at me walked by and stared at Lou. Lou erupted.

"Sir, what is happening?"

"No, Mary, I think I'll have to reschedule the meeting."

"Are they right there, sir?"

"That's right, Mary," I said, Lou straining and barking, spittle flying, the guy five feet away, his gun now tucked into the front of his waistband.

"Units are almost there, sir. Are you safe?"

"Don't be silly, Mary."

He looked at me, then at Lou. I felt idiotic, and terrified. The guy stepped closer. I wanted to ask if he was in the Culver City Boyz.

Lou was all that stood between me and a bullet. I felt like Gary Cooper drawing down on Frank Miller, not with a Colt .45 but with my beautiful, smart, lovable black-and-tan year-old Rottweiler mix, ready to spring, able to judge in an instant who was good and who was bad.

Lou was enraged, and fearless. The guy looked me in the eye and closed the gap, giving Lou a chance. Two more steps and he'd never have the chance to pull his gun in time. I loosened my grip on Lou's collar. He begged me to let go.

"*Venga!*" the woman said, getting into the Pontiac.

His hand rested on the grip, his eyes on Lou. I'm not sure what went through his head—he probably wondered if it was worth killing a dog and a man, or if he even had enough time to aim and fire before the brawny dog three feet away grabbed him by his skinny neck and throttled him. If he'd shot me first instead of Lou, he would have been dog food.

He sneered, let go of the grip of the gun, and headed for the car. I dropped the receiver and dragged Lou around the corner of the store, expecting a white-hot stab in the back. Nothing. The Pontiac rumbled to life and pulled out. No shots. I was alive. Lou was alive. I leaned against the wall and hugged Lou. His tension ebbed. "Jesus Christ, Lou. Jesus Christ."

A cop came around the corner, gun drawn. Tall, tense, chest puffed out under his vest. I sat there hugging Lou, who smiled at the cop and began to wag his tail. He didn't seem to mind the cop's gun at all.

"Are you Steve Duno?" he asked, gun still drawn.

"Yes, sir. And this is my dog, Lou. He saved my life."

Other units pulled up; soon the place was alive with officers. Lou pranced around. I rubbed his neck. Happy Lou was back.

After explaining to several officers what had happened, a plain-clothes detective handed me a coffee and questioned me.

"Did anyone get hurt inside?" I asked.

"No shots were fired," he said, his hand finding Lou's head. He definitely owned a dog.

"Did they rob the store?"

"I can't go into details. But you did great. And your dog, too," he added, cupping Lou's face in his hands and looking down at him. "Good-looking dog."

"He saved my life."

"Maybe he did."

I told him what had happened when the three came out of the store. He looked down at Lou again. "Maybe *he* should work for us."

A uniformed officer came over and spoke to the detective. In a moment he came back over to me.

"The suspects you described were pulled over on Venice Boulevard. a minute ago. We need you to ID them. Can you do that?"

"Can I drop Lou off at the house first?"

"No time. Just take him with you in the unit."

"I see Culver City Boyz around here all the time. I don't want to get shot buying a burrito on Sepulveda."

"They're not Culver City Boyz. Their plates ran back to Torrance. And the Culver City Boyz would never rob a 7-Eleven on their own turf. If they found out, you and your dog would be heroes."

"Okay, I'll do it," I said. *I'll rat out the rival gang, those bastards.*

"You'll be in the unit the whole time, and we'll shine the spotlight on them. They won't see you at all."

"Let's do it."

Lou and I climbed into the backseat of a black-and-white. We headed east on Washington to Overland, made a left, then turned east onto Venice. A few blocks up, in the median, I saw police activity.

"They didn't get far," I said to the cops. Lou sat beside me, ears perked, sniffing at the shotgun, looking like a rookie K9 officer.

"Not many old Pontiac convertibles around," the driver said.

"They should have taken the freeway," I said as we pulled up, the Pontiac on our left.

Lou became animated and attentive. When he saw the three suspects cuffed and leaned up against the convertible, he woofed a few times and started to grumble.

"That's proof enough for me," said the driver.

"He really does not like them," I said.

The three looked scarcely out of high school. An officer outside had them line up and face our car. Lou flexed, growled, and wedged his wet nose out the cracked-open window as the driver of our unit turned the car's spotlight onto the suspects, who seemed undaunted, almost bored. The skinny kid tried to turn from the light, but the cop shook his head and pointed to our car.

"Are they the ones?"

"Oh yeah. And the skinny kid on the left—he had the revolver."

"Are you sure it was a revolver?" asked the passenger cop.

"Chrome- or nickel-plated, big caliber, black grip."

The cops looked at each other and smiled. "That's it. Good job. We'll take you back to your car now."

Back at the 7-Eleven, Lou and I said our goodbyes to the two cops. "You'll probably get a call from the detectives in a few days," said the driver.

"Will I have to testify?"

"I doubt it. They got caught red-handed, and they were armed. The clerk indentified them, too."

"Thanks, guys."

"Great dog. He's still young; he could be a great police dog."

"I think today's experience will suffice."

They both shook my hand and gave Lou rubs on his head. He grinned and licked at them.

"*Rower,*" he chortled, sniffing intently at both cops' legs.

"You guys must have dogs at home."

"Shepherd."

"Lab."

"He knows," I said. "Thanks."

We got in the car and drove home. I canceled my tutoring sessions for the evening, then got down on the floor with Lou, who chewed lazily on a bone beside me, as if nothing had happened. I felt like calling Nancy but decided to wait. I wanted to be there with Lou for a while.

6

Rocky Mountain Lou

He claims you're his secret weapon," said Noah's mother, Judy. He'd finished up the school year with great grades, and everyone was stoked.

"Stealth tutor."

"My stepsister Page is also grateful for your help with her college-entrance paperwork."

"You should adopt me," I said.

In the homes where I tutored, I often melded into the family routine, and often was treated like an uncle or big brother. I'd walk in unannounced, raid the fridge, wander the house. I had even been trusted with the security codes to gated mansions in

Bel-Air and Beverly Hills, and got fed almost every night. It was cush.

"The spare room awaits."

I could get used to living in Daryl Hannah's stepsister's house. I'd wake up early and make coffee and Daryl and Page would come over and we'd chitchat about the business and dogs and Lou would *rower* and do tricks and flash his Garbos and star in Daryl's next film about a superhuman dog hero from Canis Major; he'd support me and let me write my great American novel.

"I told Noah he has to read at least one book over the summer."

"Speaking of summer, would you like to borrow the keys to our condo for a week?"

"What?"

"As a perk for helping Noah."

"Condo?"

"In Telluride."

"Get out."

"We ski in the winter but the place goes empty for much of the summer. What do you think?"

"Sure," I said, dumbfounded. I knew I could use a vacation, and a road trip with Lou, Nancy, and some friends would fit the bill. "That's so nice of you."

"I'll get the keys."

We rented a Ford station wagon, stuffed Lou's crate into the back, and took off for a ten-day adventure. Nancy liked road trips as much as I did, and Lou, with his cast-iron bladder and calm, curious road manners, was nearly trouble-free in the car. And this time he was flea-free.

The plan was to drive north on Interstate 15 to Barstow, then east on Interstate 40 all the way to Flagstaff, Arizona, where we'd meet up with my friend Dean and his wife, Kim. They'd fly into Pulliam Airport from Houston, and we'd pick them up and head northeast, through Four Corners and on into Colorado.

Dean and I had taken many a road trip together over the years, but we hadn't been together since a motorcycle trip to Yellowstone in 1988, at about the time that lightning started a forest fire that would crisp over a million acres of the nation's first national park. We'd shared many strange times on the road, including driving a school bus filled with biology students and live reptile specimens through thirteen inches of snow in northern Arizona, nearly getting shot by a state-patrol officer in Texas, and almost getting arrested at the El Paso/Juarez border for refusing to pay duty on two bottles of Johnnie Walker Black Label. I hoped we'd have better luck at the Hannah condo in Telluride.

Past Barstow, the traffic thinned; we made good enough time and weren't worried about making our rendezvous with Dean and Kim the next day in Flagstaff.

"You think he's okay back there?" asked Nancy, looking back to Lou's crate.

"He loves his crate. We'll stop enough to let him stretch and take care of business."

"He loves to do his business."

"That he does."

Lou still had his "equipment." It was 1990: the drive to neuter dogs hadn't quite gone viral yet, and people weren't as aware of the pet-overpopulation problem. And except for the two-month fostering of a terrier mix named Betty in college, I'd had no dog experience, and really didn't know any better. There was also that visceral "guy" component—men simply do not like to emasculate their dogs. Lou was clearly the swashbuckling, adventurous type, and after the incident at the 7-Eleven I felt that castrating him would have been a betrayal of our brotherly union. He'd wait until he was almost three to get his eunuch endorsement.

We stopped often to let Lou out and to enjoy the high-desert scenery. Lou befriended truckers (perhaps as an homage to that first jittery long-hauler who'd nearly taken him on that first day) and families with kids at rest stops. When a cute toddler and his grandfather walked up to him near a restroom, Lou sat politely, then gently laid a paw atop the little boy's head, as if to proclaim, "You are now my friend." The boy giggled, took a fast lick in the face, then looked at Lou and said, "You so silly!" Lou *rowered* and licked him again, his granddad looking on.

"Nice dog you got there. Looks like Victor Mature."

"He gets Tyrone Power a lot, too."

"Yep, yep. Not Bogart, though."

"No," I agreed. "Lou's way better-looking than Bogart."

"He did get the ladies, though. Darndest thing."

He and the boy walked back to their car. Lou watched them go.

"Yes, yes—you're just a big flirt," said Nancy to Lou as she walked over from the ladies' room. "Let's hit the road, boys."

With its high-desert feel mixed with scrub-pine forests and rich red-rock cliffs, northern Arizona fit my eye. As we entered Flagstaff, I recalled how, fifteen years prior, Dean and I had driven that old blue school bus packed with drowsy college kids and desert reptile specimens north into Flagstaff during a spring blizzard that would dump thirteen inches of snow in four hours. One of the best drivers I know, he'd steered the old bus around overturned semis and stranded cars. A few hours earlier, we'd been roasting in the Sonoran Desert.

"Duno, I can't see the road."

"Can you see the mountains on each side of it?" I asked, sitting beside him on an old milk box.

"Barely."

"Just steer in between them. And don't slow down."

"It's like nuclear winter out here," Dean said as we drove by a trucker struggling to chain up his rig, ice hanging like tinsel from his beard.

A motel appeared. Dean swerved into the parking lot and slid the bus into a foot of new powder.

"We're very stuck," he said, shutting it down.

Everyone on the bus sprang to life and made for the motel office. Dean and I were left to fend for the snakes, toads, geckos, and tortoises that would have died out there in the cold.

"This sucks," he said, sliding a near-comatose Sonoran whip snake into a gym sock and wrapping it around his waist.

We stuffed our pockets with socked reptiles and lay head-to-toe, one atop the other, in the only bunk on the bus—a slab of cushioned plywood. Covered by a dozen abandoned sleeping bags, we fell asleep in a bus in the Arizona snow, our pocketed creepers writhing in appreciation.

That adventure rushed back to me as Nancy, Lou, and I drove through Flagstaff on our way to Pulliam, a neat one-runway jetport nestled in the burnished Arizona hills, the garnet mountains against the azure sky, the air pure and dry.

"You're late," I said to Dean, who was a head taller than any other passengers at baggage claim. His wife, Kim, a fit, pretty Texas native, muscled their bags off the conveyor belt.

"Anything to delay the inevitability of spending a week with you," he said, giving me a brotherly shove.

'Where's Nancy?" asked Kim, appalled at the possibility of having to spend the week with two college buddies telling the same mummified stories over and over.

"At the car with Lou."

"What did you rent?" asked Dean, ever the Jersey gear head.

"Sable wagon."

"Joy."

"Needed room for the two of you and the dog."

"So I finally get to meet the destroyer."

"He's a different dog now—just wait," I said, knowing that Dean would appreciate Lou immensely.

I told them about the armed robbery and how Lou had protected me. Approaching the car, Nancy let go of Lou's leash; he ran for me, then veered toward Dean and Kim and began his prancing-stallion greeting dance.

"Hey, Luigi!" said Dean, playing a quick game of tag with him. Lou liked Dean instantly; for his entire life he could judge people faster than any other dog or human I've ever met, as if character were a cologne.

"He's handsome," said Kim, unable to avoid a stealthy lick to her face.

"This dog stared down a .357?" asked Dean. "Thought he'd be bigger."

"He changes size from moment to moment," I said. "One minute he's guarding the gates of hell, and the next, he fits into the palm of your hand."

"Looks like a guy in a dog suit," said Dean, staring into Lou's eyes. Lou slapped a paw down onto Dean's size-thirteen Converse. "I am chosen."

The drive to Telluride improved with every mile. Dwarf pines gave way to lodgepole, fir, ponderosa, spruce, alder, larch, and aspen. Rolling red hills turned into toothy, snowcapped mountains. As we climbed, pockets of snow appeared by the roadside, the runoff from them trickling onto the sunlit road in glistening streaks. As we passed an oblong hollow of snow, Lou shuffled around and whined.

"Has he seen snow yet?" asked Dean, scratching Lou through the crate window.

"Not unless it snows in Mendocino," said Nancy.

"He might just be one of those snow-crazed mutts," said Dean as we climbed higher up into the mountains. It was true:

some dogs had a blissful fixation on snow and would leap and buck with joy when given the chance to play in it.

I pulled over at the next turnoff and parked. We got out to stretch. I ducked Kim's snowball and let Lou out. He made a beeline for a crescent of dirty, wet snow and pranced through it, tossed snow up into the air, bit at it joyously.

Like marshmallow to a baby, snow was a new element to Lou, and he played in it the way Kansas kids do on their first trip to the sea. Lou leaped and pounced, did 360s in the air, grabbed mouthfuls of snow, flicked them up high, then batted at them with a paw on their way down.

"He's blissing," said Kim,

"Having a snowball fight with himself," said Nancy, trying to snap a photo.

"Get a job!" yelled Dean, tossing a snowball at Lou.

Sooner than I knew, he would.

The Hannahs' second-floor Telluride condo had mountain views straight out of a John Ford flick. "Where do they keep the oxygen canisters?" asked Dean, panting like an asthmatic. I had trouble catching my breath, too. We all lived at sea level, and Telluride's elevation of eighty-seven hundred feet was literally taking our breath away.

"How are we going to hike up to Blue Lake?" I asked, guessing that at the lake's elevation of 12,200 feet, the air would hold half the oxygen we were used to.

"Big baby," said Kim, flicking my shoulder. She'd been putting in three days a week at the gym, including aerobics classes and miles of jogging; her legs and wit were both hard as teak.

"Yes, I am a baby. Babies require air."

We settled into the Hannah condo. I claimed Daryl's room for the sole purpose of being able to declare for the rest of my life that I had in fact slept in Daryl Hannah's bed. With Nancy, of course, if anyone pressed.

Lou sniffed out every corner and lingered on a few spots, surely left by dogs or cats that the Hannahs had brought up. I watched him scent and stare off pensively, as one might while swishing fine cognac around in the mouth.

"Pomeranian or bunny?" I asked him. He gave me a look, then followed a scent trail into the kitchen, where he deftly slapped open a pantry cupboard. Inside sat a near-empty bag of dog food.

"Good call, Sherlock," I said, stowing the bag up high. He looked at me, incredulous that his tracking expertise had not been rewarded. "You don't eat this stuff. It'll give you the runs."

But I found it, he surely thought, irritated. When Lou got annoyed, he'd lie down with his face on his paws and just stare at you. So I got out a big cookie from his food pack and tossed it to him. He snatched it out of the air, then went over into a corner to crunch it down, still miffed, I gathered, from the sullied look.

Nancy and I lay in bed that night (Daryl Hannah's bed), talking over the big hike we'd take the next day, up to the alpine Blue Lake, nestled nearly four thousand feet above Telluride.

"It's nearly a mile-elevation increase over an eight-mile trail," I said, picturing the geometry in my head. "That's got to be a seven- or eight-degree incline the whole way, with half the oxygen."

"Steep," she said as Lou crawled under the bed, his favorite new sleeping place.

"It's suicide. Kim is going to kill us all."

"It'll be fun coming down," she said, ever the optimist.

"Only Kim will make it down. The rest of us will perish."

"Kim and Lou," she said. Lou stuck out his head and peered up at us.

"Even he might not be ready for this."

"He's a year-old dog. He'll be just fine."

"At twelve thousand feet?"

"It won't even faze him."

Lou crawled out and sat beside my side of the bed. *"Roo."*

"Whose turn is it?" I asked.

"He chose you," she said, pulling the covers over her head. "Come on, Lou."

Outside, it was crisp and clear and colder than I'd expected, with a scent of something clean in the air, evergreen or river water—something fresh and big and soaring, as if everything sweet and fragrant in the world started up high then drifted down the Colorado mountainsides to the rest of us.

Lou reveled in the new scents. He sniffed at every bush, tree, and patch of grass, anointing all, scratch-marking in the dirt and stopping a downy feather with his paw as it drifted down the street on an invisible wisp of mountain air.

Near a dirt path on the outskirts, I unclipped his leash and he trotted up the path toward a stand of aspen and alder. Watching him laze into the tree line, I recalled when I'd first seen him, his feral pack slipping into the forest like ninjas, Lou tagging along as he'd always done, then stopping and listening to a flash of intuition inside his puppy head, an idea that perhaps his future lay elsewhere. I watched him now in the woods of Colorado, confident that I was his family now and that we would be joined at the hip for a dog's life. And I knew he felt the same.

Kim stormed up the fire road as if prodded by a bayonet. Though just as winded as I, Dean's thirty-six-inch inseams helped him keep pace with his aerobically enhanced wife. Nancy and I did all we could to keep up, while Lou happily alternated between couples. He kept an eye out for all of us.

I ducked down behind a boulder. Lou stormed back to find me

amid Kim's admonitions for us to keep pace. Later, Lou darted off-trail, then returned with a repulsive residue all over his lips. "What did he catch?" asked Nancy, wiping off his mouth.

"We're on a need-to-know basis."

"His breath smells like liver and garbage."

"His favorites," I said, brushing dirt off his back.

"Duno!"

"Coming, Satan," I called out to Kim.

She granted us a five-minute rest every twenty. After only fifteen minutes of hard hiking, I felt sure that I had altitude sickness coming on: headache, nausea, exhaustion, and breathlessness. It felt as if I had a bag of bricks on my back.

"Why am I carrying his food and water?" I asked Nancy, pointing at Lou with a granola bar. Lou had been carrying a stick for a few minutes but had dropped it when he realized that no one had the strength to throw it for him.

"I told you to buy that dog-backpack thingy."

"He was mortified by it when I tried it on him at the store."

"How do you know?"

"You know—when he stares at the floor?" If Lou felt that you were being unfair, he'd avert his gaze and wander off to stew. He'd behaved like an eight-year-old in church clothes that day, so I'd saved myself the thirty bucks and left without the pack.

I had to cart nearly a gallon of water, two sandwiches, an apple, a bag of trail mix, a windbreaker, binoculars, a camera, maps, a bird book, a compass, a knife, a first-aid kit, and a pound of dog food, all at nearly ten thousand feet. I quit wondering who the domesticated animals were.

Kim was relentless. I wanted to hobble her, ball-and-chain her, tie her to a log—anything to slow her down. She was right, of course: if we didn't keep such a harried pace, we'd never get back before nightfall. But those five-minute breaks took forever to come and a minute to go.

"I hate you," I declared during the next break, breathing so hard that I couldn't drink from my canteen.

Kim smiled. "You're weak."

"You're a Klingon."

"You're a hobbit."

"Orc."

"Germ."

"Quiet, you two," said Dean. He and Nancy would clearly play the parents on the trip.

I poured water out for Lou into a small plastic dish. He lapped it up, then dribbled all over me.

"You should be more like Lou," said Kim.

"You should be less like him."

"Stop," said Dean. "Come on, let's get to the falls."

The trail leading up to Blue Lake passed by Bridal Veil Falls, a stunning, four-hundred-foot-high, two-pronged waterfall about an hour's walk from Telluride. During the summer, many hiked, biked, or even four-wheeled up there to catch a glimpse of the cascade, which in early summer swelled with snowmelt. The trail consisted mainly of Jeep tracks and old mining roads tied together in a loosely maintained, winding path, allowing quite a bit of traffic. Past the falls, though, the crowds thinned and the trail to Blue Lake got serious.

Rounding a switchback, we came into view of the falls, its waters pouring down, the mist cooling us. Lou licked at the air.

"That's wild," said Dean.

"Worth the trip," said Nancy, carefully walking atop rocks wetted by the spray.

"Like a Brooklyn hydrant in July," I said.

"What?"

"Never mind, Kim."

Lou trotted up to a group of three coming down the trail, all staring at the ground like haggard soldiers. The lead woman let the back of her hand brush across Lou's back as she walked by. He sniffed at her legs, then *rowered* happily.

"Nice dog," she uttered, the two men with her quiet, mournful.

"Thanks. He's just a good-time Charlie."

With a weak smile, she walked on, the men in tow.

"They're finished," I said. Lou followed them down the trail for a few yards, then came back and stared while I bit into my first sandwich. "What?"

"He wants to keep going," said Kim.

"He wants my turkey sandwich."

"Can't you eat and walk?"

"Let's enjoy the view for a second," I said, looking at Dean, who shrugged. "Look at the old power plant up at the top."

"Blue Lake," she said, hoisting her pack. "Come on, Lou."

She and the dog bolted off. "Kim's a cyborg," I said.

"Don't piss her off, Duno," warned Dean. "She's on a mission."

Lou walked with Kim for a while, then unexpectedly shot up the slanted trunk of a downed fir tree, hot after something. He could climb like a monkey.

"How does he do that?" asked Dean, watching as Lou shimmied and sniffed his way up the coarse, ridged bark of the big tree. A tiny red pine squirrel scurried down the underside of the trunk right below Lou, who did an amazing 180-degree turn atop the fir, then reached down with one paw while holding on to the trunk with the other three.

"He almost got him," said Dean, the squirrel leaping down into the brush and Lou hot on his tail.

"Lou—leave it!" I said. He put on the brakes and glared at me.

"He thinks you're nuts," said Dean.

"He's eaten enough squirrel meat in his life," I said, tossing Lou a cookie.

.   .   .

On we went on our march of doom, led by Darth Kim and the squirrel hunter up into the tall trees. The fire roads and Jeep trails narrowed and turned into woodland switchbacks on the way to the alpine area above, the air bonier with each step. Kim and Dean widened the gap between us; Nancy and I trudged on, wondering if we were still technically having fun. Lou kept up his hiking diplomacy, alternating between couples.

"I think I'm bleeding internally."

"You're not," Nancy said, gasping.

"You don't look so good."

"Neither do you. You look like a heroin addict."

"I feel like I'm climbing up a down escalator."

"I'm so thirsty."

We took an unscheduled break. Lou trotted back to us and sat, expecting food.

"Duno!"

"Don't answer," whispered Nancy.

"I can't—I'm too tired."

Lou sidled up to me and plopped his head onto my thigh. "Spin right," I asked. I'd been working on the trick for a day or so. He thought about it, then spun gracefully to his right, so I gave him a piece of my crust. "Good spin."

"When did he learn that?" she asked.

"His light went on last night. He and I couldn't sleep, so we worked on it. He'll do it in either direction, and with a hand sign, too. Try it."

She took a piece of my bread. "Spin left! Good boy. Spin right! Good boy, Lou!"

I showed her the hand signals for "spin," small, fast clockwise or counterclockwise movements of my hand. She motioned to him silently and he spun both ways.

"When is he going for his learner's permit?" she asked.

I thought about it.

"Duno!"

We hiked for what seemed like days. Switchback after switchback until the tree line came into sight. Even Kim had slowed down.

My legs felt like sacks of mud. Only Lou seemed undaunted: he'd begun to question why I was moving like a sloth up a ladder. He trotted over, dropped into play posture, and dared me into a game of tag.

"Go tease Kim," I said, so he did, bolting off and circling Kim and Dean, then walking backward in front of them.

"How'd you get him to do that?" asked Nancy.

"He understands English."

"No, really."

"I don't know; it's Lou, for God's sake," I said, taking note of his backward walking, which I would end up teaching him to perform on command. That's how Lou learned most things: he'd do something on his own, then I'd just watch for it and strengthen it with food and praise.

Dean turned to look at me. "Duno, what is he doing?" he called out, bent over and sounding like an emphysema patient.

"He's teasing you."

"There's a command for that?"

"Evidently."

At almost twelve thousand feet, the trees surrendered to the alpine meadows. Wildflowers and lichen and boulder fields artfully strewn, the sky a piercing blue, and the air so lean that your lungs could barely get a grip on it.

The beauty overcame our fatigue and lightened the mood. Even Lou, who had tired of the asphyxiating temper of the last hour, came alive again, trotting ahead, sniffing everything, scouting marmot holes and mounting car-size, sun-bleached boulders.

Fat, chestnut-colored marmots played hide-and-seek with him but disappeared permanently when they saw how keen he'd gotten at catching one of them.

"We're almost there," Nancy said, gasping, the end of the trail now clear. Ahead lay the egg-shaped lake cradled within stony mountain walls, the pure white snow lacing down their steep sides gracefully melting down into water cold as steel.

"It's unreal," said Nancy.

"Worth the trip, right, Duno?" asked Kim.

"Yeah—too bad my vision is blurred," I said, wheezing.

The only other dog we saw on the climb appeared, a Greater Swiss Mountain Dog, older than Lou but still young, and thirty pounds heavier. His owner sat by the water's edge, skipping stones.

Lou bolted off to greet them. I wasn't worried at all, as he was all but invulnerable to harm from other dogs, who simply couldn't catch him.

"Is that wise?" asked Dean.

"He'll be fine. Watch."

Instead of bolting right up to the big dog, Lou did a strafing run to lure him into a chase, which let him judge the dog's strength, speed, and intent. I watched as he flew by; the woman's big dog took off after him, protective at first, his hackles raised ever so slightly. But quickly his hackles flattened and his tail and ears came up. Lou let the dog catch up and give him a whiff and a shove. Then Lou splashed into the frigid waters of the lake, tempting his new friend in.

"They'll be fine now," I said to Dean. "He's gone to school on him."

"What do you mean?"

"Figured him out. Knows he's friendly enough. He just needed to separate the dog from his master."

"Why?"

"Because otherwise he'd have been too defensive. He wouldn't have been himself. Look at them now."

The dogs boxed by the shoreline, teasing, splashing, and cutting hard, sand and pebbles spraying up in all directions, the new dog barking happily and Lou smiling and teasing. I greeted the owner, who seemed happy that her dog had someone to play with.

"They're perfect for each other," she said.

"And we don't have to run around," I said.

"It's exhausting even to watch," she said. "It's taken me half an hour just to stop panting."

"So you're not from here, either."

"Portland."

"L.A."

"We have normal air to breathe."

"Well," I said, "that's debatable, at least in my case."

We rested, drank water, and ate a bit. I felt better. Lou and the other dog played themselves out, then each fell asleep beside his owner. Kim and Dean took photos and strolled the shoreline together.

"We should head back soon," I said to Nancy, resting my hand on Lou's chest, his breaths strong and deep. He'd been dreaming and running in his sleep.

"What do you think he dreams about?" she asked, rubbing my sore back.

"Squirrels," I said.

He'd just about come out of his dream; only the tips of his front paws flitted now, like the fingers of a pinball wizard. Then he opened his eyes and lifted his head and looked around, stupefied. He touched me with a paw, then got up, stretched his back legs out one at a time, then bowed deeply to stretch out his front legs and shoulders. He'd been doing that a lot; next time, I'd remember to reinforce this "bow" move, name it, give it a hand signal, encourage it.

"Did you catch the squirrel?" I asked, his ears perking up on "squirrel." Another word he'd learned on his own.

Lou looked around excitedly, then gave me the eye, as if to say, "Dude, don't kid around about squirrels or cats."

"*Rower,*" I said, rubbing his neck.

"Are you teasing him again?" asked Nancy, brushing her hair.

"He thinks the marmots are gigantic mountain squirrels. He's been dreaming of them."

Lou looked out across the lake at Dean and Kim. He stared for a time, then let out a sweet, wavering little yodel, one he sometimes made while thinking. He wondered what they were doing way over there and considered a trot over. But instead he just stood there looking out over the lake, its surface rippled now from a gentle wind blowing cool through the canyon, bouquets of lupines, columbines, and wild blue irises shivering in the breeze.

Lou was lost in thought, and it was fun to watch. He gazed out like a sated lion on the Serengeti—calm, pensive, introspective. Dog gears, turning.

"He is not a normal dog," I said to Nancy, who'd stopped to watch Lou.

"Looks like he's calculating pi."

"It's his thousand-mile stare."

"You love it."

"Yes, I do," I said, and meant it.

In the beginning, I'd just wanted a dog—that's all. But I'd gotten something else, something wilder and more able, like a trained ape. I'd only just begun to sense what he was about, how much he could learn, what he could accomplish. And I didn't feel up to the task.

Then the puppy in Lou came storming back. Lou realized that his cool new dog friend had left. He trotted over to where they'd been, sniffed about, peed, then wandered around, whimpering.

"Sorry, pal. You slept right through it." He looked at me with bright amber eyes. "You were dreaming and I wasn't going to wake you up."

He gazed down the trail as if to say, *I can still catch him.*

"I know."

"What do you know?" asked Dean as they walked over. Lou sidled up to him and stepped on his foot.

"Lou wants to go after his dog buddy."

"Why does he step on my toe?"

"I call it the 'Rottweiler game.' Part love, part possession."

Dean slipped his boot out from under Lou and placed it atop the dog's paw. Lou waited a few seconds, looked up at Dean, then slipped his paw out and placed it back atop Dean's size-thirteen boot. The exchange went on for a good minute before Dean laughed and ran off, luring Lou into a game of tag.

The trip back down was thrillingly fast. Each step afforded richer air to breathe, and gravity helped move us along like a mechanized airport walkway. Lou sniffed at and peed on trees and deadfalls that he knew his dog friend had visited, an invisible game of dog tag they could play forever, as if the volume of a dog's bladder knew no bounds. They could pee and pee and pee. I'd tried to keep up with his output on hikes once or twice but always ran out of fuel after my third or fourth contribution. He'd just give me a condescending look and move on.

We passed three hikers on their way up who, from the looks of the gear they carried, intended to camp overnight near the lake. The stout, short-faced little Lab mix with them instantly fell for Lou and had to be leashed to keep her from deserting her people. She was almost small enough to walk under his chest.

"Cute," I said. "What is she?"

"Lab/pug mix," said the young guy.

"No."

"Oh yeah. Pug dad, Lab mom."

"Stepladder?"

"He was persistent."

"She's adorable," I said, the dog snorting and sneezing in excitement.

"She's Sadie. We call her a Lug."

"Lab/pug . . . got it."

"Come on, Sadie," he said, towing the love-struck little dog away. Lou watched her chubby little tush sashay up the trail.

"Come on, Romeo. There'll be others."

Kim and Lou took the lead again. We were so tired that as we passed Bridal Veil Falls, we barely gave it a glance. A family of German tourists in shorts and sneakers watched us go by; their boy offered Lou a chip or something and he ate it without even stopping, like a swallow picking a mosquito out of midair. He was tired, too.

At sunset we came out onto the dirt road that led into Colorado Avenue, on the west side of town. Our water and food were gone. No one spoke. My feet felt like tenderized pork loins. Lou loped along in front, turning every so often to see what the holdup was. I leashed him up. "Sorry, bro; back in civilization."

"That wasn't so bad, was it?" said Kim, visibly tired.

"I'm very, very tired," said Dean.

"Need bath," mumbled Nancy, a glazed look on her face.

I put an arm around Kim's shoulders. "As God is my witness, I will never hike with you again."

"Liar."

The Hun was right. After a few more days in Telluride, we drove up to Snowmass, where our good friend Lisa lived. Despite our sore muscles, she hiked us up to another alpine lake, not nearly as tough a climb as Blue Lake had been. Lisa fell in love with Lou, as did everyone else he'd ever meet in his life, save a few armed robbers, a handful of bully dogs, two kidnapers, and a reprehensible fellow whom Lou would subdue a few years later.

I'd watched him like a hawk that week, but my worries about his running off and getting lost in the wilds of Colorado were put to rest. If anything, he'd been more concerned about losing me. I'd catch him staring at me when he thought I wasn't watching, coveting or fretting over my safety or wondering why I kept breathing like a bulldog on a treadmill. He was just so at ease in the wild—a fluency that made it almost au courant, as if he'd taken us into his garden and was hosting a guided tour.

It's hard to understand why, but Lou became so—reliable. It's a freeing feeling to know your dog won't run off, dash into the street, or go off with another person. Lou was that way from the start. He never disappeared—except on one exceptional occasion, which I'll talk about later on.

"How old is he again?" asked Dean, saying goodbye to Lou at the airport.

"One."

"Are you sure?"

"Yes."

"I think you've missed your calling, Duno," he said, searching Lou's eyes.

"What?"

"If you can teach a dog to be this cool at a year old, then what the hell are you doing teaching humans?"

He was right, of course. Dean was always right.

7

Lou Gets Me a Job

Lou led a dozen dogs on a race around the perimeter of the Culver City park. He'd been toying with a rag tag bunch of retrievers, hounds, and mutts, but now a ripped Weimaraner flew by the rest and nipped at Lou's heels.

Lou glanced over his shoulder at the brawny dog. A male, deep in the chest and taut in the waist—the color of steel. From the look on Lou's face, I knew just what he was thinking: *bring it.*

They poured it on and left the rest in the dust. Lou had a graceful running style, like a Thoroughbred on the backstretch biding his time. But now he kicked in that extra gear he had and accelerated like a car on nitrous, whipping his spine and extending his legs until he became a black-and-tan blur.

A length in front of the charging Weimaraner, Lou approached a hard left turn in the course the dogs took around the park—a loose collection of fields, basketball courts, and playgrounds separated from the neighborhood by low fencing and sidewalks.

A sand-filled play area with a swing set lay just beyond the turn. Lou ran for it full bore, then dug hard into the grass, cut left like a slot car, and kept going. I'd always kept his nails a bit longer than other owners did with their dogs, for situations like this, and now it paid off. The Weimaraner blew through the turn, spun out, and tumbled into the sand like a Sunday afternoon NASCAR wreck.

"Oops!" I said, as Lou rounded the homestretch. Shaking off the sand, the Weimaraner gruffed off a chummy little beagle and limped over to commiserate with his owner.

Since we got back from Colorado months before, my confidence in Lou had soared. Though I still kept a lead handy, he'd been off-leash almost exclusively for months, and would look at me with disappointment if ever I clipped him up.

Few of those park dogs could be trusted to obediently stay within the bounds of the big park once they were more than twenty yards off. But that wasn't the case when Lou showed up; he was the mesmeric "shepherd" of the group, and when he ran the border, every dog there had only one thing on his or her mind: *catch that son of a bitch.* Their owners knew that as long as Lou stayed on the course, their dogs would, too.

Getting Lou to run the perimeter of the park on his own took some work. I'd taken him around the boundary a few dozen times, first with him jogging off-leash by my side, then heeling next to me while I rode my bike. I worked long off-leash recalls along each edge of the park, then taught him angled recalls around fence corners, lengthening them a bit each time. Finally, I pieced it all together, and on one early morning before sunrise, amid cheers of *"Vayate, Guapo!"* from a group of Culver City Boyz who'd partied in the park all night, he ran the entire half-mile course on his own. With the addition of other dogs, it became a self-reinforcing game for Lou, and a schooling for the others. At not quite two years of age, he'd begun his mentoring career.

"I'm selling the business," said Phyllis, the owner of Academics Plus, the tutoring agency I worked for.

"Don't kid around."

"No. Seriously."

"Why? It's gold."

"I've got a newborn, I'm getting divorced, and I don't want the headache anymore."

I'd been making upward of forty dollars per hour and had never worked more than twenty-five hours in a week. In my spare time, I wrote and trained Lou—the life of an L.A. ascetic. But my relaxed routine was about to change.

When I first moved to Los Angeles, in 1986, I landed a substitute position with the Compton Unified School District, where one didn't exactly teach so much as protect and defend. On my first day, while taking roll and trying to settle down a rambunctious little seventh-grader, a titanic black man in a long white lab coat stormed into the classroom sporting a polished wooden fraternity paddle in his meaty hand. Before I could react, he yanked the kid out of his seat and *whack! whack! whack!* paddled his behind. Then he dropped the kid back into his chair, smiled creepily, and disappeared.

"What?" I said, the kids cheering, the paddled kid bowing to his fans.

"That's Mr. Charles," said a giggly little Hispanic girl in the front row. "He goes around with his paddle, looking for trouble-makers."

The Compton school district still practiced corporal punishment in 1986; Mr. Charles's job was to peer into classrooms and mete out retribution when "necessary." Of course, I hadn't been notified of this when I took the job, and thought him a psychopath. I got the tutoring job with Academics Plus a week later and went from paddle whacking to Poitier putting in a week.

Now, Phyllis had made up her mind to quit the business. Not many agencies paid as well, which left me few options. Any way I looked at it, something would have to change.

"What about moving?" asked Nancy.

"Seattle?" I asked. We'd visited the Northwest a while back and had enjoyed the novelty of trees, and weather.

"I could buy my house up there."

Though only in her midtwenties, Nancy was the most frugal person I'd ever known. Between saving every dime she'd ever made and living with her parents for most of her life, she'd saved enough for a respectable down payment. Unfortunately, in Los Angeles, the most she could afford was a one-bedroom condo. But in 1991, a decent three-bedroom home in a quiet Seattle neighborhood cost less than a condo in L.A.

"Let's think about it," I said.

Then two things happened that would change our lives and push Lou and me to the next level.

"Duno, I need you to do this," pleaded Billy, another college friend who'd lived with Dean and me in New York in the 1970s. He'd graduated with a degree in marine biology, then moved to San Francisco in 1979 to start a shellfish company. I'd lived with him for a time in the early 1980s and helped him with deliveries;

the company's first truck was a rusted 1975 Datsun pickup. He worked out of an apartment over a pizzeria, in a building owned by a man named Mr. Kwan, who was ever befuddled by the number of roommates Billy had at any given time in his small place.

Big, boisterous, and without artifice, Billy was a force of nature, like a beehive in a clothes dryer. A true American success story, by 1991 he'd built his company into a multimillion-dollar corporation with offices in San Francisco and Los Angeles. Now he wanted to open an office in Seattle, close to the oyster growers who supplied him with much of his product.

"I need someone I trust to drive one of the refrigerated trucks up there, help set up the office, deliver to the airport, and keep an eye on stuff for me. I'll pay for your move and for six months of you working for me up there."

"I don't know. It's a big move."

"Don't be a pissant. You said Nancy wants to move there and buy a house. They got plenty of houses up there, cheap as cars. She works in insurance, right? They got a million insurance companies in Seattle. People have accidents there *constantly*. It rains all the time, like in the Bible. Cars slide into each other. And they got forest fires and mudslides and cougar attacks and depressed people. Parkinson's, palsy, vitamin D deficiencies. *Lot* of insurance companies up there."

Six months earlier, Nancy had had to persuade me to take Lou on that day near Willits. Now came Billy's turn to break through my aversion to change. He was a relentless tidal wave of wheedling and rationalizations, and he'd assail you until you surrendered. It didn't matter what he asked you to do; eventually, you'd give up and do it just to escape his ranting and raving.

In the past Billy had persuaded me to: fake a liquor-store holdup with a balloon gun, wearing a balloon mask; call every flower shop in San Francisco to locate a woman he'd met briefly at a party the night before, knowing only her first name and the fact that she sold flowers somewhere; go on a nudist fishing trip to Lake Shasta; eat a raw oyster the size of a pith helmet; sell aspirin for a buck apiece at a Jefferson Starship concert.

And many, many other equally insane acts, all rendered reasonable and necessary at the time by Billy's irrefutable Brooklyn brand of logic.

Resistance was futile: I agreed to go. I'd switch from teaching rich kids in Bel-Air to schlepping bivalves in Seattle. But I had the germ of a long-term plan, and it didn't involve being a fishmonger for very long.

What Dean had said to me about teaching Lou had struck a chord: I *was* good at training dogs (or at least at training Lou). Why not do it for a living? But not the way Chandra the Wiccan priestess or Uri the Marxist grifter did; I wanted to do it right, and learn from the best. And with a little luck and some help from Lou, I could do that in Seattle.

"Wow," said Nancy, surprised that I was on board. "Really? So we're actually going to do this?"

"He's giving me six months and paying for the move. But he wants me to leave next month after training here with Jeff and Angel."

"I can't leave that soon. I have a million things to do first."

"I'll go up first with the truck, and you'll drive up when you're ready. We can put all my stuff into the truck, and yours, too."

"What about your car?"

"Tow it up with the truck."

"And Lou?"

"He finally gets to be a truck dog."

"Where will we live?"

"I'm in touch with an apartment complex just north of Seattle, in Bothell. They take small dogs. I've already sent them a deposit."

"He's *three* small dogs."

"I'm going to audition him."

"Audition?"

"Apartments always specify 'small dogs' because they're easier to manage and less dangerous. Once they see how well trained and sweet Lou is, they won't have the heart to say no."

"That's a big assumption, even for you."

"I talked to the manager, she's a dog fan. I told her Lou is a little bigger than small, and that he's trained for television."

"Oh God."

"Don't worry. He'll shape-shift if he has to. You know how he changes size."

"I'll have to give notice and put together a résumé. There are some big insurance companies up there."

"I know, Billy told me."

"I've been looking at home listings. They're so cheap!"

"I'll have to sign a year lease; that'll give you plenty of time to find the right house."

"I'm not even old enough to rent a car."

"That is so cool."

I'd never surrendered to the tripe about Los Angeles being a cold, pitiless place to live. I'd been friends with plenty of celebrities and struggling actors, and though they could sometimes be difficult and desperate, I called many of them friend, and respected their dreams. Narcissism, arrested development, betrayal—certainly. But L.A. is a magnet for people on the edge of success or failure, and if you choose to live there, you take it in stride.

I would miss the hills and mountains, the desert, the heat, the Santa Anas, the history, and the sense of expectation you felt in the air just walking down the street. In L.A., you could run into stars at the most unexpected times and have regular, decent conversations. In my years there, I'd talked to Rob Lowe about vintage Corvettes, to Michael Keaton about dogs, to Cher about her family, to Eddie Murphy about Stevie Wonder—memories of distinctive people just shooting the breeze. I would remember Sidney Poitier offering me juice, and my teaching Alyssa Milano how to find the area of an isosceles triangle; drinking coffee with Daryl Hannah, Carl Weathers rubbing Lou's ears, and seeing Miles Davis's hawk-eyed scowl while I helped to vaccinate his Shar-Peis. I'd stepped in miniature-pony poop *inside* a famous sitcom star's home, taken a loaded pistol away from the son of a South African diplomat, and gotten my butt kicked by a kangaroo at a Palos Verdes animal sanctuary. I'd done slammer shots with Christie Bono on the fractured marble bar of her dad's restaurant, spoken to brazen coyotes in parking lots, and watched "Dr. Smith" from *Lost in Space* talk baby talk to my dog. I would even miss the Culver City Boyz, and the earthquakes. It was a cool place to live.

I would miss Los Angeles most for being Lou's first stepping-off place out of the wild. As hard as his first few months had been, I treasured those memories now. He would never have become the dog he did without the experiences we'd shared there together, the neighborhoods, the people, our independence, the training and tutoring sessions together, the walks to the taquería, the runs on the beach, the camaraderie. A boy and his dog in the City of Angels. Most of all, I would miss our quiet hikes up into the Santa Monica Mountains, and the doting way he'd look after me while we roamed the hills together, like brothers.

The trip north to Seattle took three easy days, with two nights spent in dog-friendly motels. I'd loaded the truck with my stuff and much of Nancy's, and even had my motorcycle wedged in there. The Civic, its front wheels lashed to a U-Haul tow dolly, followed behind the Isuzu refrigerated truck. And beside me rode Lou, my trusty truck dog, sitting pretty and smiling for the people passing by, getting a taste of what life might have been like with that crazy little trucker we'd met on that first day in Willits.

I started to sing "On the Road Again" for the fifteen or sixteenth time. Lou looked straight at me and let out a long, remonstrative *rower!* Then he just stared, daring me to try it again.

"But it's Willie Nelson."

"Rrrrr-oww-row-row! Rower!"

"Okay, okay."

He aimed his nose out the window, sniffed, then opened his mouth and let his tongue flag in the wind. Lou loved to savor road air, which to him must have been turbocharged with scent, a million different flavors force-fed up his nose at sixty miles an hour, like me at a Vegas buffet.

North of Fresno, on Interstate 5, we passed through farming country, the summer air rich with the saccharine smell of fertilizer that, moments after you smelled it, you tasted. Lou surely scented cattle, too, and sheep and hogs or whatever they raised there. Perhaps he could smell the giant sequoias to the east of us, or the Pacific a hundred miles to the west, or the diesel burned in the John Deere combines. Whatever it was, he blissed on it.

North of Sacramento, I'd been tempted to detour west on Route 20 to Highway 101, to revisit Lou's Mendocino birthplace. But Billy expected me in Seattle in less than two days, and pissing off Billy was akin to sticking your face into a hill of red ants. To this day I regret not going; Lou and I would never again return to Willits, at least not while he was alive.

We stopped for the night at a cheap motel near Red Bluff, California, a small town in the shadow of Mount Shasta, known for its rodeos and bull competitions. I thought about camping out that night, but the truck had no air conditioning and the day had been a scorcher. I needed a shower, AC, and a bed.

That evening we watched television, shared Chinese takeout (he liked spring rolls and chow fun), and practiced a few tricks. I'd been working on linking together behaviors in preparation for his audition with the apartment manager, and he'd nearly nailed it that night. With a series of discreet hand signals, Lou would now sit, lie down, roll over, sit up again, spin left, spin right, bark, wave, and play dead, then return to my side. With this, plus a long-distance recall and a sit/stay in the middle of a field, I thought we were a shoo-in for the apartment.

"Just be sure to bat your eyes, Romeo," I said, admiring his long, dark lashes and "eyeliner."

"Ahoo-ahoo," he chortled, coveting the last spring roll. I bit it in half, then said, "Beg."

Lou balanced back on his haunches, put both front paws up and together, then licked his lips. He looked like a monk at prayer. "Who are you dogs praying to these days? Gog?" I asked, tossing the half roll to him. He caught it with a neat snap of his jaws. "*Gog,* get it?" I said. He walked over to the door, touched it with a paw, and looked at me, his signal that he wanted out. "It's a joke, hair face."

The next day we rolled up I-5 into Oregon. The terrain changed and the air became lusher, less parched. "Trees, Lou," I said, pointing to a green belt of tall pines beside the freeway. Lou sniffed the air and licked his lips. Then, staring out above the tree line, he whimpered the way he usually did when seeing a cat.

Above the trees a brace of huge birds rose gracefully, soaring higher and higher in concentric circles, their wings barely flapping.

"Eagles, Lou," I said, the birds gliding through the air like sailing ships easing their way through calm seas. With wings the size of coffee tables, they could soar effortlessly all day on thermals as they searched for food.

"Bald eagles," I said, their white heads barely visible. Now that the eagles were too high for him to see, Lou lost interest and lay down with his head in my lap. He was tired of being a truck dog and wanted to be earth-bound again. As I caressed his face and rubbed the inside of his ear, he yawned and draped a leg over my knee, as if trying to get me to push down harder on the throttle.

"One more day, pal."

Bothell's welcome sign said FOR A DAY, OR A LIFETIME. I wondered about those who'd stayed for only the one day. And what of the lifers? Were they incarcerated in Bothell? What if I wanted to stay for two years, then move on?

"We're here, pal," I said, pulling the truck up in front of the Beardslee Cove apartment complex. The sun shined and the flower gardens were in bloom. The units looked new, freshly sided, and nicely landscaped.

An older couple walked by with their grandchild and a toy poodle with a summer cut. Lou whimpered. "Too small for you, Romeo," I said as they walked off.

We walked over to a grassy area, where Lou let out a prodigious torrent of steaming pee that seemed to have no beginning or end. "God, man, where do you put it?"

After an eternity, he finished, then raked his back paws across the grass a few times to lay claim to his new home. I clipped on his leash (for which I received a scowl), then headed for the manager's office.

"Okay, pal. This is it. It's all you," I said. "Time to earn your keep. Just be yourself. Do your tricks, be happy, and shoot her your best Mother Teresa."

I put Lou on a sit/stay outside the office window and lay down his leash. "Good stay, Lou," I said, looking him square in the eye. Then I walked in the door, which was held open with a brick.

At the desk sat a pretty young blond woman dressed like a summer Realtor. She had bright blue eyes and a pen held sideways in her mouth.

"Hi, I'm Steve Duno, the guy from Los Angeles. Are you Kathy?"

She looked at me for a second, then took the pen from her mouth. "The guy with the dog?"

"That's me."

"Oh, hey, you're early! Welcome to Bothell."

"For a day or a lifetime."

"You saw the sign," she said, coming around to shake my hand.

"I did."

"Corny, huh?"

"Actually it's sort of existential."

She looked at me for an uncomfortable second, as if I'd spoken in Aramaic. One should never use the word *existential* during any kind of interview, no matter how appropriate.

"Where's the dog?"

"Right there," I said, pointing out the window. She looked out to see Lou sitting like the sphinx, staring in at us, smiling.

"That's him?" she asked, transfixed. "Why is he just sitting there like that?"

"I asked him to."

A fat robin ran by Lou in the grass. Lou didn't budge. *Good boy, Lou, good boy.*

"He's that obedient?"

"He's the smartest dog I have ever known."

"He's a *big* boy," she said, still staring at him, trying to comprehend why he wasn't chasing after the two kids peddling by on bikes.

"He's calm and sweet and he loves everybody."

"Can I meet him?"

I clapped twice. Lou trotted in, sat in front of her, then raised his paw and waved.

"Oh my God. He's so—beautiful," she said, bending down to shake his paw. He shook, then sat beside her and shot her the best Mother T look I'd ever seen, a smiling, eyes-half-closed, blissful gaze that would have warmed the devil's heart.

"He works it pretty well."

"He looks like the guy in *Scarface*."

"Pacino?"

"No, the other guy."

"Yeah, I guess he does."

I put Lou through all his tricks, all without saying a word. When he sprang up from playing dead, instead of sitting by me, he cozied over to her, then gently laid a paw atop her shoe.

She caressed his head and smiled. "Can you move in today?"

Lou's career as a truck dog ended as fast as it had begun. I couldn't take Lou to work with me; evidently the airport had regulations against it, as did the health department. I'd have to leave him at home while I drove down to Sea-Tac Airport and schlepped oysters, clams, and mussels for Marinelli Shellfish. For the first time, Lou would have to be by himself much of the day.

The job entailed packing boxes with fresh bivalves, then air freighting them out to retailers all over the world, as well as delivering them to local-area restaurants. What I didn't know was that I'd be working with "Big Bob," the largest man I have ever known.

Six foot eight, 380 pounds, hands like pelican maws. Bob was so big he needed a custom seat in his 1972 Monte Carlo, mounted eighteen inches back of normal. When he climbed into his car, it groaned and hunkered down like a low-rider. Bob breathed big, sweated big, ate big, moved big. Working with Bob was like having a small planet beside you in your truck, its pull influencing everything you tried to say or do.

Bob was a good-natured, friendly giant who walked a fine line, as if all his dreams were the forgetful kind that bled into real life. He'd moved to Seattle from San Francisco after getting some Marinelli work experience there.

I'd work with Bob each day for the next few months. I'm five foot five and 135 pounds on a good day—Bob was nearly three of me. The airport-cargo people began referring to us as Mutt and Jeff. When I'd see our reflection in office-building windows, I couldn't help but laugh myself.

Once I had helped Billy set up the office and find a company apartment, I got busy packing shellfish in the mornings, then riding to the airport with Bob to ship our precious cargo out on the right flights. After our first early-morning run, we'd stop at the local Jack in the Box, where Bob would order three breakfasts to my one and eat them all in half the time.

"Why do you eat so much, Bob?"

"Ever see an elephant strip a tree down to its roots?"

"No."

"Big man's got to eat."

Bob forgot stuff. Flight schedules, bills-of-lading, customs paperwork, packing supplies—you name it, he'd forget it. This led to tragicomic episodes, during which the big man would panic and go into hyperdrive in an attempt not to miss a flight. He'd fling 150-pound boxes of shellfish onto pallets at loading docks like they were playing cards; I'd try to keep up, but the physics just wasn't on my side. Three months into the job, it caught up with me.

A shipment of Manila clams bound for the East Coast needed to be on the United Airlines flight twenty minutes ago. As soon as we pulled up to the loading dock, Big Bob leaped out of the cab, rolled up the back door, and began flinging boxes of clams onto a waiting pallet.

"Come on, Duno, we got five minutes!"

I climbed into the truck box and started moving boxes to the tailgate, where Bob would grab and toss. On the third box, I bent, grabbed, lifted, and screamed.

"What?"

"My back!"

"Look out!" he said, grabbing the remaining two cartons and carrying them like cake boxes to the pallet, a forklift operator already poised to cart it off to a waiting cargo container.

As soon as I'd lifted the box, an electric shock had exploded from my lower back and coursed down into my butt and legs. I collapsed in a heap in the back corner of the reefer box, unable to stand.

Bob came back after signing off on the shipment.

"You okay?"

"Not at all."

Bob picked me up like a baby, deposited me into the cab, then brought me an ice pack from the back of the truck. "Can you finish out the day?"

"Take me back to the warehouse, Bob."

Health insurance hadn't been part of the deal. I drove home that day in searing pain, then spent the next few days in bed, icing and self-medicating with ibuprofen and an old bottle of Sambuca, the only alcohol I had in the house.

Lou sat beside the bed and sniffed at me, wondering when I was going to stop resting. Thankfully, my neighbor Sabrina worked evenings and graciously agreed to walk Lou for me during the day.

"Sorry, Lou. I need to take it easy for a few days."

Lou was always tuned in to my physical or emotional state;

now he knew something was seriously wrong, and thought that sniffing, licking, and staring would aid in the recovery.

"Don't be such a yenta. Go lie down, pal."

For the next few days I rested, iced, read, and watched a lot of television. "Daytime TV sucks," I said to Lou, who *rowered* and touched my head with a paw, as if to take my temperature.

Billy called and told me to get back to work, that Big Bob was screwing up and he might have him killed or deported.

"He was born in San Fran, Bill."

"I don't care. I'll get him Cambodian citizenship, then deport his ass."

"Huge ass."

"Can you imagine the poops he must take?"

"Got to rest now."

"Okay. But be back to work on Monday."

A day later, I was able to drive to a clinic nearby. They thought it was muscle strain and gave me a prescription for Vicodin. "These are better than ibuprofen and Sambuca," I slurred to Lou later that evening.

Sometime during the night, though he'd never slept in bed with me before, Lou quietly crept up onto the bed and curled into me. I awoke in the early morning to find his front leg draped across my shoulder and his face an inch from mine. When I opened my eyes, he painted my face with his tongue.

"Gross!" I said, wiping it off with the sweaty, hairy bedsheet. About to command him off the bed, I had a change of heart and let him stay. He sighed, aware for the first time in his young life that I was not some mythological character but a mere mortal like himself.

Years later, I would discover that I'd herniated two disks in my lower back that day. The incident would cause pain for the rest of my life and hasten the master plan I'd formulated back in Los Angeles months before.

. . .

A week after arriving in Bothell, Nancy landed a customer-service position with Safeco Insurance, earning a better salary than she had in Los Angeles. My days with Marinelli Shellfish were numbered.

"Think you can live with Lou and me full-time without killing us?" I asked, the apartment already taking on a more organized feel.

"I could never kill Lou," she said.

As much as I needed the paycheck, I couldn't work for Billy anymore without ending up in a wheelchair or an insane asylum. He was my bro, but working for him was like having your grandfather teach you to drive.

Enter the master plan. While still in Los Angeles, I'd researched dog-training facilities across the nation and discovered a prestigious one right in Bothell—the Academy of Canine Behavior. Owned and operated by Jack and Colleen McDaniel, the academy had a reputation for taking on problem dogs no one else would touch; profoundly aggressive, intensely fearful, outrageously dominant, neurotic, handicapped—whatever the challenge, they would take it on. People would ship their troubled dogs to the academy from all over the country. For many dogs, the academy was the last-ditch stop on the train of life: if they couldn't turn over a new leaf there, the next stop was euthanization.

The academy's secret weapon was its board-and-train program, an intense one-month course of behavioral modification in which every aspect of the dog's day was managed and evaluated. Recalcitrant dogs were boarded for an entire month; removed from owners and home environments where bad behaviors were formed and reinforced, the dogs were "rebooted," so to speak—taken back to basics and taught manners, sociability, and obedience, and to be responsive in a positive way to human interaction and intentions.

Following a thorough evaluation and diagnosis, the dogs were assigned a primary-care trainer, who saw to every aspect of a dog's care. After working with that dog exclusively for several days, the primary-care trainer would then place the dog into the trainer rotation, allowing it to be worked by a different person each day. This taught each dog that manners and obedience applied to all humans, and not just a select few.

But it was more than just doggy boot camp. The best-trained dog in the world could be ruined in no time by an owner with little knowledge or dedication. To prevent this, owners had to be trained, too. They came in for weekly visits, during which they learned the basics of behavior and obedience and just how to maintain the training their pets had received. After four weeks, the dogs and owners were usually ready to get on with their new lives.

"You can't just walk in there and ask for a job," said Nancy.

"Why not?"

"What's your experience? Where's your résumé?"

"Right here," I said, petting Lou.

"What do you mean?"

"Know a smarter, better-trained dog?"

"No."

"Who trained him?"

"You and my mother."

"He's proof of my potential. If you were going to hire a photographer, wouldn't you first check out his or her portfolio?"

"Is that what Lou is?" she asked.

"He *is* my portfolio. He proves that I can teach dogs to learn. If a kid comes into a class in handcuffs and leaves with a diploma, that teacher knows his stuff, right?"

"Don't prisons do that anyway?"

"Seriously."

"You are good at it. But I also think that *he's* good at it. How much is you and how much is him?"

"That's what I need to find out."

When you pulled up in front of the Academy of Canine Behavior, you felt like you were entering the grounds of a monastery. Past the high brick wall and the abandoned guard booth, the drive wound past tall cedars and firs bordering the many fields and buildings on the twelve-plus-acre property. Exercise pens, kennels, residences, and expansive fenced fields dotted the landscape. It was pastoral, and quiet.

Lou and I drove through the gate and followed the drive up to the main office. I hadn't made an appointment but simply called ahead anonymously to find out if Colleen McDaniel was in the office that day. She was, and in a moment she'd be ambushed by two unexpected visitors, a red-blooded American dog trained piecemeal by me, a self-taught, presumptuous New York native bent on changing his career.

"This is it, man," I said to him. "Your last audition got us an apartment; this one has to get us a job."

"*Rower.*"

"Yes, yes, *rower*, I know. I'm serious—be a good boy and do your best. You are a good boy, right?"

"*Aroogla.*"

"Arugula? That's a new one. I like it. Let's put that in the rotation."

I opened the back hatch and clipped on Lou's leash. He pouted. "They'll want you to walk in on leash first, fur ball. Besides, they train crazy dogs here; we don't know what to expect."

We'd practiced the routine all week and had it down solid. All

I could hope was that there would be no other dogs in the office to distract him. It was now or never.

I stood outside the door, frozen. I'd put so much energy into training him, and all my hopes were riding on this one bone-headed move. If we didn't pull it off, I'd be stuck in Seattle selling clams or wearing that "kick me" sign they gave out to all substitute teachers.

Lou gazed up at me and smiled his sweetest smile. I palmed his head. "Thanks, pal."

I loved him big. We walked in together.

I put Lou into a sit/stay in the middle of the office. An Irish water spaniel bitch lay in the corner, eyeing Lou, chocolate Rasta bangs obscuring her eyes. She looked like eighties' funk master Rick James. Lou flashed her a flirty little look but kept his stay. "Good boy," I said, eye-to-eye, so he knew I meant business.

"Hi," I said to the receptionist. "Is Colleen here?"

A petite woman with a thick mane of chin-length auburn hair walked up. "I'm Colleen. Can I help you?"

When Colleen looked at you she looked *right at you,* unblinking, taking in what you had to say, analyzing it, then answering without facade, and always with a comment you didn't quite expect. Part marine colonel, part mystic, part teacher. She would become one of my most important role models.

"I'm Steve Duno. I'm looking for a training job."

"Oh really?" she said, as if to say, *Oh yes, and you're also an astronaut in your spare time.*

"Yes, I am. To show you what I can do, I've brought Lou with me today, to audition."

'Is that him sitting over there so patiently?"

"It is."

"He's a handsome young fellow, but he's getting a bit impatient. I think you'd better get on with it before he strolls over to my dog Deuce and finds out whose office this is."

She and the receptionist grinned at each other, as if this sort of amateur spectacle happened every day, to the performer's embarrassment. They were surely expecting us to fall flat on our faces, like a contestant on *American Idol* whose talent began and ended inside his own mind.

I walked out into the middle of the room. Lou had been getting fidgety and sloppy, but now he snapped back up into a soldierly sit and locked on to my face.

"We're waiting."

Our *Flashdance* moment.

Using subtle hand signals, I spurred Lou into action. From a sit into a fast down, then back up into a sit—quick, precise. *Good boy, pal.* Spin left, spin right—360-degree corkscrew turns, feet barely touching the carpet. Wave left, wave right—holding the pose like the smart kid in the front row.

Lou hit his cues like a gymnast. Bark, then *rower*, a quick down followed by play dead, roll left, roll right, stand, back up two steps, come, around me, to your spot, come, wait halfway, wait three-quarters of the way, down, stay, catch a treat.

No applause. Colleen and the receptionist looked at each other, tight-lipped. She came out from behind the counter and walked over to Lou, arms crossed. Lou kept his down/stay but thumped his tail. Deuce walked over to sniff him. Colleen waved her off, then rubbed Lou's neck and spoke softly to him. He looked up at her. Bang—Mother Teresa.

She walked over to me, arms still crossed, an unreadable look on her face, like a drill sergeant about to praise or punish.

"Nice."

"So . . . can you use a trainer?" I asked.

She smiled at my cockiness. "Teaching tricks to a smart, willing dog does not make you a trainer."

"But working here sure would."

She smiled again, eyed the receptionist, and shook her head.

Then she looked me straight in the eye. "Except for my husband, Jack, all the trainers here are women. We've been talking about adding a man to the rotation, to expose the dogs to both genders. It's very strange that you happened by today."

"Destiny."

"You'd be our first apprentice trainer, and work under the tutelage of Nancy Baer, our manager. The pay's not great and the work is tough. And most of the training dogs aren't at all like him," she said, gesturing to Lou, who came over to sniff at the fifty or so different dog scents on her pants leg.

"You're hiring me?"

"You have no idea what you're getting into."

The pivotal moment in my life had been choreographed by a mutt.

He'd helped me teach kids, and chased off two surly dognapers. He saved my life at a 7-Eleven, won me an apartment, and now a job. He was two years old. I'd found him in the woods.

"We're all square on that rug thing, pal."

8

Lou the Teacher

The first academy dog I got to train was a 170-pound ter-rorist remembered only by the nickname Jughead. A dom-inant male Newfoundland, if you tried to take him out of his kennel he'd storm the gate, rise on his hind legs, grab you by the arm, and drag you around like a rag doll. Not Cujo, but close.

Nancy Baer took me under her wing. Though equally as skilled as Colleen, the two women couldn't have been more different. Tall with wavy dark hair, Nancy was, well—merry. Even when things got tough she kept a smile on her face and a lilt in her voice, and always had something positive to say. If Colleen was my Yoda, Nancy was my Glenda.

Nonetheless, it was a baptism of fire. It was like boot camp, with Colleen seeing to it that Nancy did not ease me into the fray. If I wasn't up to the task, she wanted to know soon.

"Open the kennel gate and grab the short blue lead hanging from his collar," said Nancy, unable to restrain the giggle brewing inside her. "Then slip this training collar over his head, clip up your leash, and ask him to sit before taking him out."

"Does he know how to sit?"

"We'll see."

Jughead was a classic example of a dog who used size and strength to intimidate and control. He'd come to the academy for mauling his owner's girlfriend and terrorizing everyone with his size and barbaric behavior. Whenever the girlfriend cracked open the door to Jughead's room, he'd lower his head like a buffalo, plow through the door, then *mount* her. The poor woman was being sexually molested by a dog.

Jughead had begun his month of board and train the day before; no one else had yet worked him. He had a head the size of an army turkey and the body of a burro. Picture a shaggy baby buffalo in your living room and you had Jughead.

"Why is he here?" I asked, the dog pressing his bulk against the side of the gate, loading it up, watching me reach for the handle.

"Because he's a completely untrained dog who's learned to use his power and size to get whatever he wants," said Nancy. "He mounts the girlfriend and drags people down the street like cartoon characters whenever they try to walk him. And he uses his mouth. A lot."

"He bites?"

"Not exactly. He *uses* it. Like a hand. A very drippy, powerful hand with teeth."

Jughead drooled and gazed at me almost pitiably, as if to say,

Sorry, rookie, but I gotta be me. The second I lifted the gate handle, Jughead plowed his way through like an Abrams tank and lumbered off for the north kennel door. I grabbed his short blue lead as he stormed by and got dragged like a toboggan down the hallway. Laughing, Nancy crept up, slipped a collar onto the brute, and clipped on her leash.

"Welcome to my world," she said, as Jughead planted his front paws atop my shoulders, looked down at me, then lacquered my face with a tongue the size of a Ping-Pong paddle.

She walked him up and down the narrow hallway a few times, reversing direction without warning, handling the leash with grace and style. Watching her, I noted parallels between dog training and martial arts: how physical mastery was balanced by attitude, understanding, and mental discipline. Within moments, Jughead began paying attention and responding to her movements, instead of trying to dominate the walk.

"Keep them guessing about what you're going to do," she said, making a sharp left turn in front of the beast's face, using her body to facilitate the turn. "Keep changing speed and direction and they'll start paying attention. They realize it's easier just to stay with you than keep getting left behind."

It was similar in style to how I'd trained Lou to walk. But she was way better at it.

"Shouldn't we be using treats?" I asked.

"Not with him, not yet. We use treats to initiate behaviors with a willing dog. With him, treats would not address the abiding issue but just mask it."

'What's the issue?"

"He's a barbarian."

When Nancy took him outside, all hell broke loose. As soon as we got out the door, he leaped straight up, getting a good four feet of air beneath his yeti-size paws. Nancy looked as if she was breaking a horse.

"He is going to bite me," said Nancy. Right on cue, Jughead grabbed her wrist but did not break the skin.

I watched as this monstrous dog sprang high up into the air, slobber flying in all directions. "Get your leash on him," she pleaded, knowing that the only way to gain control was to double leash the brute.

I made a loop with my leash and lassoed his head in midair. A moment later, the two of us were able to contain the beast, and with Jughead now sandwiched between us, we began walking him around the property, perhaps the first time humans had ever managed to exert their will over the cantankerous creature.

We quickly discovered another of his amazing talents: Jughead could perform a flawless leg sweep. He'd wrap his front paws around your leg, then, fast as Bruce Lee, yank hard and sweep you off your feet. He swept me twice before we wised up and put at least three feet between us and the canine karate expert. It was comical and fascinating; how had he learned to do that, and how on earth could anyone *live* with such a dog?

The next day, Nancy let me take over with Jughead. He tried to jump and sweep, but by then I was wise to him. I kept reversing, turning, adjusting speed, and using my body the way he might, to control the dance. I felt like I was sparring with a giant.

By feeding and grooming him each day, working his obedience, and rewarding him when he behaved, we became friends. It would be the first comical step I'd take toward becoming a trainer, and toward understanding things from a dog's-eye view.

Most good dog trainers I've known have had, well—doggish personalities. They focused well, listened, used their senses, and had an innate sense of fairness. But they were also a bit tribal, and slow to warm up to a new person. And, almost to a person, they said exactly what they thought, without pretense or any hint of political correctness. Sort of like—well, dogs. Such was the case at the academy.

"Who's the dude?" asked Tracy as she walked into the trainers' room. Young, pretty, and athletic, Tracy had a natural talent for training, and she was someone you definitely had to prove yourself to. She and her husband, Neal, the kennel manager, were good-hearted hell-raisers who, once they trusted you, would give you the shirts off their backs. But for an East Coast loudmouth who'd just weaseled his way into a job, winning them over would take more than a few days.

"Tracy, this is Steve," said Nancy. "He's the new token male. Be nice and don't let him get eaten."

"He'll probably get that done all by himself," she said, shooting me an elfin grin.

"Just watch out for the cocker spaniels," said Julie, looking up from her paperwork and smiling. Elegant and quick-witted, Julie could talk Rottweilers, Dickens, or NASA, depending on the crowd. She had a sharp sense of humor, but, like the others, she took a while to warm up to the new guy.

"I hear cockers can be trouble," I said.

"They're not of this earth," she said, straight-faced.

"A Roger Corman classic," I said, referring to the 1950s sci-fi film of the same title.

"I'm not a big Corman fan," she said. Nancy and Tracy looked at each other.

"I knew his foley artist in L.A. Same birthday as me."

"Okay, then," she said. "I think I'll go work a dog now."

The difference between working with Lou and working at the academy was like the distinction between high school and major-league pitching. In high school you could sense the arc of the ball, and had a moment to decide what to do; in the majors, the ball comes at you like a beam of light, wobbling like a palsied aspirin, hissing past you and cracking into the catcher's mitt before your neurons could even tell your arms to swing.

I'd never seen so many disobedient, maladjusted dogs before. If Lou was an honor student, the dogs at the academy were dropouts, ADHD kids, truants, toughs, terrorized mental patients, killers, and martyrs. It was the big leagues, and I had to learn not just to train but to retrain, modify, ease, calm, convince, control, and teach. You had to teach manners, confidence, discipline, and self-reliance to the dogs, while assuring their owners that it wasn't all their fault (even if it was), and that hope was right around the corner. You had to think through unique problems, come up with novel solutions, and stay alive. I had a lot to learn.

Each day I worked six or more dogs of varying breeds, ages, and temperaments. Big, small, scared, nasty, dangerous, hyper, silly, grumpy—all different, all problematic. Most had issues larger than simple disobedience. Many were aggressive, and all were confused at being away from home. I moved from one to the other, working on socialization, obedience, attitude, confidence building—whatever was needed to advance the dog. Fear-aggressive cocker, hyperactive field-bred Lab, suspicious Saluki, deaf Dalmatian—you never knew what you'd get on any given day.

It could be draining, not only physically but emotionally. Most of the dogs there had high levels of stress that you could feel, waves of emotion that to a great extent determined what your next step would be.

The best part of working at the academy was that Lou got to come to work with me every single day. As long as a trainer's dog didn't cause problems or take up boarding space, they were welcomed at the academy. We were a team again.

It became clear to everyone there that Lou had a special gift of working his way into the hearts and minds of dogs who normally wouldn't have given other dogs the time of day. Befriending and mentoring antisocial, fear-aggressive dogs became his signature. Strong and dog-smart, Lou drew upon his feral roots, lightning reflexes, and unruffled moxy to win the respect and trust of even the most dangerous of dogs. Quick and tough, he'd wear them down and eventually get them to tolerate, then even like him.

For these troubled dogs, it was a huge relief to finally know a dog they could rely on. He'd take the worst they could dish out without losing his cool or holding a grudge. *Who is this crazy dog?* they must have thought, their aggressive tirades failing to scare off the big black-and-tan.

You could see their eyes soften when Lou walked into the room; once terrified or enraged at the sight of another dog, their tails would slowly begin to wag the moment Lou danced into the room, chortling hello or leaping up onto a piece of agility equipment. This was Lou's lasting genius, and it gave me entry into the hearts of scores of troubled animals who, with no other hope of rehabilitation, would otherwise have been euthanized. I was a good trainer with an extraordinary dog by my side.

If Lou is remembered, it should be for how he helped hundreds of dogs find peace in their troubled souls. He taught them to let go of their fears and showed them how good life could be. Their families, grateful for the new lease on life we'd given their pets, were especially thankful for not having to make that fateful decision, one that would have haunted their consciences for years. I didn't give them that; Lou did.

Solo looked like a dog, ran like a dog, and sounded like a dog. But others of his kind terrified him, made his skin crawl. He sensed kinship but couldn't speak their language. He was terrified of his own kind.

He got his name from being the only pup in his litter. A beefy retriever/pit cross, he'd never gotten to play, wrestle, or contend for status with kin. Now an adult, he didn't know what to do around other dogs. Solo was miserable, and dangerous.

During the innocence of litter play, pups learn how to socialize with other dogs. Body language, pecking order, bite inhibition, communication skills—these things get worked out naturally during that three-to-ten-week period. This give-and-take is how dogs learn to behave among themselves. Without it, a dog can become a pariah among his own kind.

Though good-hearted and earnest, Solo simply didn't have the social skills to be at ease around other dogs. When near them, he would get overexcited at the prospect of interacting, but then quickly become terrified of the escalating contact. He simply did not "speak dog." It would have been like having a crowd of people on the subway yelling and pawing at you in ten different languages. For Solo, it was untenable.

His owner, Megan, came to us in hopes that we might help. If we couldn't, she would have to give him up. Few shelters adopt out aggressive dogs, so Solo's next stop would have been the veterinarian's needle.

Solo became my primary-care dog. That brought into play the only individual capable of surviving his anger, calming his fears, and helping him reenter dog society. That was Lou.

Megan and her husband were new to dog ownership and hadn't taught Solo much basic obedience. Without it, there was no way to communicate with, control, or focus Solo. That would be our first goal.

The first thing I often did with fearful dogs like Solo drew laughs from the other trainers. I'd walk into the dog's kennel with a book, sit down, and read aloud. That's it. I did it a lot with Lou in the beginning, to help him settle down before bedtime. Now I used it at the academy. It was nonthreatening and could soothe even the most worrisome dog. When starting with a particularly aggressive dog, I sat outside the kennel with my back to the animal, reading calmly and slipping treats through the fence separating me from the beast. Within minutes the dog would give up growling and posturing, then lie down and listen.

I read *The Hobbit* to Solo. He seemed to like it, especially the parts about Beorn, the shape-shifting man-bear. Each day before taking him out of the kennel, I'd read four or five pages; by the second page he'd wander over, and by the third he'd be licking my neck and sitting beside me like a kid.

I liked Solo. His personality was admirable, and kind of fun. He was strong and virile and affectionate, like Lou, and if you hung out with him without other dogs around, he'd calm down and be your buddy.

But he could also be a butthead. Strong, reactive dogs without adequate training are rolling stones, crashing and breaking through things helter-skelter without self-control. And so, I began to teach Solo his canine ABCs.

I chose an empty classroom to begin teaching him basic obedience. Even so, Solo was nervous because of the smells and sounds of a hundred dogs in the surrounding buildings.

We worked on sit, down, and walking manners first, using treats and praise. I used my body like a dog's, turning fast, leaning, keeping my posture, looking him in the eye. I was fair but stern, and after a few sessions he began to appreciate it.

He liked peanut butter. A lot. So, to teach a decent heel command, I'd often dab a bit onto the tip of a wooden dowel, then hold it in front of his nose while walking, allowing me to fine-tune his position and reward him in real time, without having to stop and reach for a treat. Carrot-and-stick 101.

On the third day, I brought Solo into the classroom as usual to work on basics. He responded eagerly and lapped at the peanut butter when offered. After a few minutes, he stopped and sat without prompting and began to sniff the air and scan the room.

Dogs have great vision for spotting movement but don't always spot something if it's perfectly still. But he knew something was close-by from the smell.

Lou lay motionless atop the ramped agility walk at the far end of the room, his coat blending in with the paint on the wall, his muzzle hanging off the walk, and his golden eyes following our every move. I'd put him up there a few minutes before; now, watching me work the big, edgy dog, Lou knew what I wanted of him, and he wasn't afraid at all.

Solo barked, whined, and refused the peanut-butter offerings. When a dog feels threatened, it's not food it wants, but safety. Those who think food can conquer fear haven't worked dogs like Solo.

I continued to work his obedience as if nothing had changed. After a minute, I flashed Lou the sign to sit, which he promptly did, atop the walk, a good four feet above the floor.

Solo growled. I ignored him and walked the big dog around the room. Lou began waving at us on his own. "Right back at you, pal," I said to him.

"Rower."

I let go of the leash. Solo bolted over to the elevated walk and began pacing back and forth beneath Lou, who cocked his head at the big chestnut-colored dog. Then Solo growled and snapped up at Lou, who pranced back and forth atop the walk, eager to play the game. Each time Solo snapped out at him, Lou gracefully leaped to his left or right, then stood there waiting for Solo to make up his mind what to do next.

I picked up Solo's leash, walked him over to a tie-out spot on the far wall, and tethered him there. Then I returned to Lou and loved on him a bit in full view of Solo, who sat and looked at us quizzically.

"Good boy, Lou," I said. "You too, Solo—good boy!"

As I walked back over to Solo, Lou made a graceful bound from the walk to an agility A-frame in the corner, then climbed to its apex. Now nearly six feet off the floor, he commanded the room.

I released Solo, who ran to the base of the A-frame, sat, and stared. No growling. Lou did his little prancing-pony routine, then waved at Solo.

"Aroogla."

"Good boys," I said.

That was the end of the session. If only for a moment, Solo had endured another big dog without freaking out. Perhaps for the first time in his life, curiosity had trumped fear. It hadn't taken a week's worth of treats, but just a few minutes with the right dog.

After a week of this, Solo and I once again walked into the classroom to find Lou lazing atop the walk, waiting to play the bizarre game. Solo saw him right away and did not whine or growl. I gave him a special treat—a piece of jerky. He gobbled it down. I walked over to Lou and continued to feed Solo jerky along the way. Then I gave Lou a piece, which he inhaled.

I walked to the opposite side of the room. Solo couldn't decide whether to follow me or stare at Lou.

I crouched. "Lou, come here!"

Lou leaped off the walk, over Solo's head, and onto the matted floor, then sprinted over to me. I flicked him a treat and he caught it. Then the drama began.

Like a goldfish on the bathroom rug, Solo just didn't quite know what to do next. As Lou frolicked around the room, Solo made a dash for my burly Rott mix. His short hackles up and tail pointed straight out, Solo meant business.

Lou cut, ran, and leaped around the room, avoiding Solo's wrath. It was like watching an albatross chase Tinkerbell. Up the ramp onto the walk, over to the A-frame, down onto the matted floor, keeping to the rubber mats for traction while Solo slipped and slid across the bare floor.

I let them go at it for ten minutes. I wanted Lou to make the call and knew he would, soon.

Finally, Lou stopped and stood his ground, tail flagging, muscles flexed. He was calling Solo's bluff. Tense as steel, Solo came over and touched his nose to Lou's, who turned to sniff at Solo's rear. Solo growled and snapped at Lou, who ducked the bite and did a bucking 180-degree turn to face Solo, who sneered and came at Lou again. It was like watching *Enter the Dragon*.

He'd had enough. Unlike the eight-month-old dog who'd happily avoided the ire of other dogs, the two-year-old Lou had decided that if a dog still wanted a fight after all this, he was welcome to it. Though I was taking a big chance, I knew that this was the best medicine for Solo, and that Lou would practice proper restraint.

Lou slammed Solo down onto the mat. A rumble emanated from Lou that I hadn't heard since that day at the 7-Eleven— rolling and low like an earthquake far below the surface. Standing astride him now, Lou shook Solo by the neck, then let go and walked off a few paces. Solo sprang up and trotted around in small circles, astounded. No dog had ever been gutsy enough to do that before. Lou followed him for a bit, then came over to me.

"Good boy, Lou," I said, giving him a tear of jerky. To my surprise, Solo wandered over, too, and sat for a piece, close beside Lou, who held no grudge. "Good boys," I said, rubbing both their heads.

It hadn't been cutting-edge training techniques. No clickers, bells, whistles, or human psychology. It'd been school-yard justice, plain and simple. Solo was on his way.

Over the next few weeks, I trained them together and let them play and roughhouse. They spent lots of time in each other's company. Lou had to mix it up with him a few more times, but eventually Solo realized that his fears had been somewhat base-less; he began to trust Lou and would soon actually wag and smile whenever we all got together.

They'd do long down/stays beside each other in different places, including the front office, where people and dogs passed in and out like a train depot. Solo's improving obedience, com-bined with his trust in Lou, helped him stay calm and under control; instead of erupting in reactive fear, he'd just look to Lou and me. Solo was learning to relax and be a dog.

I worked them in an outdoor exercise pen and then a big fenced field, where they romped like pups together. The extra space there actually helped depressurize the situation for Solo; when he'd begin to feel tense, he'd just trot off a ways while Lou and I played a game of fetch or tag.

Solo let Lou introduce him to other dogs, ones that I knew had the ability to convey the same confidence and poise as Lou had. I did so in the field first, then gradually took it into smaller areas until Solo could be trusted on-leash with just about any other dog. Down/stays, regimented heeling exercises, tandem walks—he handled it all with little objection. After two weeks with us, he'd turned a corner.

It meant nothing if I couldn't transfer control to Megan, his owner. An earnest person with a heart of gold, she understood the seriousness of Solo's situation and was ready to get the job done.

After the two-week mark, owners came in for the first visit, to observe their dogs' progress and to reunite for a time. It was al-ways an emotional visit; often the dog temporarily reverted back to its old ways when seeing its people again.

To forestall that, we had the owners sit quietly in the corner of the busy office lobby. Then we'd bring the dog up there to work its obedience, as we had each day for weeks. Often, the dog wouldn't even notice the presence of its family, letting us show what it had learned. This worked quite well with most dogs, except scent hounds and German shepherds, who would smell the presence of their owners even before we'd bring the dogs up front. To throw these dogs off, we often dabbed a minuscule amount of Vicks VapoRub under their noses, to temporarily short-circuit their scent abilities.

Megan and her husband, Curt, sat quietly on the sofa while I brought Solo in. Lou and another dog were already there, doing down/stays. I walked Solo around the room on a loose leash, weaving in and out of the other dogs. Then I put him on a down/stay beside Lou, facing away from the sofa. He licked him. Megan stifled a cry.

I released Lou from his stay and walked him around off-leash. Solo thought about getting up but caught himself when I stopped and pointed at him. After putting Lou into a sit/stay beside Solo, I stepped over Solo a few times. He kept his stay.

Megan's face was a study in joy and disbelief. Looking into her eyes, I saw what she'd been holding out for: hope.

Then Solo started sniffing the air and getting squirrely. He smelled Megan and Curt. Before he broke on his own, I released him, walked him around the room, gave him a tear of jerky, then brought him over, signaling Megan and Curt to stand to prevent Solo from jumping up into their laps. Lou stayed where he was and watched.

"Solo, sit!" asked Megan, as per an earlier request from me. He did sit, but then broke down emotionally, spinning and whimpering like a kindergartner on his first day. I let them love on him. Megan teared up; Curt looked stunned.

Now I had to prove what Solo had learned. With Megan and Curt back on the sofa, I took him back to Lou, where, after several tries, I got Solo back into a shaky down/stay. Often, at this point, a dog will fall to pieces and redirect his frustrations at the nearest target, which in this case was Lou. But, instead, he just whimpered and commiserated with his big friend lying there beside him.

"Are you sure that's Solo?" she asked. "He's right *next* to that dog."

"That's my dog, Lou. He's the reason Solo is doing so well."

"They like each other."

"They do now."

"It's a miracle," she said, barely able to hold it together.

"It's a beginning," I said. "The hard part will be teaching you."

Megan and Curt came in for two more visits, during which time I taught them the basics of obedience and leash work. Though she had started out knowing very little, Megan learned fast and became a great student. By the end of the month, Solo would obey both Curt and Megan with the same enthusiasm as he showed me.

But Solo wasn't done yet. They understood how crucial it was to keep socializing and working him, and how they needed to be there as mentors rather than littermates, servants, or apologists. To keep him alive, they knew they needed to stay on top of it.

Megan became so confident in working Solo that, a short while later, she decided to get a new dog, Sasha, whom Solo, with help from me and Lou, took to quickly. Shortly after that, another rescue mutt named Java came into their lives; abandoned at the age of five weeks, Java never got the right attention from her mother and littermates. But Java would be just fine; Solo and Sasha would take care of that.

Solo lived to the good age of thirteen. Not only did he retain what he'd learned from Lou, but he used it to help socialize Java, who would otherwise have turned out to be as frightened and antisocial a dog as Solo had first been. Solo had "passed it on."

And now for a little spooky stuff. While working on the first draft of this chapter, I had searched in vain for contact information for Megan and Curt. I'd wanted to tell Solo's story, but my faltering memory wasn't filling the gaps very well. Then (I kid you not about this), at the *precise* moment I was looking over some old photos of Lou, I received an e-mail from who else but Megan! Here it is, unfiltered:

> *Hi, Steve:*
>
> *Just wanted to say hi to one of my first dog training mentors! My husband Curt & I had the pit/Chessie mix Solo who your Louie taught to play with other dogs, which allowed us to adopt the Australian shepherd/Border collie mix Sasha from PAWS—you introduced Solo & Sasha at the Academy. Thank you for training me & Curt, for training Solo, and for finding Solo an appropriate dog friend to join our family.*
>
> *Sasha and Solo both lived to about thirteen years of age. We now have Java, Tex, and Tommy, who are shown in the attached photo. (Java is the black Lab cross in the front with the gray muzzle, Tex is the spaniel mix Curt is petting, & Tommy is the Dobie/GSD behind Java, next to me—Tommy reminds me of Louie.)*
>
> *I'm in the process of building a swim spa for dogs (I'm an animal massage practitioner and got hooked on canine water therapy when Sasha needed it for her arthritis). I'm building it gradually, & I'll let you know when it's finished.*
>
> *Megan Anderson*

After reading the e-mail, I looked at photos of Lou for a while, then went out for a walk. I thought about how, without Lou's help, Solo would probably have been put down. Curt and Megan might have shied away from further dog ownership, or at the very least not learned the right way to train troubled dogs like

Solo. Instead, they got to enjoy a happier Solo for many years, and even used him to do for others what Lou had done for him.

Megan now helps dogs recover both physically and emotionally, because of Lou, because I'd driven by that stretch of Highway 101 at that exact instant instead of ten seconds too soon or too late.

Pass it on, Lou.

9

The Quick, the Young,
and the Old

In one year at the academy I'd trained more dogs than most trainers do in a decade. But the real key to my success was having a good rapport with the owners. In fact, I think my teaching experience and East Coast gift for gab might have been one of the reasons why Colleen kept me around. I could talk some trash.

Colleen soon let me loose in the classroom. I taught seven-week basic and intermediate obedience classes, and used Lou as my assistant in them all. He'd lie in his favorite spot atop the ramped agility walk while I taught, lording over all the "store bought" plebes. When I needed to show the class a new technique or behavior, I'd call him over to demonstrate. And any antisocial dogs in the class of course got special attention from Lou, the warrior-diplomat.

During the first week of a class, Lou and I would put on a little demo, most of it off-leash. He'd even begun to throw in a few impromptu tricks of his own, using the agility equipment stored in the same classroom. He'd leap sideways up onto the four-foot-high ramped walk, jump through hoops and over jumps, balance himself on the seesaw, and stand atop the apex of the A-frame, then wave to the class. The owners loved it; their dogs acted like they wanted to brain the show-off.

I'd been teaching Lou a backward heel when Colleen came into the empty room. "I need someone to teach beginning agility."

"I don't know how."

"Hasn't stopped you before."

"Good point."

"No one else has the time. And anyway, you two seem to like messing around with the equipment," she said, watching Lou sniff his way across the ramped walk.

"I sat in on Julie's last agility class. Lou likes it."

"She can show you the basics. You work owners on gaining directional control over their dogs and then on mastering each piece of equipment. Then you just link them together."

"I suppose."

"Yes or no?"

"When?"

"Next week. You already have eleven sign-ups."

"All right then."

I felt like the Boy Scout on a lifeboat asked to perform an appendectomy with a Swiss Army knife and a bottle of vermouth.

I knew Lou was quick. But I didn't know how quick.

Fast dogs signed up for my first agility class. A Border collie, an Australian shepherd, a whippet—all manner of quick dogs. Even a speedy little Jack Russell and a Shetland sheepdog showed up. All had been through some basic obedience, and a few even had decent off-leash skills. I knew half of the dogs already; it was more of a reunion than a class.

I'd practiced with Lou beforehand and had picked Julie's brain. "Most won't care how fast their dogs go through," she said. "But just that they can put it all together. And they want their dogs to have fun."

"Do they?"

"Oh, it's wild. And a Border collie always puts in the fastest time anyway, so it doesn't really matter."

A lanky male Border collie named Tex or Rex (I really can't recall) looked like the speedster of the bunch, though the female whippet and the male Aussie looked quick, too. Though I was teaching the class, I wanted to see if Lou had it in him to compete. Hell—I wanted him to burn that Border collie.

The class went well. I taught them directional control—how the placement of your body and the use of hand and verbal signals can facilitate a dog's performance around the agility course. We familiarized the dogs with the equipment—weave poles, jumps, tunnels, the platform, the ramped walk, the chute, the tire jump, the seesaw, the A-frame—everything a competitive agility class would have.

Each week, after familiarizing the dogs with a new piece of equipment, I'd add it to the course. For the last twenty minutes, each dog got a chance to put it all together and run the expanding course.

Though he was the same height as a tall Border collie, Lou tipped the scales at nearly seventy-five pounds at this stage of his life, heavy for this kind of competition. Lou was NASCAR; they were Formula 1.

He reveled in it. We practiced after-hours until each step, jump, and cut became second nature to him. After he'd run the full course eight or nine times, I didn't even have to direct him—he just ran it on his own, while I simply stood in the middle of the room, calling out the obstacles. The weave poles took him the longest; he didn't quite have the same speed through them as did the snake-backed Border collie.

But Lou couldn't be touched on the rest of the course. I actually had to slow him down on certain pieces of equipment, especially the five-and-a-half-foot-high A-frame, which he tended to leap up onto in one bound, then leap off in the same manner. Under AKC agility rules, the dog must climb one panel, then descend the other, and must touch a specified "contact zone" on the down side with a part of one foot prior to exiting the down side of the obstacle. Leaping clear off the A-frame to the next obstacle was a no-no.

On the final day of class, we ran the dogs. Though the course was a hair shorter than AKC regulation, due to the limited width of the room, it contained all the required obstacles and came close to the proper square footage.

Everyone had prepared so well that none of the dogs missed a single obstacle. Even the pug had a ball, giving the spunky Jack Russell a run for his money. But among the small dogs the JRT ruled, beating the sheltie by a good two seconds.

I timed each dog with a stopwatch. The JRT ran the course in the low thirty seconds; the whippet ran it in a very fast twenty-eight, and would have done better if she hadn't paused at the seesaw, her least favorite obstacle. But the two fastest dogs in the room came in dead even at twenty-seven seconds flat. You guessed it: the lithe Border collie and the barnstorming Lou. We'd stage a runoff to determine the champion.

Lou was stoked. If I hadn't kept his leash on, he would have gone out and run the course by himself. But the Border collie

won the flip of the coin, and the owner, a retired Boeing machin-
ist, chose to go first.

"You're going down, big guy!" he said, pointing playfully at
Lou as he brought his dog to the starting line.

"Rower."

"Ready . . . go!"

Off he went, like lightning. He couldn't run as fast or leap as
high as Lou, but, true to his birthright, the Border collie could
cut and weave faster. And he did, snaking through the weave
poles and cutting into obstacle entrances like an F-16.

"Wow," said the JRT's owner, standing beside me and petting
Lou, who, drooling onto the floor, watched raptly.

"He's got it beat," I said as he came into the stretch, the pause
platform just ahead, the stopwatch ticking past seventeen seconds. All that remained were the seesaw and two more jumps.

"Aroogla!"

"Damn straight."

Off the platform, over the seesaw, and over the second-to-last
jump. Twenty-two seconds. Everyone caught their breath as his
back legs momentarily slipped out from under him. But he recovered, launched himself over the last jump, and blazed through the
finish.

"Twenty-five seconds flat."

The room erupted. Lou chortled and spun like a top, as if to
say, *Let's go, man!*

"You're the best," I whispered to him, as I always did before
he ran the course. I gave the Jack Russell owner the stopwatch,
brought Lou up to the starting line, put him in a sit/stay, and took
my position close-by, ready to pull his trigger. When he saw me
take my position, tremors began running through his foreleg and
thigh muscles. He had that wolfish, kill-the-reindeer look, and
was tensed like Carl Lewis in the starting blocks. For an instant, I
could have sworn he'd glanced over at the Boeing guy and his dog.

"Ready . . . go!"

Lou exploded out onto the course like a sidewinder missile. Over the first jump, he cut to the ramped walk and flew across it, then cut hard through a series of jumps. He vaulted over the long jump, cut to the tunnel, blew through, then cut to the tire jump.

"Batman!" yelled out the whippet owner's little boy.

I could hardly keep myself in position as Lou powered his way through to the weave poles, his Achilles' heel. But we'd worked on his getting that disjointed, Border-collie cadence, where the front and back legs worked contrary to each other, creating the illusion that the dog's body is simultaneously going in opposite directions. He streamed through like a champ, then cut hard over to the chute, one of his favorites.

Bursting free of the shoot, he veered fast to the A-frame. Up and over with a perfect step-off toward a hoop jump. He flew through it and dipped hard right to the pause platform.

"Seventeen seconds!" yelled the JRT owner.

I saw Lou look up and scan the rest of the course, without slowing down. It was pure Lou.

"Heya!" I yelled, his time on the platform up. "Run, pal!"

Lou soared off the platform like an eagle. I watched him in midair, stretched out, smiling, eyes glistening, muscles rippling, a faint glance my way. I could almost have reached out and touched him as he flew by and made for the seesaw and the last two jumps. I remember feeling proud.

Lou tap-danced across the seesaw and cut hard for the last two jumps, set at near-right angles to each other. At the same spot where the Border collie had slipped, Lou reached out with his back legs and caught the edge of the textured mat for traction, his body leaning like a racing motorcycle. The mat rippled but held.

Over the second-to-last jump. Set, turn. Soar over the last jump, turn, race across the finish line and into my arms.

His heart jack-hammered. I lifted him in my arms and nuzzled his neck. Everyone looked at the JRT owner.

"Twenty-four point five seconds!"

Lou ran back out on the course, leaped over a jump, then pranced up onto the ramped walk. The other owners let their dogs join him out on the course, while the Boeing guy came over to me.

"I want him drug tested," he said, smiling, grabbing me by the neck, his dog frolicking with the others.

"You just need to feed that skinny sheep lover a steak or two," I said.

It'd all been unofficial and unsanctioned. Plenty of "professional" agility dogs could have beaten Lou in his prime. But on that one day, he showed everyone what he was made of, including that spooky, slinking little sheep herder.

That night I stopped at the market, bought a big sirloin steak, seared it on the grill for a minute, then brought it in.

Lou looked at me. "Your trophy, sir," I said, forking it onto a plate, placing it down with great ceremony. Incredulous, he got to work.

"We're having a preschool and kindergarten class come in tomorrow for an impromptu little demonstration," said Colleen while she worked one of her Irish water spaniels on some directed retrieving. "Tricks and obedience plus some dog safety tips for the kids and teachers. Simple stuff."

"Lou loves kids."

"That's why you're it."

"Just me?"

"You and Lou, Tracy and her pit, and Nancy with her golden. Just be entertaining."

"Aren't I always?"

"A laugh a minute."

Lou always had great affection for and patience with kids. He'd let kids touch and stroke him, look him in the eyes, hang from his neck—anything they wanted. He knew they were puppy humans and deserving of some understanding. And just as he'd become the perfect dog to help bring fear-aggressive dogs back from the edge, Lou would turn out to be the go-to dog to help ease the fears some kids felt when around big pooches.

As the kids marched into the classroom single-file, holding hands, they couldn't help but notice the beautiful black-and-tan dog lying atop the agility walk on the far side of the room. Some oohed and ahhed, while others went quiet and wide-eyed.

At nearly three years old, Lou had filled out nicely; with his deep chest, muscular legs, and strong shoulders, he reminded me of a petite version of his herculean Rottweiler dad, last seen lying by the side of the road, gnawing on his beloved deer snout. Lou's neck and head had filled out, too; his forehead had a hint of Rottweiler "dome," with a muzzle longer and more elegant, like that of a German shepherd. He'd grown into a truly stunning dog.

The teacher introduced me to the kids, who clapped and squirmed in their seats. Before I could start, one brave little soul popped up off his bleacher seat.

"I have a dog!"

"What's his name?"

"Rudy!"

"Is he a nice dog?"

"Yeah, but he poops in my closet a lot!"

The kids laughed, then went quiet when I signed Lou into a sit.

"How did you do that?" asked a red-cheeked little blond girl sitting against the wall.

"That's my dog, Lou. He knows sign language. Watch."

I signed him into a down, back into a sit, then had him spin left and right atop the walkway. The kids started to come alive. Then I signed "bark," an upward left fist pushed forward at him.

"Ruff!" he barked out. Lou used his big-dog bark only when I asked him to, or if something bad was happening. It echoed through the room.

"Whoa!" said the kid with the pooping dog.

I called Lou off his perch and had him sit by my side, signaled him to stay, then went over to sit with the kids.

"What would you like Lou to do?" I asked a shy little girl with red pigtails and a runny nose. She'd sidled up to me and was staring at Lou as if he were a fairy-tale creature.

"Wave at me."

I signed him to wave right. He lifted his right paw and waved at us, then chortled. The kids cheered. The girl smiled and pushed her face into my sleeve.

"How about you?" I asked the poop kid.

"Make him go up on that thing again!" Everything he said ended with an exclamation point.

I gestured to the ramped walkway and said, "Lou, hup-hup!" He trotted over to the ramp, climbed up to the walkway surface, walked across it, then leaped from it to the apex of the A-frame and stood atop it like Sir Edmund Hillary.

"I love Louie!" said the poop boy to a freckled girl beside him.

'So do I!" she said defensively.

The kids started repeating it like a cheer. "I love Louie! I love Louie!"

"Aroogla!"

"Yay *Aroogla*!"

"Who wants to learn about dog safety?"

"Me!" said the entire class of munchkins.

"How about you?" I asked pigtails.

"Okay."

I called Lou down, then froze him in a wait position halfway over. The kids with dogs giggled, while the kids who clearly had no dogs in their lives went silent. It was one thing to watch him from afar and quite another to have him advancing on you.

"Is he going to bite me?"

"No, honey, he loves you."

"My kitty bit me."

I advanced Lou again, then stopped him ten feet off. He stood there marching in place, chortling to himself, dying to love on the kids.

"He's pretty," said a little Asian girl with a bright red ribbon in her hair.

"Who knows how to say hello to a dog?"

"Me!" said the poop kid, now the official spokesman for the group. The teacher looked at me and shrugged.

"Okay, tell me how."

He stood up, faced Lou, and said "Hello, Louie!"

Everyone laughed. They were composed now, and clearly fascinated by Lou. But some of them still felt uneasy, and embarrassed because others weren't scared.

"Come here, Lou."

Lou walked over and sat in front of me. The poop kid came right over and wrapped his arms around Lou, who licked him from chin to brow.

"Ha-ha!"

"He loves you, but that's not how you say hello to a strange dog, right?"

"Right!"

"First, if your mommy or daddy is there, you let them say hello first. Then you listen to what they say. But if you are by yourself and a strange dog comes over, what should you do?"

"Run away!" said a skinny black-haired kid with a crooked smile and his hands in his pockets.

"Is that right?" I asked.

"No!" said poop boy. "You stay still, like with a bear!"

"That's right. Just stay nice and calm, and don't look at the dog. Let him smell you. If he likes you, he'll let you know. Otherwise, he will probably get bored and just walk away."

Lou luxuriated in the attention from the kids near him. "Okay, now I am going to let you all say hi to Lou!" I grabbed the short lead I had on him and walked him down the line, letting them run their hands through his fur. Lou smiled and licked. Some kids reveled in it; others were still scared.

A dark-haired little girl smiled and giggled when Lou licked her face, but couldn't bring herself to pet him yet. "Do you think you can get Lou to do a trick for you?"

"I don't know."

"Let's try, okay?"

" 'Kay."

I took her by the hand and brought her out in front of the others, then sent Lou out to sit atop a small rug in the middle of the room. I had them face each other, five feet apart. She giggled nervously. "When you are ready, look at Lou, then move your hand in a quick little circle like this and say, 'Lou, Spin!' at the same time. Can you do that?"

" 'Kay."

I stepped back. "Okay, hon."

She looked to her friends, then got a scrunchy look on her face, like that of a kid drawing a picture of her house. She lifted her right hand a bit and looked at Lou, who knew a sign was coming down the pike. He watched her, not me.

"Lou, spin, spin!" she said, twirling her hand around like she was waving a flag. He immediately did a 360 to the right, ending up in the same position. The kids all cheered. Lou yodeled and marched. She made a Bill Cosby O with her mouth.

"Good job!"

"Lou, spin!" she repeated, cocky now. He spun again and I tossed him a treat. "Lou, spin!" He spun left this time, twice, did a funny little "Urkel" dance, then came over and placed a paw atop her shoulder. She laughed while he slobbered her face.

"Good job," I whispered to her, leading her back to her seat.

I used Lou to show them what never to do with a dog. No screaming or running away, no grabbing ears, tails, or feet, no sneaking up, and no staring in the eyes. No teasing, no rough-housing, no crouching down and slowly reaching your hand out (a threatening mistake made by nearly everyone).

"What *can* I do?" asked the poop boy, ever the pragmatist.

"You can be gentle and quiet and let the dog smell you before you touch him. You can stand tall and pet gently on the head or neck, and walk slowly when near any dog."

"My dog likes chasing her ball," said a chubby-cheeked, blue-eyed girl.

"That's a great game to play," I said, walking over to a Kong toy on the floor. "Lou, fetch!" I said, tossing it into the far corner. He jetted over, pinned the wildly bouncing Kong to the mat, grabbed it, and returned it to me. "Good fetch! Here," I said to the red-ribboned Asian girl. "Throw it for him."

She gave it a kid's toss; it bounced once before Lou grabbed it out of the air and brought it back to me. "Good job, hon!" Then I backed Lou up all the way into the middle of the room. "Lou, catch!"

I threw it high right, and he launched himself up, did his best Willie Mays imitation, then brought the Kong back. "Atta boy!"

"Yeah!" said the poop boy.

"Okay, we have to say bye-bye to Lou now."

"Ohhhhhh."

I placed him in the middle of the room in a sit, then stood with the kids. "Everybody wave goodbye!"

As they waved and shouted, "Bye-bye, Lou!" I gave him a

subtle sign for wave, and he lifted his paw and waved bye-bye to them.

"Aroogla!"

Tracy went next with Gator, her beautiful brindle pit, more intimidating than Lou because of his breed's infamous reputation. His mighty jaws and ripped body worried the kids at first, but they soon warmed up to his obedient and sweet ways. Nancy went last with her bubbly golden retriever, in training for advanced obedience competition.

By the time we finished, the kids were tired, happy dog experts. They filed out with their teachers, petting each dog along the way. Some of the kids touched the dogs as if handling fire, while others (like the poopster) gave the dogs hugs. Lou obliged with hugs and kisses of his own, and some throaty yodels.

"He should work at the school," said the kindergarten teacher on her way out, caressing Lou's head. "He's remarkable. Looks like that guy from that show *Wiseguy.*"

"Kevin Spacey?"

"No, the other guy."

We had preschools and kindergarten classes in on a regular basis after that. The kids loved it and so did the dogs. Lou seduced them, taught them about dog safety, and got many anxious children to loosen up and start enjoying every kid's birthright—the love of a good dog. Parents even called to thank us and ask for help in finding a dog for their once-apprehensive children, who, after meeting Lou, learned that dogs weren't so bad after all.

That night I sat with Lou on the floor and thought back to my cranky parakeet, the dog books I'd read by flashlight under the covers as a kid, and Sabino the unbribable, dog-hating landlord. Thinking of the kids that day, I knew it had all led up to this.

"Better late than never, huh, pal?"

"Roo."

Years later, after my private life would take an unexpected 180-degree turn, an older, more dignified Lou would get yet another shot at teaching little kids. This time he'd inspire them to learn a new language, one used by many millions of Americans every day. In his sixteen years, that feral fuzz ball would end up clocking more actual classroom teaching time than I did.

The very young live from instant to instant, unaware of the memories they build. But the very old, thinking that little worth remembering can happen while they fade away in nursing homes, have banked their old memories and survive on them like pension checks, drawing upon them when needed for support and succor.

But sometimes unexpected things happen that can rouse an old memory, something seminal, a past event so momentous and strong that, like a rare old book, it dare not be touched too often for fear of tearing its brittle pages. Shelved and dusty, only its resonance remains, until something special comes along to yank it down from its ledge, open it to the proper page, and wrest the reader back to that exact moment in time, to the experience that, like a bolt of lightning, singed the reader's heart forever.

For one such man, waiting on a forgettable death in a clean, forgettable nursing home, a very special thing would bring him back to his moment in the hot Pacific jungle, back to his comrades, his revered young friends forever frozen in time in his old heart, like painted angels to him now. That special thing was Lou.

The preschool kids had loved the dogs and learned from the experience. But some of us wanted to bring joy to those on the other end of the journey, to those who'd led long lives, raised kids and dogs, fought for their countries and made an impact, but who now, cowed by age and illness, found themselves missing the simplest pleasures. We could bring them one simple thing: the friendship of a good dog.

Back in the early 1990s, the therapy-dog phenomenon hadn't yet taken off. But the idea was self-evident: close contact with a calm, loving pet could improve the mental and physical health of persons of all ages. Medical studies have shown that people with regular access to dogs visit the doctor less often, have lower blood-pressure levels, and suffer fewer incidents of heart disease and dementia. Pet companionship can even motivate seniors to increase daily activities and socializing. But for many in nursing homes, a pet just isn't possible: they simply do not have the physical ability to care for one. We decided to do something about that.

After contacting a few local nursing homes, we found one that was more than open to a visit from well-behaved, calm dogs.

"Any joy we can bring to our residents is more than welcome," said the activities director, herself a dog owner, who on occasion brought her own little dog in for the residents to fawn over.

But we would be bringing in larger dogs. "As long as you guarantee them to be safe, there shouldn't be a problem," she said. "Just be sure they aren't too frisky, and that they can take *lots* of petting."

Lou fit that bill to a tee, as did Tracy's pit bull, Gator, who was an ambassador for the breed. Though not the typical dogs used today by pet therapists, Lou and Gator loved people and had calm demeanors that made them perfect for the job.

The residents were brought into the community-events room. Most used wheelchairs or walkers; two in hospital beds had to be rolled in. Luckily, the academy had a wheelchair and a walker on site, which we used to desensitize dogs; Lou and Gator had been guinea pigs for this early on and couldn't have cared less about either.

We spent the afternoon demonstrating obedience and trick behaviors, then brought the dogs around to the residents, letting them interact and enjoy. They loved it. To a person, you could see them remembering dogs from the past, pets they'd had as kids, as parents, as grandparents. They told me about farm dogs they'd had growing up in Minnesota and North Dakota, bird dogs who could flush out the most secreted covey of quail, companion dogs who'd spent years snowbirding across the nation— many memories, all heartfelt. Then came the story that touched my heart and brought its teller to tears.

He hated his wheelchair. You could see it in his eyes, and in the way he manhandled its wheels and brake. If he'd risen that day, he would have stood tall and shown hints of who he'd been— an athlete, a roustabout, a soldier. What he'd done in his long life had been etched into his face like scrimshaw. Though he'd lost his youth, his blue eyes remained bright and filled with life and remembrance.

When Lou walked in, something in those blue eyes kindled. He smiled broadly, cradled Lou's happy face in his old hands, and said, "Hey, big feller, good to meet you."

"*Aroogla,*" said Lou, resting a paw atop the man's blanketed thigh and flashing him the Mother Teresa.

"Damned if he ain't a handsome devil," he said, vigorously rubbing Lou's neck and ears. "Looks just like Gable."

"He gets Tyrone Power a lot," I said.

"Oh hell, this dog is beefier than that," he said, a poignant look on his face, gazing hard into Lou's eyes. The two stared at each other as if remembering something shared. "Not to speak ill of the dead, of course. Power was a good egg; flew marine cargo out of Kwajalein and Saipan back in forty-five. Evacuated some of my buddies off Iwo and Okinawa. Gave it all up, right at his peak."

"I didn't know that," I said. The activities director looked at me and nodded.

"Oh yeah. Heart attack at forty-four, just like his dad. Frozen in time, just like that."

Lou leaned into the wheel of the chair, rolling it forward an inch or two. The man liked to move his chair back and forth slightly with his foot and hadn't put the brake on. He rubbed Lou's neck and kept staring at him.

"Were you in the Pacific theater?" I asked.

"I was."

"My uncle, too."

"Did he make it out?"

"He did not."

"Sorry, son."

"Where did you serve?" I asked, not sure if he wanted to go there.

"Guam, Saipan, Iwo Jima. All through the Marianas. You heard of them?"

"I was a history student in college. I studied World War II."

"You know about the war dogs?"

"No, sir, I don't."

He stared at Lou. "Well, I'll tell you. Guam was a shithole. The enemy hid in caves and bushes. We never knew when one of them would pop up and start shooting, or toss a grenade. But we had something they didn't."

"Scout dogs," I said, remembering something.

"That's right. Second and Third Platoons used them to warn of ambushes or land mines. Shepherds and Dobies mostly. I was a handler for a shepherd mix named Shep, of all things. Looked a helluva lot like your Lou here."

The room went quiet. The oldest residents nodded as they flashed back on faces from the past. Most must have known someone killed in the war. There was a kinship of strangers you could feel in the air.

"Shep and I would take point. I can't tell you how many times that dog saved our asses, pointing out ambushes, mines, or soldiers hiding in holes. It was a damn dangerous job that dog did."

He was into it now and I wasn't sure if it was good for him. But the director let him speak.

"When he'd smell or hear something, that big old dog would stop and go on point just like a bird dog, freeze and stare down the trouble. He'd get this look in his eye, like a wolf maybe or a mother bear, like nothing on earth could break him. Whenever we'd settle in somewhere for the night, we all wanted Shep close, because nobody could sneak up on his nose or ears.

"He loved us like brothers. You could feel it. He'd walk toward trouble, then freeze, walk closer, then freeze. But pretty soon it'd get to be too much for him, he couldn't take it anymore, so he'd rush right into the mess, roaring like a lion. So brave. He'd flush those bastards like quail and we'd take care of the rest. They were more scared of Shep than they were of our rifles, I tell you."

"What happened to him?" asked a woman sitting next to him.

"Oh . . . he got shot storming a cave. We buried him with the other dogs in a corner of the marine cemetery there on Guam. Saved my life a hundred times, that dog. Never got a medal or nothing."

I looked at Lou, who had his head nestled in the old vet's blanket, looking up, listening. I thought about him at the 7-Eleven that day and knew he would have been a great marine dog, like Shep. Then I thought of something.

"You trained Shep to stop and point?" I asked him.

"His first handler did. I took over for him after he got wounded. Stop, freeze, start up again, stop, freeze."

"Come here, Lou."

I put Lou into a standing position across the room from the old marine, told him to wait, then walked across the room.

Lou watched me. He knew it was time to work. I faced him,

then gave him the come/walk sign, a slight move of my fingers toward my chest. He walked toward me slowly, gracefully. The old man watched.

I signed Lou to wait. He froze in place. I signed come/walk again; he walked five or six paces before I froze him in place again, posed, tail steady, ears alert, his gaze on me. I moved him again, then stopped him right beside the man, who looked down at Lou, the dog stock-still and vigilant, muscles flexed beneath his shiny coat.

I left him there on point. I held a cookie in my hand to keep his gaze front and center.

When the old marine broke down, Lou went to him, rested his head in the man's lap, and looked up at him with compassion.

"Oh Shep, Shep," he sobbed, rubbing Lou's head over and over, boyish faces from long ago now sharp and clear, his dusty book opened to their page, the dog that saved his life, the dog that saved mine, bolts of lightning branding our hearts, changing our lives forever.

10

The Devil at the Gate

We moved into Nancy's dream house, a three-bedroom on a cul-de-sac in Bothell with a nice yard and decent neighbors. The big yard bordered a green belt that sloped down to a commercial kennel, where the owner boarded dogs and bred Bouvier des Flandres—big, powerful, herd-guarding dogs. Because the sound of barking could be annoying, the house went for a steal. Used to the racket at the academy, I barely noticed.

Lou loved the yard. He sniffed out every corner and squirrel stash, and every rat or mouse trail through the woods leading down to the kennels. He eyed raccoons in the trees and listened to the kennel dogs below woofing on and on about how their owners had abandoned them to go on vacation. He explored and marked and watched, half expecting those Bouviers to come lumbering up the hill, their massive bodies and bearded and mustachioed faces like those of Victorian gents on their way to a Dorchester smoking salon.

Now that she had a home, Nancy wanted a puppy. With Lou to serve as a role model, and with the big yard, we decided to give it a go.

"What do you want?" I asked.

"A Rottweiler."

"They're a lot of work."

" I love them."

"They get *big*."

"Want one."

"Very active."

"Rottweiler."

After a debate I was doomed to lose, I found a respected Rottweiler breeder north of us who had puppies nearly ready to go. They had good breeding stock, kept a clean kennel, and socialized the pups in and out of the home. I interacted with the parents and found them to be typical Rottweilers—busy and strong, with a hint of that gladiatorial bearing that helped define them. The father, as big as Lou's snout-crunching dad, was calm and lordly, as was the sleek, happy mom.

I convinced Nancy that a female pup would be best. In my experience, alternating the genders of home dogs helps keep the peace. And so, after two visits and more temperament testing than the breeder cared to bear, we took nine-week-old Ginger home.

Ginger was a busy pup with good focus and a friendly personality, and she lucked out in having the best role model in the world. At first, Lou just thought her another training dog to be "fixed," then returned. But when he'd awake each day to find her still there, pawing and licking at him, stealing his things, and nosing into his food, he finally grew to accept the orphan and began to teach her manners.

My job was to train Ginger in the fundamentals; Lou's job was to teach her the rest. Respect, self-control, patience, the pecking order—as the dominant dog, these were his province. When she nosed into his food dish, he growled her back to her own. When she tried to steal a bone or a chew, he batted her off and grumbled. If she played too rough, he gave her a shake and a stare. When she tried to nose out the door before him, he'd bump her aside and smirk. But he also balanced it all out, like a good trainer would: he'd lick her, play gently, and shepherd her around the property. A curious thing happened: Lou became a big brother, and he rather liked it.

At seven months, Ginger stood as tall as Lou and was nearly as heavy. She had a gliding saunter and, though unaware of it at the time, was already every bit as strong as Lou. Only when she occasionally sent him flying during play did she get a clue as to how strong she was.

She followed Lou around all day. When he sat and stared down the hill at the kennel below, she would, too, as if participating in some sort of religious dog ritual. I'd look out the back slider to see them sitting side by side, Ginger looking to Lou every few seconds as if he were an elder dog shaman awaiting some heralded event.

"They're worshiping Lou's deity 'Gog' again," I said to Nancy, half expecting Lou to wrap a front leg around her shoulders and pull her close.

I took both dogs to work with me; Lou helped with training, while Ginger got socialized and exhausted. Staying at home by herself just wasn't a good option for a young Rottweiler, who needed as much interaction as possible to become a happy, outgoing girl. She played in the fields, got tethered in the hallways and trainers' room, took crate naps, and generally had a grand old time while Lou and I slogged through the dogs of the day. Ginger was Nancy's dog, but during the day, Lou and I watched over her. But then a new test came our way, one that would side-track me from Ginger's training and test Lou and me in ways we'd never been tested before.

At two years old and nearly 130 pounds, Branka the bullmastiff prided himself on having an infamous reputation among the Beverly Hills landscaping community. Owned by a Hollywood film producer, Branka lived the lush life at a lavish Beverly Hills estate, with housebreaking and a few tricks being his only training to date. Willful, spoiled, and iron strong, Branka had begun systematically terrorizing the gardeners hired to groom the grounds of the estate. *His* grounds.

Branka's bullmastiff genes came out in spades. Historically bred to track, take down, and hold game poachers until their masters showed up, they can quietly subdue even the strongest brigand without difficulty.

Branka had decided that the Mexican gardeners who showed up in the mornings to trim, cut, and plant on the property were in fact poachers. He'd run them down, knock them over, bite and terrify them. Branka had quickly become a near-legendary character among those who made their livings tending to the plush Beverly Hills estates.

The gardeners stopped coming. Lawsuits and local authorities forced the owner's hand: if Branka couldn't be controlled, he'd have to be put down.

"This one's for you and Lou," said Colleen, smirking, handing me the paperwork.

"I love bullmastiffs," I said, looking over the information sheet.

"He flew in over the weekend, from Tinseltown. You'll need a red cape, flame thrower, and a suit of armor."

From the start, we knew that Branka would need more than the normal four weeks to be turned around and rebooted. He was strong—beastly strong. He had no manners and didn't think twice about knocking you over and gnawing on you like a Slim Jim. And he didn't discriminate between man and beast—most dogs got the same rough treatment.

'Why me?" I asked Colleen.

"Because you look like the guys he's been mauling."

"How thoughtful of you."

"Take your time. He'll be here at least two months. Double-leash him with another trainer at first if you think he's too dangerous. He needs the fundamentals but he also needs to feel leadership. You need to become his master and commander."

Bullmastiffs fascinated me. Smart and quiet, they were the ultimate home security system. When raised by competent owners willing to set ironclad rules, they make great pets who accept those you accept and vanquish those you do not. But when put in the hands of someone better suited to a toy poodle or a kitten, they can turn into a Stephen King plotline in a heartbeat.

There was just something about the breed's calm diligence and easy, authoritative demeanor that impressed me. Branka had that, but it was wrapped up inside layers of cheeky impertinence so thick that you could barely see the dog inside begging to come out and play.

I read to him for a week before feeling safe enough to go into the kennel. I'd chosen *Beowulf*; it seemed right at the time. He'd slammed himself into the gate a few times and roared like Grendel but soon calmed it down to a rumble and an occasional head butt.

Like Kong, he'd been taken from his island paradise and put into captivity. I was no Fay Wray, but I was all he had, and he was beginning to warm to me and the errant cookie tossed his way. I called my plan with Branka the Stockholm Syndrome Technique.

That morning I asked the kennel staff not to feed him any breakfast. Then, at around ten, I went in with a fistful of turkey meat. He walked over like a centurion, sniffing and staring me in the eye. He was magnificent—muscle-bound, broad-chested, and fawn-colored, with the stare of a hunter. Branka looked like a seasoned linebacker with a neck as thick as his stony head.

"Branka, sit," I said, holding the meat just above his big head. He looked at me, then at the meat, as if trying to decide if his rage at captivity was stronger than his desire for the turkey. Grumbling, he sat.

"Good boy." I gave him a slice. I kept it low-key; no phony emotion for this one. It would be bullmastiff style all the way.

I watched him for a moment without staring into his eyes. He marched in place a few times and sneaked in closer, wanting the rest of the meat. When a dog did that little marching motion, it sometimes meant that he knew "shake," so I asked, and sure enough, his big right meat hook slowly popped up and planted itself onto my chest. "Good shake, Branka." I gave him another slice and he took it softly. Good old Chandra the Wiccan trainer had gotten something right.

"You've had it your way too long, pal. You don't know it, but the gendarmes back home want to stick a needle in you," I said quietly, holding a slice of turkey at waist height, letting him wheedle it out of my clenched fist. "You, me, and Lou have work to do to," I said, rubbing his neck as he munched away, his eyes switching from the meat to me.

It had been important for us to reach detente before I brought Lou into the picture, because, despite the size difference, Lou would have come to my rescue had the brute attacked me. Lou was uncatchable, but not unbeatable.

I spent hours with Branka. He drooled so much that I had to

keep a rag in my back pocket. When I wasn't training him, he'd be chained out in the trainers' office, in a hallway, or in a spot where he could see activity but not actually come nose-to-nose with it.

He'd been wrested from his celebrity throne and was confused. We'd taken his crown, his fan club, and his victims, and put him into a world that demanded obedience, manners, and fair play, things foreign to him. He was a good dog on the inside; it was his outside that I had to deal with now.

Branka was not fear-aggressive. Rather, he had a superhigh defensive drive, defined by breed but intensified by being treated like a king by his submissive, spoiling owners. He had a taste for it; he *liked* it. When a dog develops a passion for defensive aggression, none of the usual tricks to quench the behavior, such as treats, distraction techniques, redirection, or time-outs, work.

Branka *wanted* to be aggressive, and would continue being so no matter how many time-outs, veal chops, or redirections one used. The behavior would not extinguish itself; it was self-generating, and if the normal motivators disappeared from his world, he would simply find new ones to stimulate the behavior.

It's one of the things some trainers today don't get: sometimes a dog becomes passionately wedded to a bad behavior that he has created, all on its own, and refuses to give it up unless given no other option. Dogs are not mindless automatons; they create, and initiate. Living with Lou for sixteen years taught me that. He constantly authored new behaviors entirely on his own, with no input from me whatsoever. When a dog like Branka did this, he'd want to keep repeating the behavior, because it *defined* him. It became his own personal muse.

In the same way as one can't cure an alcoholic by locking him in a closet, showing him old movies, and feeding him chocolate whenever he reaches for a bottle, so I could not distract Branka from his penchant for aggression or extinguish the behavior by restructuring his environment. I had to give Branka a new muse and at the same time make his old one problematic. And I thought I had come up with a plan.

When not being trained, dogs often got tethered out, usually on a nylon lead. Branka had to be tethered on a steel chain, as any other material would have snapped like thread during one of his harangues. In the beginning, if a trainer walked by with a dog on leash, Branka would roar, rise, and try to pounce; the chain would ring tight and stop him. After a day or two of this, he accepted his fate and calmed down.

Watching him from down the hall, I saw what I wanted to see. Branka was becoming—lonely. He had a winsome, hangdog look on his face, like the last kid picked for a team. Though he was still a young dog, even this bully needed friends.

Out of necessity, we'd denied him dog companionship. He'd never really had an honest friend but only people and dogs he could intimidate. It was time for Branka to find out how good it could be to have someone to look up to. It was time for a mentor to show him what life was all about.

Branka weighed twice what Lou did and was four inches higher at the shoulders. He made Lou look like a miniature pinscher.

When Lou first saw Branka, he turned and gave me a look that seemed to say, *Man, you have got to be kidding.* "I know, pal. This one could get hairy."

"Rower."

I brought Branka into the classroom as I had Solo, with Lou lazing atop the ramped walkway. I hadn't needed to double-leash the brute, a technique we used with very dangerous dogs, where one trainer's sole job was to simply keep the dog off the other lead trainer. The two trainers kept 180 degrees apart at all times to prevent an attack on either person. It could be tense; if you didn't know the other trainer well, someone could get badly hurt.

Branka had ceased to fire up on me and had even warmed up to petting and a little horseplay. But he could still go hot at any time, and I thought that he probably would once I began putting pressure on him.

I wanted him to feel what it was like to have a dog to look up to. I had to get him to look at Lou and me and think, *You guys are cool; what can I do to impress you?*

I tethered Branka to the wall, then went over to pet Lou. He sat up and gave me a lick, then took a cookie. Branka stood there, muscled up, staring, and grumbling.

"Quiet, you," I said, looking him in the eye. He stopped grumbling and looked at me with that jowly bullmastiff mug, like a drunken sailor after a bottle breaks on his head. "This is my dog Lou. He is better than you. Maybe one day you'll be cool, too, but right now, just be quiet and wait."

This went on for a few days. I fed Branka and Lou in the same room, tethered them in the same hallway, put Lou in the kennel next door. I made him watch Lou and me play fetch in a field. And I worked Branka like a marine recruit, every day, and had him watch as I worked Lou and other dogs, so he'd begin to think I was big medicine. I made him want to be part of my tribe.

If he'd been a fear-aggressive dog, my plan wouldn't have worked. But he wasn't; he was just a big lummox who thought friends were things you tackled and sat on. After two weeks of training and watching how friends treated one another, he was ready to grow up.

I began to walk them together. Lou could walk on either side, so I kept him on my right and Branka on my left, without letting them nose up at all. The few times Branka tried, he got a sharp reprimand from me and a quick correction.

By now, all the trainers had worked him. He could walk on a loose leash and behave himself, provided no strangers appeared.

But training was just a means for getting us closer to that change of heart we looked for in him.

When I got to the sheep field, I let Lou in first and unclipped his leash. He bolted off for a good run. Branka whined.

"Jealous? Good. You should be," I said, rubbing his head and neck, his bullmastiff body like a marble statue with a bearskin rug draped over it.

He licked my hand and leaned into me. "I'm going to let you off the leash. You are going to charge out there and try to demolish Lou, but you won't, because he is smarter and faster than you. You are a child and he is a man. Go on, find out for yourself. But if you do hurt him," I said with tone, grabbing his jowls and lifting his head to mine, "I will render you."

I unclipped him and let him go. He ran straight for Lou, who was sauntering now in the middle of the field, eating grass and sniffing out sheep dung. Branka charged out like Russell Crowe. Lou looked up and smiled.

I laughed as Branka moved in, roaring like a lion, and went for Lou straight on, like Andre the Giant trying to nab Jerry Rice. Lou waited to the last second, then cut hard left and ran for the perimeter. Branka thundered after him, dust wafting up off the dry grass as he tried to keep up.

Lou slowed down enough to keep Branka just off his tail. He toyed with him. He put some distance between them, then stopped and faced Branka, braced, then cut right, grinning, schooling the thug. Then he jetted off toward me at hyper speed, caught a cookie I'd tossed up into his path, and jetted off just as the frustrated oaf panted over. Branka looked at me in disbelief, then tried again to catch Lou, who lollygagged around, waiting for the game to continue.

Lou's rope-a-dope went on for another ten minutes, until Branka collapsed in the high grass, panting like a locomotive. I walked over and rubbed his tummy.

"You cannot catch him," I said, as Lou came over and sat a few feet off. Branka lifted his head, looked at Lou, then sighed.

We did this three times in three days, until Branka actually started looking forward to it. Then I took it into the classroom. I considered muzzling him for Lou's sake, but we didn't have one to fit his big fat face, so I let it go. It wouldn't be the same technique as I'd used on Solo; instead, I'd work both dogs, Lou off-leash and Branka on-, to build a working camaraderie between them.

Branka could manage a pretty decent down/stay by then, so I parked him in the middle of the room and walked off with Lou. I sat on a bench, rubbed Lou's neck, and watched Branka, whose hangdog look belied his desire for companionship.

"See his tail wagging?" I said to Lou. "He's starting to like us. But he's got a mean bite; think you can duck it?"

"Aroogla."

"Okay."

I put Lou into a down/wait two feet away from Branka then crouched down and cupped the brute's face in my hands. "Stay *right* there and do not hurt my dog. Savvy?" He looked up, licked drool off his chops, and slapped a human-size foreleg atop my arm. "Yes, yes, I like you, too. Just stay there."

I took big chances with Lou and Branka. I was working without a net. But Lou was the key to saving this numbskull, and I trusted his judgment and skill more than any person I have ever known. And he reveled in it.

I sat close-by, ate a banana, and tossed an occasional cookie out to each dog. They looked at each other. Branka yawned then lay on his side. I let him get away with it. He took a peek at me, then ever so slowly reached out to Lou and pawed at him, then stretched out his thick neck and gave Lou's paw a lick. Lou sniffed him and *rowered*. Branka went belly up and reached his paws out to Lou, who stood up, licked Branka's face, then sniffed at his big fat butt.

I gave Branka a touch on the butt to release him, then called both dogs over to me. They shoved their heads into my lap and inhaled the rest of the cookies I had in my hand. I bonked their heads together like Moe in the *Three Stooges,* then walked around the room, both dogs right there with me, tails wagging. The danger had passed; we were a pack of three, the least among us the size of a loveseat.

We began taking Branka out to a park close-by to generalize his obedience and new attitude to public surroundings. At first he tried to "manage" things, but he quickly gave that up when tasked by me. Lou came with us several times. Seeing how carefree and sociable Lou was made it easier for Branka to relax and let go of his attack-and-hold mindset, and eventually he took treats and pets from strangers. And not one of the Hispanic men on the park's landscaping crew got knocked down or mauled.

"I like this dog," said a short, dark-haired man who was trimming a dogwood. "Can I pet him please?"

"Ask him to sit, then give him this piece of jerky."

"Sit, sit," he said. Branka looked at me as if to say, *He's carrying clippers; you want me to knock him over?* I stared at him with a gaze he'd come to know as the "don't go there" look. "Sit, sit," the man repeated, waving the jerky around. Branka sat and the guy fed him the meat. "Good boy."

He didn't know how good.

"I have two round-trip tickets to Los Angeles," said Colleen. "One for you, one for me."

"Colleen, this is all so sudden."

"We're taking Branka the bullmastiff back."

"His owner treats him like Lord Fauntleroy," I said. I was fond of Branka and had actually entertained the thought of adopting him. "What good will it do to just bring him back?"

"We aren't just bringing him back. We're going to reintroduce him to the home, and train the owners to treat him the right way."

"We're both going?"

"Yes. Together."

"Can you handle it?"

She laughed. "Don't flatter yourself, kid."

The idea was simple: reintroduce Branka back into his home turf, this time using our rules and leadership skills, while at the same time showing his owners what needed to be done to prevent the beast from reverting to his old ways.

Of course, nothing is ever that easy.

We got to LAX on time. Colleen and I had only one checked item—Branka. He, of course, took forever to show up, and was fuming in his crate as the baggage handler wheeled him over.

"What is it, a baby lion?" he asked, as Branka slammed his face into the crate door so hard that the crate jerked across the floor.

"Knock it off," I said, squatting in front of the door. He quieted down and licked my hand. The crate smelled of pee. "Anywhere I can hose him off?" I asked the handler.

"There's a car wash on Sepulveda," he said.

"Want to tell him that?" I asked, opening the crate door. The guy hurried off.

Colleen rented a station wagon, and we loaded Branka in and drove him to his home, a plush estate near North Canyon Drive. Three years earlier, I'd tutored a few kids just a block from there, the young Lou in tow. It was a strange homecoming for us both.

Norman was a piece of work, fast-talking and tan. The first thing the small man did was to call Branka over and give him a big bear hug, the dog standing toe-to-toe with him and a head taller. "I missed you, big guy!" he said, Branka buttering his face. "You smell like piss!"

"He peed in his crate," I said.

"I'll sue those bastards," he said, smiling, shaking my hand. Branka went to his water bowl and drank and drank.

"I'm Colleen, the owner. Steve here was Branka's primary-care trainer for the last three months."

"So show me what he learned."

"Can I hose him down first?"

"Yeah, sure, come on."

We hosed him off and dried him down. Then I let him wander a bit to see what he'd do. He patrolled the property like a good bullmastiff, sniffing out all his Hispanic gardener friends.

We spent a while with Norman and his family, discussing what we'd done with Branka and what the new rules would be. They were impressed at his new obedience skills and couldn't believe that Branka actually had a brain in his head.

"This is great!" said Norman, moving Branka from a sit to a down and back again with just hand signals. "It's like steering a yacht!"

"I guess," I said, realizing that to them, the big dog had been more of an uncontrollable force of nature than anything else. "I'll show you how good his recall is."

I showed them Branka's charging recall, then put him into a down/stay on the patio. "Let's all sit down."

"You want iced tea, or a beer maybe?" asked Norman, grabbing my shoulder.

"Iced tea would be great."

"Sure," said Colleen.

She let me take the lead on showing them what Branka had learned, partly because I'd spent so much time with him, but also for the experience. I think she knew that I felt right at home with the "Hollywood types," who'd all been born in New York anyway. Colleen had planned on leaving me there for a day or so while she visited some breeders she knew in the area, and she wanted to be sure I could handle the situation.

"Rosita, *dos* iced teas *por favor*. So why is he just lying there like that? Is he upset?"

"No . . . he's obedient," I said, wondering if Branka had been Norman's first dog, as Lou had been mine. Norman was like a sixteen-year-old with a new driving permit who jumps into a Ferrari and lights it up. "Branka *wants* to do it. That's the trick."

"You seeing this, honey?" he asked his wife.

"I'm right here, Norman."

"Marsha," he said to his twentysomething daughter, who was busy listening to a pirated copy of the newest Blues Traveler album on her Walkman.

"What?"

"Look at Branka."

"Mind-boggling, Dad."

Branka sneezed. A string of drool threaded from his mouth to his forehead. He tried to paw it off, but it stuck there like Silly String.

"Gesundheit," said Norman.

I told them how Lou had helped me over the months. Norman stared at Branka like a kid at a new bike.

"That Lou sounds pretty great. Glad Branka didn't eat him. They made friends, huh?"

"Lou was my ace in the hole. They got along like George and Lennie."

"Huh?"

"Steinbeck, Dad," yelled Marsha, rolling her eyes.

"Oh, right. Wasn't he retarded, though?"

The gardeners' truck pulled up at nine thirty. The three guys sat in the cab, waiting to see who had the courage to get out first. I could see the driver argue with the front passenger, a stout young Hispanic man holding a cup of coffee, his last pleasure on earth before being rendered by the dog lion of Beverly Hills. He lost the argument, got out, and walked to his disembowelment.

Norman watched from the window. I didn't want him involved this time. I wanted to see Branka in his element without Norman's influence stacking the deck.

Branka and I left the home by a side entrance, walked past the parked truck, and sidled up to the terrified man at the gate, the murderous gardener-slaying dog on leash, a bag of jerky in my pocket. I'd dressed in scrubby clothes and played around in the garden with a rake beforehand to get into character, and to plant the idea into his thick skull that gardeners were to be obeyed, not turned into compost. And I hadn't fed him since the day before.

Branka grumbled a bit out of habit. "Knock it off, beef brain," I said, looking him in the eye.

"I am very afraid of this dog," whispered the gardener, his eyes like saucers. Branka sniffed at his pants leg, then stared up as I handed the man a strip of jerky.

"He knows. He can smell it. But he is hungry. He wants food. Tell him to sit, then give him this."

"Sssit."

Branka sat and licked his chops. The gardener dangled the strip of meat out and Branka inhaled it.

"Good boy, Branka," I said, motioning to the man to repeat what I'd said.

"Good boy, Branka. Very good boy." He looked at me. "He bite me bad, this dog. He no like Mexicans, I think."

"Don't worry," I said, opening the gate and walking in with Branka and the young man, then motioning to the others to come in. "He's a different dog. No more biting."

As the other two came over, I flipped the bag of jerky to the driver, an older man with a limp. He caught it. Branka watched the flight of the bag, then stared at the man as if trying to remember him.

"He no like me much, this guy," he said.

"Give him some meat."

He held a strip out to Branka, who slurped it down like spaghetti, then looked for more.

"You, too," I said to the third man, an impossibly thin guy with a straw cowboy hat. He took out a strip of jerky and gave it to the dog, who by now had put aside his grievances in favor of the food.

"He like us now?" he asked, giving Branka more.

"Not yet. He just wants food more than blood."

They looked at one another like city kids at a zoo, excited to be near a big animal that did not want to kill them.

"Okay," said the driver. "We can work now?"

"Yes. Get your tools and start work. I will work with you."

With Branka's leash tied to my belt loop, I worked with the gardeners, trimming shrubs, edging a lawn, and pruning a small maple. Every few minutes I walked over and had one of the guys ask Branka to sit, then give him jerky. Eventually I let each of them walk him around on-leash, and even had him sit in the truck for a few minutes between me and the driver as the man took a cigarette break.

"He is better now, I think," he said, petting Branka. "But before, he was like a lion. He knock us down and bite us many times. You want to see?" he asked, going for his belt.

"No, that's okay. I believe you. He is better now. But you have to give him food and walk him a little each time. Be his friend, okay?"

"Sure. I bring him some good food next time."

"Bring him some cheese enchiladas," I said, grinning.

"He likes those?"

"All dogs do."

"Sure. Every time, then."

"And never meet him at the gate. The owner will come around

with him like I did today, and all of you go in together. No gate, okay?"

"Good, good. No gate. He was like the devil at the gate."

I spent time walking Branka around from man to man, letting him sniff each, take food and pats on the head. Other than a few dirty looks at the skinny man, he seemed fine.

The stout man dropped a spade onto the patio behind Branka, who wheeled and went for him. "Hey!" I roared, stopping his bulk in midair with the leash, then poking him hard in the chest, the signal I'd worked out with the brute to let him know he'd crossed the line. Branka was unbelievably strong; had I not seen the spade drop to the patio before Branka had, I wouldn't have been braced for his lunge. He grumbled at the man, then looked at me as if to say, *Come on, bro; he deserved it.* I'd been able to stop him only because of our three months together; anyone else would have gotten creamed.

"Not cool, butthead. Down." I kept him in a down/stay for a minute and had the man come over to me and shake my hand.

"That is what he used to do all the time," he said, looking down at Branka. "Like a panther."

"Take his leash," I said.

"No, no, no."

"Here," I said, handing it to him. "You walk him with me. Everybody. *Todos.*"

I got Branka up, and together we all headed for the gate, the stout gardener holding Branka's leash like it was on fire. I saw Norman looking out the window and motioned for him to come with us.

"Where we going?" he asked, a cup of coffee in one hand and an onion bialy in the other.

"Hey, where'd you get the bialy?"

"I got a guy on Fairfax," he said, smiling.

"Norman, we are Branka's new pack, and we are all going for a walk in Beverly Hills."

I gave everyone a strip of jerky. We walked down the sunny street, Branka sandwiched in between the stout guy and myself, looking at me like I was nuts. The gardeners moved along like kids on a frozen pond while Norman drank his coffee and waved at neighbors with his bialy.

"This is great," he said, watching as Branka towed the stout gardener over to a hydrant to pee. "We should take him for walks like this every day."

"You don't walk him?" I asked, taking the leash and handing it to the skinny gardener. He took it and nodded gravely, as if asked to sacrifice himself.

"Never."

"He's not a cat, Norman, he's a dog. He needs exercise and he needs to get away from his fortress of solitude."

"Superman."

"If he just stays on the property, he will guard it like Fort Knox and hate anyone who comes near it."

"Not good."

"No. Luckily, he's still young. We may have caught it in time."

"Damelo," said the driver to the skinny gardener. He took the leash and with a surge of confidence trotted out ahead with Branka, who lumbered off with him. "Sit, sit," he said, holding out a tear of meat. Branka sat fast and inhaled the treat.

"Great job," I said, taking back the leash, thankful that Branka hadn't taken the guy down in front of the whole neighborhood.

"I have a poodle," he said proudly.

"She is the size of a hamster," said the skinny gardener, holding his fingers apart.

"But you are still scared of her," he said, laughing.

"She is nasty, like you."

We walked around the block, the whole lot of us, waving at people and making Branka sit, lie down, and walk nicely. Norman offered the rest of his bialy to Branka, who inhaled it, then looked around for more. He pushed into the skinny guy and knocked him into Norman, then pawed at him.

"What?"

"He wants the rest of the jerky in your pocket."

"I should give it to him?" he asked, still scared.

"Make him sit, then say, 'Branka, shake.'"

"He knows how to shake?" asked Norman.

"Evidently. And I taught him to spin, roll over, and bark on command."

"That's great!" he said. "I'll get him on Letterman."

"Branka, sit, sit," said the skinny guy. Branka sat and stared. "Branka, shake, shake." The dog dropped his paw into the guy's open hand. They shook for a few seconds, dog paw in man hand, both the same size.

"Great job. Now let's go home."

"I like him," said the driver.

"These walks have to happen once a week minimum, Norman," I said.

"No prob. I like this walking thing. Maybe we'll start jogging, huh, Branka?"

I gave Norman the leash and took his coffee cup. "Walk him around a little more. Be like a third-grade schoolteacher with him. Tough but fair."

"That's me!" he said, trotting off with the big dog. The four of us looked at one another and shook our heads.

"When you go, he will treat him like a baby again," said the driver. "And we will all be killed."

"I want to live," said the stout gardener.

"I like him," said the skinny guy, watching Norman and Branka saunter down the street with the same lumbering gait.

"He threw you in the air like a little bird."

"He is better now."

I shook their hands. We walked back through the gate and they got back to work. As I opened the patio door to go inside, the driver looked at me. "Maybe he will change his mind, that dog. But maybe not, yes?"

"It's up to Norman," I said.

"We will all be killed."

As far as I know, Branka never did kill anyone. That week, I taught his family to work him the way I did and went over the importance of leadership and social interaction. Norman actually followed through with the walks, and the gardeners brought him enchiladas. They toured the neighborhood like a Barnum & Bailey side act, trading the leash off from man to man and greeting anxious neighbors, postal carriers, dogs, and squirrels.

I never did see Branka again, and though that probably was a good thing, I found myself missing the big lug and wondering if Norman had held up his end.

But I had missed Lou more. Since finding him three years before, we hadn't spent more than a night apart. I had Lou withdrawal. At home with Nancy, he'd been busy schooling Ginger on the ways of the world, as I'd been doing with Branka a thousand miles away, both of us teaching dogs how to be dogs, with Lou always better and faster at it.

Norman couldn't know what he owed Lou. Branka had been a lonely bully whose only passion had been defending his kingdom from three gentle Oaxacans in an old Ford pickup. But even the toughest and meanest dog needed a friend he couldn't intimidate. In Lou, Branka had found a big brother to impress, someone immune to harm. The months we'd spent with him in Bothell had taught him what it meant to be a real dog, and how good it could feel to let somebody else take over. He grew to love Lou and me, not because we'd kissed his big fat ass but because we'd stared him down, been honest from the start, and given him peace for the first time in his life.

Branka was just one dog. Over the years, hundreds like him would come just as close to the needle, only to be pulled back from the edge by me and the other talented trainers at the academy. Nasty pits, junkyard shepherds, doubting Dobies, ferocious American bulldogs, edgy wolf hybrids, sullen Akitas, nervy Jack Russells—the list of saved dogs was long.

Every one of them—every single one—owed its life to Lou. For every night spent with their families, for every walk, each pat on the head, every morsel of food, there was Lou, working without a net. For their years of life, for the dignity of old age, for the chance to smell and run and catch a ball and make a child laugh—Lou was there, alive somewhere in that dog's heart, like the fading scent of Mother in a puppy's memory.

He knew how lucky he was. I could see it in his eyes each morning, like the people we know who love their work and can't wait to wake up and get to it. He couldn't wait to run a mad dog tired, then lick his face, or dodge a killing bite, then teach a foolish young dog how to look forward to things. Lou was brave and sure and he didn't care if some tormented meathead of a dog tried to rip out his throat because he knew he was too fast, too smart, too linked in to wilder sympathies. Lou knew that sooner or later he'd find a dog's button, discover what it needed in order to feel that it was part of something, part of the world again instead of that friendless, dogless place where it couldn't help but feel afraid or angry or lost.

Lou was old school. He had the heart and soul of the dogs of old, who'd rather work than eat. And the work he'd chosen was drawing dogs back from their visits with the dead.

On the plane back to Seattle, I began to understand some

things about Lou. He wasn't like other dogs. He was rare. He wasn't just a product of good training; he was the perfect happenstance of genes and timing. What had happened in Mendocino County had been a shot in the dark—that two dogs from such notorious circumstances and conditions could come together and create him, that among his flighty brethren only he would have the inspiration to stop on the hill that day the way he had and look down upon me, look me in the eye, and choose.

I tried to read a magazine on the flight but kept thinking about how different life would have been had my car passed down that stretch of highway ten seconds earlier or later, and how the veterinarian that day had said that Lou would have died of infection in a month without our rescuing him. An ignominious death, a thing of crows and vultures and ants, a nameless, defiled dog never given the chance to become the best friend I would ever have.

Our friendship defined us. These days I can't think of myself, or of life before or after him, without imagining him here forever, like an inscription carved into my heart.

He was the perfect storm. And I know now that, no matter how hard I try, it will never happen again. But back then, he was young and alive and different each day, better, wiser, clearer. We were a team, and time seemed to stand still. Now, without him, the incredible odds of him, the chaotic miracle of him—it just makes me wonder.

11

The Errant Knight

Lou could read dogs better than I could people.

Nancy came home late. I'd been up with the dogs, watching a movie. She'd been out dancing with friends. I hadn't worried about it. If I'd been as smart as my dog, maybe I would have.

Over the years, I've mulled over both versions of the blame list. First in my favor—a self-righteous list. Then, years later, more fair to her. But, for whatever the reason, when she got home that night she'd already made up her mind to move on, and it hit me like a lead pipe.

Five years is long enough to think you know somebody. So, when Nancy asked me to move out, I sort of, well—flipped. Bawled like a child, then stormed out of the house with Lou, a bag of dog food and a sleeping bag, drove around the state of

Washington with my big-hearted dog, sleeping in the car or out-side under the stars. I had no destination in mind save forest and trail, save the birds and whatever expletives I could let fly into the wind.

Driving down Route 97 through the Teanaway range, I saw a sign that said simply RED TOP. I thought, *What the hell, sounds about right*. I took the turn and found myself crawling up a rut-ted dirt road, my Civic none too happy about it. But I wanted to find out what Red Top was and I didn't care about anything else. I had a goal and this was it. Lou and I in the car, driving up to Red Top.

A half hour later, I found out that Red Top was a fire-lookout tower stuck smack in the middle of the mountains near Blewett Pass, five thousand feet up, with views of Mount Rain-ier, Mount Adams, and Mount Stuart, pine forests thick as fur and sun and sky and agate fields and stray cattle and hawks overhead, wondering how I'd been able to get that silly car up that road. But I had, and at the end of the road I parked and let Lou out and together we looked at the lookout tower perched above us atop a rocky outcropping beyond the tree line, an ele-vated wooden structure abandoned for much of the year except for the fire season.

"Come on, Lou," I said. "Let's go up there."

"Aroogla," he said. He was eager to cheer me up. If I was up-set or blue, he'd dote on me, put his head in my lap and chortle, throw a paw over my leg, or follow me around the house.

When I'd bawled the night before, he'd stuck to me like glue. He'd even tried to distract me by bringing over a ball, then grab-bing his leash and dropping it at my feet. Now that I was willing to do something other than blubber or complain, he bucked like a horse and led the way up the rocky path.

The rocky trail wound past agate fields, then emerged out of the tree line onto vast slabs of rock bathed in sun and swept by wind. The lookout tower sat above us; Lou barked out, then ran to it.

"Be careful," I said, sure of his agility but pathetic from emotion. One bad step up there would have meant certain death, and losing Lou at that moment would have pretty much guaranteed me a month-long stay in a rubber room.

The wind blew hard. I climbed the steep stairs along the side of the tower, with Lou right behind me. He had no problem climbing stairs and could even go up a ladder if asked to.

I pushed open the unlocked trapdoor and climbed up into the structure. Lou popped through and sniffed his way around, smelling out old lunches, rat droppings, and whatever else waited up there, then lay down to clean himself. I had a box of mini-doughnuts and a bottle of water in a butt pack; we each ate a doughnut, then shared some of the water, mine from the bottle, his from my palm.

I had a panoramic view of the Cascades and of a sharp blue sky with saucer-shaped clouds flying by above. In the distance, a hawk soared fast above the tree line. It couldn't have been more beautiful.

I was miserable, but the beauty didn't care. Lou felt it, but being a dog, he focused on things at hand. I did my best to copy that, to just look at things, to move from second to second like a dog.

We stood above the forest, mountains all around, the trees below reaching up to the sky. Sunshine bleached the world. I tried to think of nothing but sun and wind and the time it had taken to make this quiet place, the passage of time like the broken spine of a mountain that heals slowly, from the inside, without ever being seen.

I found an apartment in the city, close to the University of Washington. It was cheap. The busy neighborhood reminded me of Queens, New York, where I'd lived for years. Lou and I went from a rural house and a backyard perched above a dog kennel to a ground-floor shithole with bad plumbing and a homeless guy living in a lean-to behind a toolshed outside my living-room window. Lou passed another apartment audition and we moved in.

The big old house was partitioned into six small, dysfunctional units. Most of the tenants were college kids who didn't care if the toilets exploded or the heat didn't work. My apartment had odd little rooms and cubbies; the kitchenette was a converted walk-in closet and the bedroom was part of an old garage, with a cold, painted concrete floor. But the big living room had hardwood floors, huge windows, and a nice nook for an office area, which I'd use to begin work on my first book, *Choosing a Dog*, a study of dog breeds that I coauthored with Nancy Baer.

Lou liked the place. I think it reminded him of our first apartment, in Los Angeles, where he'd gaze out the window at pigeons and traffic. Here, he looked out the window and saw and smelled our homeless neighbor cooking beans and franks on a Sterno stove beneath an army-surplus tarp held up with coat hangers and lumber salvaged from a construction site down the street. In the mornings, he'd wave to us while he washed up in an old marble birdbath surrounded by weeds that flowered purple in the summer. Lou met him a few times early on and got fed and petted. They liked each other right off.

"Nice-looking dog. He bite?"

"Defended me a few times. That's all."

"I got a metal plate in my head."

"How come?"

"You know," he said, lowering a cup of beans to Lou, "I really can't recall. Woke up in the hospital with it. One moment I was down in Pioneer Square, drinking with some pals, the next

I was waking up in Harborview with a shaved head and a tube stuck in my dick."

"I'm Steve. This is Lou."

"Nice to meet you. I'm Henry. I won't remember your names; hope you don't mind."

"No problem."

"I ain't no trouble, in case you're worried."

"No. I got the dog and all."

"Nice dog, nice dog. Looks like Marcello Mastroianni."

"Does the landlord know you live here?"

"He don't come around much. I hear he's one of them slum-lord types. I move around a lot anyway. Got another setup under the freeway."

"Nice."

"Got a lady friend, too. She's in treatment now but she usually stays with me. She *loves* dogs. Don't worry, we ain't gonna rob you or nothing. I'll keep an eye out if you'll help out a little sometimes."

"You want a beer?"

"Hell yeah."

Henry and I drank beers and talked about things. I poured a little into a bowl for Lou and he lapped it up.

"He likes beer?"

"Loves beer."

"Smart dog."

I showed Henry some of Lou's tricks, then had him fetch an empty beer can. He laughed and stared into Lou's eyes for a while. Henry got fuzzy sometimes, as if the plate in his head were an AM antenna that got lousy reception. He'd get stuck between stations some of the time, but every so often when he'd come out of his tunnel it all got crystal clear for him, he could hear it all perfectly. Then he'd turn his head the wrong way or dive down into another rum tunnel and the static would drown it all out. "Like Hiroshima in my head," he called it.

Nancy Baer and I wrote the proposal for *Choosing a Dog,* then sent it out to twenty agents. The book gave readers candid insight into all the breeds and helped them pick the right dogs for their lifestyles. Too many people choose a dog for its looks instead of its behavior; we wanted to help them make better choices.

To our surprise, three agents got back to us. One, Toni Lopopolo, said she could sell it in a week. She lied: she sold it in two, to the same editor who, fifteen years later, would ultimately make it possible for me to sell this book to St. Martin's Press. As my relationship with Nancy Banks ended, my career as a writer began.

I worked dogs, wrote the book, lost weight, gained weight, and lived with Lou in a ramshackle apartment with a homeless guy outside guarding us while we slept. I shared more than a few beers with Henry and even became something of a barfly for a few months. I'd walk down to the Blue Moon Saloon with Lou, tie him outside, then go in and shoot pool, squabble with regulars about who was better, Hendrix or Clapton, win a few bucks and lose a few, then go home smelling of Pall Malls and spilled ale. Once home, I'd sit down and write in the dark, then go to sleep, and start it all over again the next day, Lou there, my shaggy psychiatrist, watching me for signs of melodrama, ready to catch me like a tennis ball. He was a good friend. He got me through.

Real heroes are not pompous or bigheaded. They're accidental and sweet and good-hearted, with nothing to prove. Farm kids called to war, cops and firefighters rushing into eternity, plain folk when the dykes break. They are uncomfortable with attention tendered for simply doing what seemed right at the time.

When faced with danger, some folks fold like napkins, then live with themselves in a penitent place, never to be the same again. But others find their courage and step up to the call.

Lou did not fold.

I walked home from the Blue Moon after a few beers and some pool. A summer night, warm enough for shirtsleeves. Lou greeted me at the door, leash in mouth, *rowering.* "Okay," I said, taking the leash and letting him out without clipping up. He walked to a far corner of the back parking lot and peed on the hubcap of an old Ford, then sauntered over to look for Henry, probably at his freeway location. Sniffing out an empty Hormel can, Lou whined, then came over to smell me, his way of guessing where I'd been. "Come on, Lou. I'm tired. Let's go to sleep."

I'd taken to sleeping on a foldout foam sofa in the living room instead of in my bed in the garage bedroom. I preferred to wake to morning sunlight sneaking by the blinds instead of the cavernous, cold darkness of the bedroom.

I shut the light and crawled into bed. Lou lay on a rug in the corner. He licked his chops, yawned, and settled in. I fell asleep thinking of a sweet double-bank shot I'd made to win a game of 8-ball.

Screams, at first in my dreams. Real-world sounds can burrow their way down into a dream, co-opt it, wake you slowly from the inside out, then persist into wakefulness, as if the nightmare has the power to claw up from the underworld, burst through your skin, and live on.

I awoke to find Lou in the middle of the room, staring at the ceiling, growling, coiled and hard like a black belt ready to smash a board to kindling. The screams had stopped, but there was moaning and the deeper sound of a man's stern voice.

Through the apartment's thin walls I heard college kids bumping headboards all the time; I'd become accustomed to falling asleep to the rhythms, screams, squeaks, and groans. But these were extraordinary voices and different sounds—unfriendly, unwanted.

Upstairs lived a young woman in her thirties, blond and pretty, a bit of a loner who surely thought the same of me. We'd pass each other at the mailboxes and at the local Safeway. I might have known her name for an instant, then like a dream had forgotten it. She hadn't seemed the type to bump headboards, at least while I'd been there. And my dog had never stared up at the ceiling, snarling like a werewolf, in the dead of night before.

Homeless Henry and his wife could laugh with strangers in the parking lot at three in the morning and Lou wouldn't care; his tail would wag slowly and he'd look out the window with anticipation. Headboard bangers down the hall, whom Lou had never met, could screech and moan, and he'd just cock his head and swivel his ears and wonder what he was missing.

Lou could distinguish.

She'd come home sometime after we'd fallen asleep. She'd had a bit too much to drink. He'd followed her home from the party, and when she'd put her key in the door, he'd pushed his way in, and that was that.

Weeks later, I learned that he'd been up there with her for almost two hours. After abusing her, he'd shoved her into a closet, then sat outside the door, talking to her, chastising her for being so careless. She'd panic every few minutes and scream and plead, and when he'd threaten to take her out of the closet again, she'd quiet down.

For two hours he terrorized her. Then her screams reached in and pulled me from sleep and changed sweet Lou from a giver into an engine of reprisal.

As I made for the telephone, I heard the sound of an old counterbalanced window sliding open above us. Each time Lou barked and growled, his body levitated off the ground. Then, outside my living-room window, I saw construction boots and then legs and then an enormous body shimmying down the drainpipe, then jumping to the walkway below. For some reason, he'd decided to climb out the window rather than leave by the door.

The woman screamed again. We could hear her more clearly now because of the opened window. Lou threw his full weight into the door. I heard the wood crack. Twice more and he'd have smashed right through it. There was no stopping him. I didn't want to stop him. I opened the door.

The man was four times Lou's weight. He wore overalls and tan boots and a ragged brown cap with fold-down earflaps. Ruddy skin, hulking, sweaty reddish brown hair sticking out of the hat. That's all I remember of him.

Lou caught him on the sidewalk two doors down, in front of a private shelter for abused and homeless single mothers. The irony of that still pleases me.

He knocked him down like a bowling pin, then bit him on the ass. I ran to the sidewalk in time to see Lou hanging off the man's backside like a rabbit's tail, the back of his overalls ripped open. He shook Lou off, ran a few yards, then got knocked down again, Lou flying through the air like Superman, going for his neck and arms, wanting to kill him. This is what nature designed dogs to do.

I shuddered. Lou wanted to kill. He hated him. I didn't know at the time exactly what the brute had done to my neighbor, but I was sure that he needed to be stopped.

The man strong-armed Lou off him again and stumbled down to the parking lot of a local YMCA, where Lou again tore into him. The man fell, slammed his head on the asphalt, and lay prostrate. Lou tore at his clothes and stood atop him like a mountain climber at the summit. Each time the man tried to get up, Lou slammed him back down.

"Better get your dog out of here, pal," said Henry, rushing up, scaring the hell out of me.

"Why?"

"Don't matter what the guy did; the cops'll shoot the dog or send him to animal control."

"You heard the screams?"

"Woke me up."

In a flash I saw that Henry was right. "Lou!" I roared. He looked at me, then stared back down at his prey. I heard sirens getting close.

"Lou! Come *here*."

He snapped out of his trance and trotted over. The cops were almost there.

"Come on, man!" said Henry, pulling on my sleeve.

Lou came over in a daze, threads of denim on his mouth, pink saliva on his lips. I grabbed his collar and Lou and Henry and I ran home.

I got Lou's leash, locked the door to my apartment, then went with Henry into his shelter behind the toolshed. Lou shivered beside me, then licked at Henry's dirty hand. I was terrified of losing him.

"Nobody seen nothing, man," he said. "Coulda been anybody's dog."

"That's right. Only we know. I'll put him inside and walk down there."

"And you don't know *nothing* about no dog."

"Thanks, Henry," I said. He'd been crystal clear this time. He'd heard it all perfectly.

I walked out to the sidewalk in time to see two police cars in the YMCA parking lot, the villain in cuffs spread across a hood, sobbing, the back of his overalls gone. Women in bathrobes from the shelter stood outside, watching.

They had him in cuffs, so someone must have called the police to report the attack. I went back to my apartment, leashed Lou, and took a long walk down to the ship canal, the eastern sky turning pink, the neighborhood quiet except for another siren, probably from an ambulance. I wanted to tell them all what Lou had done, how he'd hunted the bastard and put him down. But Henry was right—he was smarter than I was—they would have taken Lou, euthanized him maybe, or even let the guy go because of Lou's wrath. He'd have sued me and gotten on cable.

It was a crazy world. It wasn't a dog's world, where scent and truth ruled the day, where things were frank and honest and beastly. Somehow, he'd known what the man had done, and it had enraged him, made him invincible, made what he'd done at the 7-Eleven years before seem like child's play. Lou made sure that sack of crap would be tried and convicted, and if he'd been a K9 officer instead of a civilian, he probably would have gotten a medal.

The woman upstairs disappeared for a time. A day later, an officer took statements from all the tenants and neighbors. I told the truth about everything except the part about Lou giving the guy a colonectomy.

"Did he rape her?" I asked the officer.

"I can't comment on that," he said. Lou cozied up into him, smiling sweetly, playing the Rottweiler game.

"But you caught the guy."

"Well," he said, closing his notebook and grinning, "something did."

"Good thing," I said, smiling.

"Yeah. Good thing," he said, fondling Lou's head.

. . .

I've told friends about it over the years. This is the first time I've written it all down. What could they do to Lou now? I wish we'd stayed up a bit longer that night and run into the rogue before he was able to do what he'd done. But everything, for good or bad, was timing, was chance. Except one's intentions, and one's reaction to crisis.

After that night, I saw Lou differently. If only for two minutes, he'd turned into a raging beast, showing a wild side that had frankly shocked me. I'd seen dogs show that kind of untamed aggression before, some of it directed at me. But those dogs had been flawed by nature and were untrustworthy in everyday life. Lou's nature remained as sweet and loving as it had ever been, but now I knew what lurked inside him, perhaps another legacy of his days in the wild. It made me love him all the more.

I've thought of her many times. I'd wanted to confide in her about what had happened, how Lou had taken down her attacker, debased him, hurt him. How a woman he'd never met became part of his pack just from the sound of her pain, how Lou hadn't been able to take it, how something inside him had snapped and set free the beast. He'd sensed it all through a ceiling, from the scent of fear or hate or whatever it was in the air that night. I'd wanted her to meet Lou but she'd disappeared, and when I finally did hear sounds from upstairs I decided that it was better to leave it alone, that bringing it up again might have been untenable, and dangerous for my dog.

The only person in the world who knew the entire story, who knew what had happened inside that apartment and outside on the street, that cur who to this day tells the tale about the mad dog who took him down—whenever he parks his big fat ass down into a chair, I hope he can still feel where the fangs ripped in, hope he can still feel the fire of my dog in his scarred skin. I hope the memory of Lou worms down into his dreams each night and terrifies him while he sleeps, makes him cross the street whenever a black-and-tan dog with a twinkle in his eye walks his way.

Weeks later, while playing a game of "mad dog" with Lou, I recalled how he'd behaved that night. *You sweet, smart, wonderful dog,* I thought, hoping he'd never need to go there again.

"I love you, Lou," I said, hugging him, feeling safe and a little sad.

12

Change

I opened my front door. Water poured out onto the concrete stoop. Inside the apartment, Lou danced around in the fetid pool—turds, tampons, toilet paper, rotted leaves, and who knows what else floating around in it. In my *home*.

"Even you couldn't do this," I said to Lou, close to retching. "But the least you could do is not have so much damn fun."

The old pipes in the apartment had exploded. I waded through the effluvia to the bathroom and found the source of the flood bubbling up out of the shower drain.

An old sewer line outside the building had cracked and some-how linked up with a split drainpipe from my bathroom; waste from the building was literally flowing *into* my apartment. Except for a seagull dropping a warm, chalky load of goo into my open mouth in the seventies, it might have been the most repulsive thing ever to have happened to me.

The landlord didn't answer. He never answered. I left a message that included the words *health department, plumber, lawsuit, police, coliform bacteria, shit, piss,* and certain expletives not suited for this book.

He called back in five minutes.

The apartment had been a colorful place to live. I'd finished writing the first book there and was half finished with the second, another written with Nancy Baer, titled *Leader of the Pack,* a primer on the importance of leadership in a dog's life. Our agent had sold that one quickly, too; before I knew it, I was actually making money as an author.

But I was tired of busted pipes, bad wiring, drunken melees, all-night headboard banging, and the tenor of the neighborhood, where, once the sun went down, indigents, drug dealers, and stumbling frat boys outnumbered normal people just trying to get by. Good fodder for memoir, I guess, but for a burgeoning pet-care author and his wonder hound, enough was enough. I started looking for a new place.

I lived the life of a Benedictine for a while, replete with hearty ales and quiet meals with my dog. Then a six-month relationship with a wild woman from Portland began on a dance floor and ended when she confessed to an affair with a fiftysomething dentist in Los Angeles, who'd fly her down first class, gift her Harley Sportsters and free crowns, wine and dine her, then fly her back to Portland in time for her frugal thirtysomething trainer/author to schlep south in his Civic to give her whatever it was her elder dentist couldn't.

Lou and I worked hard. After training thousands of dogs, I found they'd all begun to blend together into a big, many-headed supermutt I called Pangaea. "Good Pangaea," I'd yell out the window on the way home each night, Lou yodeling away in the back, the back window smudged with nose grease.

We added sheep to the academy's big field and let the dogs have at it. Some did well, while others got into it a bit too much and had to be pulled out before sheep parts began disappearing. Oddly, Lou was one of those dogs.

Lou had always maintained a very high prey drive for squirrels, ferrets, hamsters—whatever moved fast and could be defined in the broadest terms as a meal. I'd taught him to curb his enthusiasm, but sheep touched some deep nutritional chord in him.

Rottweilers of the Roman army had guarded sheep on long marches, and German shepherds had strong herding skills, so I thought Lou's heritage and speed would make him a great herder. He did well the first few times we put him with the sheep, naturally herding them, moving them, corralling them. It was fun to watch; his speed and cutting skills had found their purpose, or so I thought.

He'd eaten a lamb-and-rice diet all his life, including raw lamb at least once each week and a beefsteak every now and then. The taste of lamb was a holy thing to him, and after he'd spent a few days running with the sheep, a switch must have clicked on in his head. *I am surrounded by a lifetime supply of dinner,* he must have thought that day. Instead of herding sheep, he began to bite them. Hard. Food hard.

And so ended Lou's short herding career, perhaps the one thing he could not master. Considering his early life as an opportunistic predator, it made sense that Lou would see sheep as Costco-size bags of lamb-and-rice dog food.

Lou kept three paws in my world and one in the other place. Sometimes when he'd stare off into a forest, or spy a mule deer crossing a fire road, or eye a raccoon climbing a spruce, I could see that fourth paw. It was part of him and I treasured it.

The one good thing the wild woman of Portland had left me was a renewed desire for live music. So on weekends I began to listen to blues bands down in Pioneer Square, which back then had blues at nearly every club. A group cover got you into eight different venues; people on First Avenue trolled from bar to bar, sampling bands and dancing their socks off. It was at one of these clubs that I met Nicki, who would restore my faith in women and give Lou a home for the last five years of his life.

"You going to nurse that beer all night?" she asked, dancing with friends to her husband's rock-'n'-roll cover band. I'd been moping around like a teenager while she and her friends sweated to every raucous song, the floor crowded and sticky with spilled beer.

"I guess not," I said, jumping into the humid fray and having a great time. Nicki was petite and fun and awfully cute—and, as I quickly learned, married with two young boys. She was simply an affable dancing fool who couldn't bear to see a guy standing around like a moax.

I got to know Nicki and her husband and friends, a lively crew who danced themselves silly on weekends. Her husband (another Steve) had played guitar and sung in the same cover band since college, and though he was in his thirties, he still played gigs around the city just for the fun of it.

I enjoyed the company and the chance to dance until my feet ached and sweat soaked my shirt. After a year of feeling sorry for myself, it felt like I was finally coming back to life.

Each day I came home to an apartment that smelled like a landfill in July. Though the landlord had fixed the pipes and helped clean up the mess, the stench had leached into the floors and walls and wouldn't go away.

While working on edits for *Choosing a Dog* (which wouldn't be published for at least another nine months), I began to create the structure of the second book, *Leader of the Pack*. Nancy Baer and I worked hard on crafting the right outline for what we feel is still the best primer on canine leadership yet written. To save money, she illustrated every AKC-recognized dog breed for *Choosing a Dog*, and did a bang-up job at it. My strategy of crafting a detailed outline would be the model for all my future prescriptive pet-care books; right down to the paragraph, I knew where the books would go.

Lou and I hung out each night in the smelly apartment. I wrote while he chewed on something or hung out with Henry, who, after my neighbor's sexual assault and Lou's vigilante action, became one of Lou's best friends. Henry's partner, Margaret, had disappeared from the scene, and he'd become terribly depressed over it. But he wouldn't talk about her, so I left it alone.

Lou brightened Henry up and kept him out of his funk. It reminded me of visiting nursing homes with Lou—how he could reach the child inside the oldest, saddest person and get him or her talking, laughing, reminiscing.

"Know why I'd never steal this dog?" he said one evening, sharing a bag of chips with us.

"No, Henry, why?"

" 'Cause I love him, that's why," he barked, as if I didn't believe him. "And cause Margaret loves him. I love my Margaret more than anybody's ever loved anyone, and I can't even take care of *her*. How the hell would I take care of this fine dog?"

He teared up, so I grabbed two cold beers and a tennis ball, tossed the ball for Lou, and gave Henry a beer and talked baseball with him, as I had with John years before in Los Angeles, another good, lonely man with a sick wife, a man who loved dogs and baseball and who didn't know where he was headed.

.   .   .

Every piece of advice, every trick, every behavior I've ever written about first got tested out on Lou. He was my test kitchen, and it gave him a great vocabulary and a big, active brain.

Check out the following vocabulary list. Though I'm sure there are a good many more words I'm not remembering, this will give you a good feel for what he knew. And most of these words had a corresponding hand signal, effectively doubling his list of understandable commands. He also knew the names of places, and at least twenty or thirty people and a good number of dogs. If you said the name of someone he liked, he'd wander around the house looking for that person (or dog).

LOU'S WORKING VOCABULARY LIST

around	comb	give
away	come here	good
ba-ba	come by	guard
back	cookie	head down
ball	crawl	heel
bark	cross	heel right
bed	dance	hold it
beer	dig	house
beg	down	hug
bone	drop	hup
bowl	eat	hurry
bring	fetch it up	hydrant
brush	find it	inside
bumper	food	keys
car	frame	kiss
catch	Frisbee	kitty
chute	gentle	Kong
climb	get	leash
close	get in there	leave it

left	reverse	stay
lick	right	steak
look	roll	stick
Lou	rope	swim
mad dog	*rower*	take it
no	rug	teeter
off	run	through
on	shake	tire
open	sheep	touch
out	shoes	tunnel
outside	sic 'im	under
over	sit	wait
park	slow	walk
pasta	spin left	water
pull	spin right	wave
push	spot	weave
quiet	squirrel	wipe
ramp	stand	

Working dogs have an unfair advantage over companion pets when it comes to developing a big vocabulary and behavioral repertoire. Their exposure to diverse environments and complex activities all but guarantees a diverse lexicon. Lou fit this working-dog model; for sixteen years he'd sweated through the rehabilitation of hundreds of crazy dogs, the proofing of more than a dozen books, the education of hundreds of kids, the entertainment of the elderly, and the capturing of four very bad people. That kind of life experience creates complex associations and a sophisticated aptitude.

Lou's vocabulary list is long. But the truth is that most dogs understand more words than owners are aware of, words used in everyday conversation that become associated with actions, like saying "where are my keys?" before going out, or "the mail is here" before checking the mailbox. Repetition creates meaning and understanding. In all likelihood, Lou's actual vocabulary was much bigger; I just wasn't aware of all he knew. I kind of like the thought of that.

Salli was a big woman who liked small dogs. She came to the academy shortly after me, first as an apprentice and then a full-fledged trainer. Her dog Oliver, a bichon frise, was a spunky little puffball with a pure white Afro. Lou thought he was a squeak toy. I liked him a lot.

I liked Salli right away, but, for some odd reason, Lou didn't, at least not right off. It would cost him his manhood.

I'd waited quite a while before seriously considering taking Lou's *huevos*. He'd behaved so well that it hadn't seemed necessary. But after being at the academy for a while he'd begun showing signs that maybe his time had come. Marking indoors on spots where dogs had been tethered, biting the sheep, and showing some mild possessive behavior with toys not his own—it began slowly.

One morning I had Lou tethered to a doorknob in the trainers' room. Salli came in while he nibbled at some breakfast kibble, and when she bent down to give him a pat on the head, he growled and lifted his lip. He'd done it to dogs before but never a person, save me the first month I owned him. It didn't matter that she was an imposing woman and new in his life; unless someone came at me or him with a cleaver, he was not to arbitrarily growl at another person, especially someone close to me.

"Teach him," I said to Salli, handing her Lou's leash.

"Can do."

I let her work Lou through his food-aggression issue for a few days, until he understood the situation. Then I made an appointment with the vet. Lou's stud days were over; life as a eunuch savant began.

When you castrate a four-year-old dog, not much changes. The marking does slowly diminish, as do possible aggressive events between male dogs. Weight can increase if you don't pay attention. But by the time a dog is four, his personality and idiosyncrasies are what they are, and aren't going to change all that much.

Regrets? In retrospect, I wish I'd frozen some of his sperm before having him castrated him. Yes, exceptional dogs like Lou *should* pass on their genes, despite being mutts, and despite whatever prejudices might exist in the breeding world. Sure, the indiscriminate breeding of dogs by amateurs and entrepreneurs is a bad thing and should be discouraged, as should the birth of unwanted pups. But when a dog comes as close to physical, intellectual, and temperamental perfection as Lou did, *that's* the kind of dog that should be bred.

Just because a breed is "pure" does not guarantee superiority, believe me. Dogs should be bred for sound temperament, generous intellect, and physiological soundness, and for the ability to do a job well. They should not be bred according to some arbitrary, inbred, time-honored aesthetic that serves little purpose save the fulfillment of some tradition.

I've trained thousands of dogs and remember the very special ones. That list is short, with Lou squarely at the top. Some were purebred and some were unidentifiable mutts. Most were magnificent dogs who were never bred. Now, does that make any sense at all?

Anne Gordon ran Anne's Animal Actors, an agency that supplied trained animals for film, television, and print work. She visited the academy every so often to buy supplies for her dogs. Instead of driving her truck, she'd sometimes ride over on Barney, her coffee-colored quarter horse. I'd walk out the front entrance to discover Anne clopping by on her gelding, the training dog with me staring up, thinking, *Holy crap, that's one big-ass dog.* Then the horse would lift his tail and drop a load of manure and the dog would be even more impressed.

Anne could train a spider to do the tarantella. A consummate Hollywood professional, she'd worked on many projects, including the films *Vanilla Sky, Legends of the Fall, A River Runs Through It,* and *The Good Son.* She'd also worked for a time on the hit show *Northern Exposure,* taped in Roslyn, Washington. Remember the moose?

I taught dogs to relax and behave. Anne taught dogs, cats, raccoons, birds, wolves, bears, foxes, moose—almost any species you can think of—to perform some abstract action at a specific time. I had to know canine behavior; she had to know a whole lot more. Hers was a different approach that fascinated me; it would lead to my interest in cats, and in teaching complex, linked behaviors to Lou and other dogs.

I'd been learning the fundamentals of cat training from her and was amazed at what she could get the right cat to do. Her cats would do just about anything a dog would—sit, lie down, come, spin, meow on command—almost anything. The secret was twofold: use an outgoing, motivated cat, and bribe the heck out of it with the right food at the right time.

"What about a book on how to teach tricks to cats?" she asked one day.

"I don't know. Cat people are, well . . ."

"I know, I know. But I think a book on cat tricks would work. The market is wide open. And it's not like you can make a cat do anything it doesn't want to do," she said, holding a hand out to her calico, who promptly lifted her paw up and meowed. Anne rewarded her with a spoonful of meat-flavored baby food.

"I'll talk to Toni. Maybe."

My agent had sold the first two book proposals in near record time. And she had quickly become a big dog aficionado,
adopting an Italian greyhound and a Jack Russell terrier. Toni
was larger than life, with a big smile and a mane of thick, wavy
dark hair, like a Puglian countess on holiday. She spoke her mind,
laughed loudly, and never soft-soaped anything.

"Write a good proposal. I'll see what I can do," she said, her
speakerphone echoing. "Maybe I know somebody; we'll see.
Tough one, though: cat people are meshuga."

Anne and I hacked out an outline and a tentative overview of
the idea. After I learned her techniques, we came up with ways to
make it easy for cat owners to teach simple tricks to their pets.
And our book proposal also played upon the age-old dog/cat ri-
valry by showing that if cats could perform the same tricks as
dogs, they must in fact be as smart. Whether true or not, it ap-
pealed to diehard cat fans tired of taking it on the IQ chin.

We wrote a good proposal, sent it to Toni, and got on with
our work. I wrote *Leader of the Pack,* edited *Choosing a Dog,*
trained dogs all day, and looked for a new apartment. Anne trav-
eled up and down the West Coast, working on films and other
gigs. Life was very, very busy.

And then it got much busier.

"Got an offer," said Toni.

"You're kidding."

"Adams Media. No other offers. I say take it and run. It's not
every day a publisher agrees to buy a book when the author has
one coming out and another in the chute. I pushed Anne as the
primary author, with you doing the heavy lifting. She'll have to
hold up her end on promotions."

"Holy crap."

"Yeah. Hope you're up for it, kid."

Three books at the same time. All because Lou had passed an
audition and gotten me a job.

. . .

Nicki, meanwhile, hadn't been so lucky. She and her husband had hit a rough patch and thought that some time apart might ease the situation. So, he stayed home while she took off with her two boys and younger sister on a cross-country road trip that would last almost two months. They disappeared into the heartland, lapping the nation in an unlimited-mileage rented Ford van. It was a trip to remember, especially for the rental company.

"I've been looking for a new place, Stevie," said Salli. She called me Stevie and I let her.

"Any luck?"

"No, but I saw a nice condo for rent in Sand Point, near Magnuson Park and the Burke-Gilman Trail. Too small for me but perfect for you and Lou."

"Yeah?"

"One bedroom with parking, storage, a little patio, and a pool with Jacuzzi."

"Rent?"

"Four hundred seventy-five dollars."

"What?"

"Lime-green counters, and the owner won't change it."

"I don't give a rat's patoot about the counters."

"It's debilitating, Stevie."

"Yeah?"

"Retina burning."

"Have you *been* to my apartment?"

"Lime green, Stevie."

"His number please."

Lime-green counters and a Jacuzzi versus crackheads, frat-boy drinking contests, and floating poop. I did the math, and two weeks later I moved in.

The landlord was a tough old cuss who balked at the idea of a big dog in his place. But in the end, Lou charmed another landlord and passed his audition with flying colors. I convinced him that having his property guarded by a big, smart dog with a cast-iron bladder would be a plus. And with an extra five hundred dollars to pad the security deposit, I was in.

Compared to my University District cesspool, it was heaven on earth. Clean and airy, in a great neighborhood. New appliances, dishwasher, garbage disposal, tiny patio. No kitchen in a closet, no bedroom in a garage, no puking eighteen-year-olds. And right out my back door was a community center with a billiard table and a meeting room, a pool, and a clean Jacuzzi kept at 104 degrees. All for twenty-five dollars *less* per month.

Lou and I walked the neighborhood. Behind the condo complex sat the Burke-Gilman Trail, a bike-and-pedestrian path that ran nearly twenty miles from Ballard, in the city of Seattle, north all the way to Bothell. And right across the street sat Magnuson Park, a 350-acre recreational area located on the shores of Lake Washington. I felt like George Jefferson hitting it big and moving on up to Sutton Place.

As he always did when we moved into a new place (our sixth together), Lou investigated every corner, every carpet fiber. "What'd you find, Lou?" I asked, seeing his nose buried beneath the refrigerator. I popped off the bottom grille to find a few dry cat-food nuggets secreted underneath.

"Nice call, pal," I said, sliding him the kibble.

I bought a humongous L-shaped IKEA desk and wedged it into the corner of the living room, near the back window. With my computer and peripherals set up, it looked like the bridge of the *Enterprise*. I got back to work.

Lou got pissy at the cyclists on the Burke-Gilman. They

would fly by, their clarion call of *"on your left!"* the only warning we'd get before they'd whoosh past, often en masse. At first, I tried to walk or run Lou down the trail on my left side, but that put him in between me and the express trains of cyclists. And I soon realized that as soon as they caught sight of Lou they would actually speed up, in case the muscular black-and-tan dog was a bike hater.

Lou wasn't at all aggressive toward them; he just didn't like them coming so close at such high speed. A reasonable concern. And it was only the serious cyclists decked out in skin-tight clothes riding featherweight race bikes that pissed him off; more than once I could feel his desire to take off after them and teach them some manners. At not quite six years of age, he probably could still have caught them, too.

He'd learned to heel on the right years before, so I moved him over, and that calmed things down. I worked positive reinforcement into the equation and even compelled some cyclists I knew from the condo complex to slow down and toss him a cookie or two while going by. He'd catch the treats and *rower* out his thanks. After a few weeks of that, he settled down and enjoyed our trail time.

A few months later, while walking Lou along Sand Point Way, Nicki's red Subaru flew by. I hadn't heard a peep from her since before she'd taken off on the road trip. I was sure she'd recognized me, especially with Lou by my side. But when she didn't call, I started to wonder what was going on.

I'd be a liar if I said I didn't think her attractive and fun. But getting involved with a married woman with two kids just didn't seem relaxing, or respectable. Even so, her not calling after seeing us on the side of the road just seemed odd.

A few weeks later, I called their house.

"Sorry we drove by you like that. We were late."

"Thought you moved to Oklahoma."

"We were there. We were everywhere. Ten thousand miles. The rental agent almost had a heart attack."

"They probably sold the van for parts, after."

"It backfired."

"The van?"

"No—the separation. You know that crap about absence making the heart grow fonder?"

"Oh. I'm sorry. What happened?"

"Long story. Hard times ahead. Just know that I wasn't ignoring you."

"Just avoiding me?"

"Maybe. I'll be in touch, but now I just have to figure it all out. Didn't see it coming. It's just—sad."

"Like years of work gone in an instant."

"Twelve years and two kids."

I tried to compare it to what had happened to me with Nancy. But Nicki had known her husband three times as long, had a home and photo albums and videotapes of kids being born or baptized, had Christmases and birthdays, vacations, traditions. I really had no idea what she was going through.

"Let me know if I can help" was all I could muster.

"I will. Thanks. Sorry about driving by like that."

"I was invisible. Happens a lot lately."

"I saw you both. You were not invisible."

"It's Lou's doing; he's hard to miss."

"Looks like Warren Beatty."

"That's what people say."

"I really did mean to call, sooner or later."

"If I can help, let me know. No babysitting, though: I'd make them sleep in crates."

"I'd gathered that."

"Glad you're back."

"I wish I was still out driving, sleeping in parking lots, watching the sun come up over the rim of the Grand Canyon, waking next to the Mississippi in a cloud of mosquitoes. It was special. It was—blameless."

"Glad you're back."

"I'll call."

She had hard things to do. We wouldn't talk for a while. People steel themselves. It seems like we are never strong enough, but we are—we are stronger than we seem to ourselves. And we are always the last ones to know what we can do.

"Somebody likes Stevie," crooned Tracy, poking me with a finger. "Nah nah nah nah nah."

"Quiet," I said, barely awake. I'd been getting four hours of sleep as I worked on three books, which at two in the morning began to intersect in strange ways, with Abyssinians herding sheep, spaniels climbing curtains, and tortoise-shell Great Danes stalking sparrows at the bird feeder.

"Somebody sent you flowers. They're up at the reception desk. *Stevie's got a girlfriend.*"

"I do *not.*" I sounded like an eight year-old.

"Scandalous," said Julie, eating something bright and vine-gary from a Tupperware bowl.

"Eat something real for a change."

In the office sat a bouquet of flowers, bright and bold. I guessed who they were from but opened the card anyway, to find Nicki's unmistakable cursive, buoyant as the daisies, asters, and chrysanthemums rising from the vase.

"When did these come?" I asked Linda, the receptionist, who was Nancy Baer's sister.

"Just a few minutes ago. She's sweet on you!"

"Short and perky with long hair?"

"That's her."

"She's just thanking me is all."

"Hah!"

"Thanking you for what, Stevie?" said Tracy, marching into the office with a skinny black Lab.

"For not flossing out your butt cheeks with my leash," I said, pinching her nose. The jumpy Lab sniffed at my leg and wagged his tail.

"Girlfriend," she repeated, poking me, that elfin, lemony look smeared all over her face.

Eventually she'd be right, as usual.

The great thing about having a dog, a pool, a Jacuzzi, and a billiard table at your place is that you needn't worry about two high-octane little kids running out of things to do when they come over to visit you with their newly separated mom.

Nicki's two boys were like terriers on meth, especially six-year-old Jake. Nine-year-old Zac had more focus but could still give his madcap little brother a run for his money. All-American boys, they brought something into Lou's life that he hadn't experienced before—unrelenting boy action.

At nearly six (the same age as Jake), Lou was now a dignified dog in his prime. He loved kids, but he hadn't had any in his inner circle before these two stepped in to rock his world.

If Lou saw Zac as an eager young Lab ever chasing an uncatchable ball, he saw Jake as an unneutered Jack Russell with a bug up his butt, impulsive, electric, and in perpetual motion until he'd drop off into a sleep deep enough to recharge every exhausted cell in his turbocharged little body. Together, they defined what boyhood meant.

The puppies I had been denied as a boy, Lou got as an adult.

It rejuvenated Lou. Though still fun and sweet, he'd attained an air of nobility apropos of the experiences he'd had. Hard to stay innocent when you've stared down the barrel of a .357, jacked sex offenders, and dodged hundreds of treacherous dogs.

Zac and Jake helped Lou get his "goofy" on again. He relearned the art of play for play's sake. Along with always having purpose in his life, it's a big reason why I think Lou lived so much longer than other big dogs. A bit of magic at work there, I think.

Nicki had a ten-year-old dog named Shyanne, a mix of shepherd, Lab, and faery nymph. A real lady, sweet as sugar, and, as her name implied, a bit bashful. A thin, leggy blonde, Shy stood as tall as Lou but was nearly greyhound thin, with a coyness my genial dog found refreshing.

She'd lived much of her life as a solo backyard pet, so, when the big black-and-tan with movie-star good looks began to visit, she didn't quite know what to think. But Shy quickly warmed to the idea of gaining the friendship of one of her own for a change.

She'd have made a good wife for Lou. Their pups would've been impossibly cute and smart as monkeys. Her modesty balanced by his bravado. Lou's strength, Shy's chic. A family of his making was the one thing Lou never got to experience.

But we were family, and he loved me. I could tell by the way I'd catch him smiling at me when he thought I wasn't watching, see him in the reflection of the television screen or closet mirror gazing at me like I was a saint (if he only knew!). He'd come over, sit beside me, and plop a mollifying paw onto my thigh whenever I got blue, or when I wept over something. If I watched Rick at the Paris train station waiting in the rain for Ilsa—boom, Lou would sidle right up. On 9/11, Lou wouldn't leave my side the whole day.

He loved me. But to this day I wonder whether being a father would have been his ultimate accomplishment. Of course, neither of us would ever find out.

. . .

"I'm a writer, Colleen."

"And a dog trainer."

"I'm a better writer."

"You've done well here. We like you. Think about it. And anyway, what the heck else would you have to write about?"

She had a point: the academy was the world's best proving ground for dog behavior. In the four years I'd worked there, I had trained more dogs than most trainers would in a lifetime. Every conceivable breed or breed mix, every possible temperament. No better source of material existed. What else *would* I write about?

I'd worked with every kind of dog owner, too, and learned to predict what mistakes they would make before they made them. The huge number of people and pets I'd worked with at the academy helped me identify patterns and work out strategies, no matter the dog or owner. If I left the academy, that vast flow of information and experience would go away.

Other things about the place had been special. For instance, Colleen bred and showed Irish water spaniels, strong, clownish hunting dogs with big hairdos and bigger personalities. When one of her bitches gave birth to a litter, she had the great idea of letting each trainer "manage" a puppy from birth to ten weeks of age. The mom still did her job; we just handled the pups, saw to their general health, and experimented with early-on training/conditioning techniques to see if having a skilled trainer influence a dog from birth would actually produce a better dog.

It convinced me of how overriding heredity was—how profoundly different dog temperaments could be right from the start. Some pups were coy and tentative; others, macho or hyperactive. And some were sweet and confident from the time they opened their eyes and began exploring their world.

I was amazed at how soon unique personality traits manifested themselves, and I learned that although human involvement from day one could affect or improve them, we certainly weren't the panacea. It was an invaluable experience that, apart from having a litter in my own home, wouldn't have happened anywhere else. I owed Colleen and the other people at the academy a lot.

The academy let Lou blossom. It was where he learned his craft, helping dogs and owners find their way. Lou had been the Dr. Drew of the dog world: day in and day out, he did what he'd been born to do—save dogs.

But writing three books was just too much. I began bumping into walls, getting bitten, missing cues, losing weight, and coming in late. So I decided to take a chance and be what I'd wanted to be from the time I was twelve: a professional writer. I had an agent, three book contracts, and plenty to say. And I had the best dog in the world by my side.

It was two thirty in the morning. I sat at my desk waiting for my dial-up connection to load a page on dog nutrition. Lou woke from a nap, strolled over, and sat beside me. He stared at me as if to say, *Hey, moron, it's time for bed*. He'd taken to sleeping beneath my bed in the new place but wouldn't go until I turned in.

"What do you think, pal?" I asked him.

"Rower."

"Yeah?"

He whacked a paw down onto my knee hard enough to swivel my desk chair 180 degrees.

"ROWER."

The next day, I gave Colleen two weeks' notice.

13

Dancing with Wolves

A washboard dirt road led to Anne's new training compound, wooded acres above the small town of Monroe, Washington—tall pines, screeching hawks, coyote and deer scat, and views of snowcapped Mount Baker, the air clean, the moat of mud around her double-wide as thick as fresh concrete.

Nicki, I, and a posse of friends helped Anne move her belongings and animals up from her home in Bothell. The caravan of cars, trucks, friends, and animals moved slowly up the mountain, like a traveling circus rolling its way to the next small town.

I got the Civic stuck in the mud for the third time. A friend of Anne's who was standing in the bed of his four-by-four pickup laughed, then came over to help push. The front wheels of my Civic spun like yo-yos in the greasy muck.

In two days, our muddy little army hauled Anne up to her new sanctuary in the woods, where the creatures she'd collected and trained could hoot, holler, bark, or caterwaul to their hearts' content without reprisal. She put in heated kennels for the dogs and suitable enclosures for the foxes, birds, deer, rabbits, monkeys, beavers, armadillos, squirrels, raccoons, and other rescued animals she'd turned into Hollywood actors. Even Barney, the gelding, had his own paddock and pasture on the back of the property.

Close-by, Anne fenced in a large tract of forest. The sturdy eight-foot fence was topped with a thin wire that held enough electrical current to knock a person silly. But it wasn't there to keep people out; it was there to keep the wolves in.

By the early twentieth century, nearly every wild wolf in the United States had been killed, out of either misguided fear or a desire to protect livestock out on the range. Today, with the reintroduction of wolves into the wild, they are making a comeback. To help in this, a number of licensed wolf breeders produced quality pups each year, not only for federally sponsored reintroduction into the wild but for supplying legitimate wolf sanctuaries with animals for public viewing. The more familiar the public got with wolves, the better chance they had of being accepted back into the wild.

Originally owned by a Washington wolf breeder unable to care for an unexpected glut of pups, the three wolves had found safe haven with Anne in her quiet, natural habitat. In exchange for the great digs, they would do the occasional photo shoot or entertain admirers eager to view wolves living in a natural environment. As they could not have made it on their own in the wild, this was the best alternative for them.

My second book, *Leader of the Pack,* was half written. The

book stressed how crucial leadership is in the dog/owner dynamic: without enlightened guidance, dogs slip into a pushy state of mind that leads to disobedience and sometimes aggression. The book taught owners simple techniques that would help to establish and maintain the pecking order in the home and make life easier for everyone.

As a model, it used the concord of the wolf pack. Though wolves are different from domestic dogs in many ways, they share a common social dynamic—the hierarchy of the pack, or "family." The dominant, parental breeding pair at the top of the group choreographs much of what goes on—hunting, mating, privilege, possession, migration, and many other facets of pack life that don't get voted on, but instead are determined by these two elders, whose experience and force of personality keep the pack alive, much as a gifted leader does in the military. Without this style of enlightened control, the pack's success as hunters could suffer.

"Think we could get a wolf and Lou together for the cover of the book?" asked Nancy Baer.

"That'd be fitting, and damn hard to get," I said, knowing that wolves and dogs wouldn't get along unless raised together.

"What about Anne's wolves?"

"I wonder."

And so began Lou's short-lived dance with wolves.

"We can try, but no promises," said Anne. "Lou's mature, strong, smart, and dominant, and they are still young. But they're *wolves;* they could snap his neck in an instant if they chose to."

"Which one has the best shot at accepting him?" I asked, intrigued at the possibility of Lou mentoring a wolf. He'd handled mastiffs, shepherds, and all manner of strong dogs before, without much fanfare. But Anne was right: these were wolves. Stronger, smarter, and wilder than anything Lou had ever dealt with, at least while he'd been with me. I thought Lou could end up on a dinner plate if we didn't handle it right.

"Definitely Timber. He is a total lamb with Queenie, my little cattle dog/husky mix. She mothered him, and lords over him now. Funny to watch."

"So there's hope for Lou."

"Timber knows her since he was a pup, but he's nearly a year now. His window for socializing is pretty much closed."

"Have you ever done it before?"

"Honestly, no. But if any dog can do it, Lou can."

The idea was to get a cover shot of Nancy and me with a wolf on one side and a dog on the other, to suggest that what worked among wolves could work for dogs and owners. Done right, it would make a startlingly effective cover for the book. Done wrong, it could mean the end of Lou.

Nicki came with me to see the wolves in their new home. Anne was down in the kennel area, preparing meals for her fifteen dogs, two red foxes, and three wolves. The fifteen house cats would eat later.

"Grab three chickens out of the fridge, will you?" she asked as we walked over.

"Nice flooders," I said. Her hip waders, gloves, and knitted cap made her look like an Alaskan crabber.

"Gets grimy around here. You shouldn't have dressed so nice," she said to Nicki, who wore nice jeans and a sweater.

"That's what washing machines are for," Nicki said, helping me carry the half-frozen raw chickens.

Anne's fifteen dogs sounded like the starting line of the Indy 500. It was unbelievably noisy and frantic, with dogs leaping up against the kennel fencing, spinning, pawing, and arguing with one another over who deserved to eat first. But Anne had the eating order worked out: she fed in order of status, starting with

Queenie, the spunky little mix who dominated not only dogs but wolves as well.

"Let's go feed the wolves."

Timber the dog-friendly male, Kwani the dominant snow-white female, and Tundra the subordinate male each ate a whole chicken for breakfast and dinner. Along with supplements and some other choice offerings, twice a day they ate like, well—wolves.

Anne carried the three plucked chickens in a big steel bucket while Nicki and I lagged behind. It gave new meaning to the phrase *a bucket of chicken.*

"Stay here. They're flighty around strangers. I'll go in and feed them; you two keep still and quiet."

She latched the gate behind her and walked into the forest of pine, alder, and maple, the bucket heavy in her hand, rubber waders squeaking, the ground dotted with sword ferns and the first dropped leaves of fall.

We lost sight of her. She whistled a few sweet, lilting notes. A gray ghost blurred through a grove of alders, then disappeared behind a big cedar where Anne had vanished. Then a white flicker and another gray stroke, like sharks circling in a pool. They yipped, the anticipation of food almost unbearable.

Anne led them back toward the fence. Bigger than I had imagined, the wolves stood tall as Danes, with full coats, wild, handsome faces, and an absurd, loping grace, the authority of it and the easy way they sauntered—no sound of footfalls, just the whining of hungry young wolves with the smell of strangers and fresh chicken in their noses, the bucket swinging in Anne's hand, the fear of us no match for the lure of blood and meat and bone.

Anne tossed each of them a chicken, careful to make sure each was far enough away from the others to avoid argument. They snatched up the birds and wandered off, the sound of tearing and crunching already begun. It would take mere minutes for the chickens to be eaten, with not a morsel left, not even the blood, licked clean from maple leaves lying on the forest floor.

She walked over to the fence. "I always try to feed them when guests come. They still don't like it, but at least they learn to connect you with meat."

"That's what Nicki always says about me."

"Ha-ha," said Nicki, nudging me with an elbow.

"If you stay quiet and still, they'll come over. No sudden moves."

Kwani came first, her white face stained pink. She made a quick pass, eyed us timidly, then came back for a gentle stroke from Anne. Then came Timber, the dog-loving male, larger than Kwani, with the classic gray, white, and black coloring of his kind. He pushed into Anne and stretched out like a cat, enjoying her strokes and gentle talk. He nosed into the bucket, looking for more food, but settled for licks of watery blood.

Tundra darted and wove through the trees twenty yards off. Smaller than Timber, he would never find the courage to come closer.

"A good start," said Anne, the fifteen dogs in the kennels barking, wondering why wolves got whole chickens and they mere kibble. "Next time you'll come inside."

"Yeah?" I said.

"You'll carry the bucket, and eventually feed them."

"When can Lou come?"

"Patience, dog trainer," she said, the wolves retreating into the woods, their gamy scent lingering. "Your board-and-train program won't work on them. Let's do this right, for Lou's sake."

Anne walked through the woods with Timber, the big wolf, ahead of her, his ten-foot-long, heavy-gauge forged steel chain "leash" dragging in the dirt. He was magnificent, with a ghostly stare that bored right into you. Little Queenie trotted ahead of them both, sniffing at trees and peeing like a male. Kwani and Tundra flitted about in the distance, too scared of me and Lou to come close.

"Today we'll just walk. No interaction. Just let them get used to each other's scent and presence. Just remember: don't look them in the eyes, and do *not* let Lou off the leash."

"Roger that."

I wasn't used to fretting over Lou's safety. But Anne was right: any of the wolves could have killed him, and all three could have torn him to confetti. It was humbling—like seeing Sugar Ray Leonard climb into the ring with Mike Tyson.

Lou was wound up. He knew that something unprecedented was happening. I tried to guess how he was interpreting the moment. *Dogs but not dogs,* he must have thought. A new smell entirely, sharper and more pungent, like a hundred dogs rolled into one, like a winter forest at night when the real killers come out to hunt down their prey. Wild dogs, wilder than Lou had ever been, wilder even than the coyotes he'd heard or seen as a pup in the hills of Mendocino. *Not dogs at all.*

Next time, we left Queenie home. Just Lou and Timber, the others trailing in the distance, Anne holding on to Timber's heavy chain leash.

"You sure you want to do this?"

"He can handle it."

"Let him off the leash."

Anne was very strong. But I was ready to grab that chain and drag that beast off my fine dog if need be. Turned out it wasn't necessary.

Lou trotted right up to Timber. My heart was in my mouth. They greeted like dogs, nose to butt, sniffing, Lou taking in all that his great nose could teach him. Timber's nose told him more, much more. The best nose on earth. Then the peeing contest, then play posturing, then Lou realizing that the wolf had thirty pounds on him and wasn't at all understandable in a doggish sense.

What a dog does not quite understand he either fears or challenges, so Lou, sensing that Timber was but a big goofy teenager, brought to bear his experience and courage and grabbed the wolf by the scruff and took him down.

"Holy crap," I said, wondering what would happen next.

"It's okay, Queenie does it, too. It won't last, but right now this is a good thing."

Even among wolves, it wasn't size that determined behavior, but perceived power and standing. At six years old, Lou knew every trick, and so put on his best poker face and played the game. Timber didn't know the rules of the game yet; he just knew that Anne and Queenie liked Lou, and that he had a way about him.

I knew Lou too well to fall for his bravado. He was edgy. He knew that this thing was more dangerous than anything he'd ever met. He took Timber down a few times, barked and growled at him, ignored him. He acted the way a henpecked alpha might—aloof, crabby, a bit bossy. But inside he was scared, possibly for the first time.

Anne and I knew that it wouldn't last. Two, maybe three more sessions before Timber caught on to the charade and tore Lou a new one. So we scheduled a photo shoot with Don Mason, a photographer she'd used before, a pro who knew how to shoot animals.

"If it's a book cover, we'll have to do it here in my studio."

"But it's *Timber*, Don," I said. I imagined Anne and me dragging a full-grown male gray wolf through the busy streets of Seattle, like a blooper reel from a Lon Chaney horror flick.

"Can't do it in the woods. I can't make the lighting work there, and I won't have the right backdrops. No—got to be here."

"Can we schedule it for a Sunday morning?" I asked, knowing that would be the quietest time all week.

"I'll do it on New Year's Eve so long as the publisher pays my fee."

We scheduled it. Nancy Baer, Anne, and I would haul Lou, Queenie, a few backup dogs, and a full-grown gray wolf down to Don's studio on the corner of First and Jackson to get a shot for the cover of *Leader of the Pack*. We'd either pull it off or make the Monday headlines.

Thanks to Timber, neither quite happened. During the next session at Anne's compound, all seemed fine between Lou and the big wolf, who'd begun to loosen up. He'd actually gotten playful with Lou, and began acting like the younger brother who, after a growth spurt, realizes he's bigger than his older sibling and can best him in a fight.

Lou grabbed Timber by the neck a few times, then ambled over to a woodsy hillside to pee. Timber followed. Then, instead of marking over Lou's spot, the big wolf teasingly shoved at Lou's rear with his muzzle while Lou had his back leg raised high. Poor Lou went tumbling down the hillside like a kid in a barrel.

"Uh-oh," said Anne. "That's not good."

A light bulb hovered over Timber's head. *Holy crap—he's a gnat,* he must have thought.

Lou ran back up the hill to give Timber some hell, but by then the wolf had changed hats and seen through the charade. As Lou made a last attempt at bluffing his way out, Timber began batting him around like a handball.

"We're done here," said Anne, yanking Timber off Lou with the chain. "Take Lou back to your car. Timber's figured it out."

In an instant, Timber's opinion of Lou had changed from

cool older crony to disposable chew toy. Had we let it go on another minute, Lou would have been demoted to a pastrami sandwich.

A wolf isn't a shepherd or a retriever. It's a wolf, and will always be one. They've never bought into the "domesticity script" that dogs and people have been writing for the last twenty thousand years. They can't, really; they're wolves.

Lou had always kept that one paw of his inside the same fierce country where Timber had kept three. But on that day at Anne's, the big wolf had set down his fourth paw squarely beside his other three and surrendered to heritage. Lou had had his dance with the wolves and survived. And he learned, as do we all, that there is always something tougher than ourselves out there, waiting.

The photo shoot with Lou and Timber together in the same shot was canceled. But we did take Timber down to Don's studio on that Sunday morning and got great shots of him alone, with Nancy and me, and with his beloved Queenie. Walking a full-grown gray wolf on the end of a forged steel chain down First Avenue on a Sunday morning past churchgoers, German tourists, and sleepy homeless men turned out to be one of the most peculiar and enjoyable experiences of my life.

Lou and some of Nancy Baer's dogs got their photo ops later in the week; we hoped to piece together a montage of wolves and dogs, for the book cover. But after we had submitted them to the publisher, they decided against using Timber, to avoid encouraging readers to think that wolf ownership might be a good idea. But Nancy, I, Lou, and two of her dogs did make it onto the front and back covers. I treasure seeing his happy, smiling face on that book, knowing how close he had come to becoming sashimi in the process.

14

The Wookie

L ou's value as a trainer lay in his gift for passing skills he'd learned in the hills onto "store bought" dogs. What Lou knew and how he used it was more real than anything I could have taught.

As capable as he was in the wild, Lou was no Timber. But to other dogs, Lou was the wolf, the wilding. And if any dog needed a serious dose of "wolf justice," it was Johnny. Cute as a cartoon, he was a busy little cobra who ruled the roost and bit anyone fool enough to touch his bowl, toys, feet, or just about anything he deemed his. Owned by a single mom, the cairn terrier mix couldn't be moved from chair or bed, couldn't be groomed, couldn't even be handled unless he'd initiated the contact. Worse, he'd bitten the woman's three-year-old daughter, who, despite the attacks, loved Johnny with all her heart. Bite a mom and you might survive; bite a mom's child and you end up on death row.

I sat in on Colleen's evaluation. The mom held on to Johnny's leash as if readying to set a hook. Her daughter played with dog toys in the corner. Johnny watched her play.

"When we got him he was so cute," she said, watching Johnny sniff the carpet. "He slept with Jenny every night. They'd been inseparable. 'The Jenny and Johnny Show.' I was happy for her to have a little buddy, what with the divorce—you know."

"When did he start biting?" asked Colleen, reaching over to take the leash. Johnny avoided eye contact with both of us; as far as he was concerned, we didn't exist. Yet.

"About three months ago. Jenny petted him during his dinner and he snapped at her hand, then went back to eating, like nothing had happened."

"How bad was that bite?" I asked as Johnny sniffed my leg. *Pee on me and be the first terrier in space,* I thought.

"Six stitches."

"And then?" asked Colleen, walking the dog around the room. Colleen was like Spock—she mind-melded with a dog, discerned what it was thinking, what it was about to do.

"Then came the face bite. Come here, honey." Jenny had curly blond hair down to her shoulders. Her mom swept it aside to show us the fresh scar on her left cheek. "Three stitches. We went to a plastic surgeon, but he said we'd have to wait."

"What prompted the face bite?" asked Colleen.

"She kissed him on the nose," she said, welling up.

Colleen reached down to touch Johnny's rump. As he turned to snap, she corrected him fast as lightning while saying, "No," then walked him around.

"He's not fearful. He just thinks he's lord of the manor," said Colleen, handing back the leash. "When he bit Jenny, he thought he was disciplining her for touching his possessions, or for getting inside his 'personal zone' without permission. He'll bite anyone who tries to take a toy, pick up his bowl, check his teeth, cut his nails—anything he deems inappropriate or demeaning to his perceived position of authority."

"You mean he's not crazy, or scared?"

"Not at all," said Colleen, looking at me. "Though this behavior often does happen when a dog is scared or unstable, he is clearly neither. He's really quite composed. Johnny is simply doing what most dogs would do, given the opportunity."

"What?"

"Take charge, and discipline his pack."

Colleen called Jenny over. She was adorable, and suspicious of being where she was.

"Jenny, you love Johnny, right?" asked Colleen.

"Yes."

"And he loves you?"

"Yes," she said, looking to her mom.

"Now I want you to tell me the truth, okay?"

"Okay."

"Has Johnny bitten you lately?"

She looked down at Johnny with a sad smile, then back at Colleen, her little face toughening up. "Not today he hasn't!"

We took Johnny in for a month of board and train. The mother made it clear that she couldn't bear the thought of her daughter being bitten ever again, and that if Johnny snapped at her one more time he'd be euthanized immediately. In any contest between a mother's love and the love of a child for a nasty little cur, the dog would lose every time.

They left Johnny with us that day. "You're his primary," said Colleen, handing the leash to me. "He won't be easy."

It would take a temporary stay of execution and a black-and-tan drill sergeant to pull Johnny's furry little ass out of the fire.

Johnny was a rat trap. Every decision he made concluded with an attempt to bite. Brush me? Try and I'll bite you. Touch my bowl? How's about I bite you instead? Pet me when I'm not looking? A biting offense. About the only time he wouldn't bite was when you came bearing edible gifts, or if you prostrated yourself to him like a religious martyr. Otherwise, if you and he butted heads, his teeth broke the impasse.

He didn't do this out of fear or because he'd led a hard life. To the contrary: Johnny had lived like a king for his first year. He wasn't down on confidence or shouldering some overwhelming dread; he was simply a dominant terrier to start with, and he'd had that dominance amplified by a mother and daughter who'd spoiled him and not taught him a darn thing. He was a crotchety cuss whose sole trick was the Cujo clamp-down.

Those days were over. Johnny was a twenty-pound barracuda, but something in me said he'd come around with the right training and follow-up. And the best mentor in the business waited patiently for his last assignment at the academy. Life for little Johnny was about to change radically, in the form of a seventy-five-pound truck of muscle named Lou.

I liked Johnny, though I never quite figured out why. He looked like a partied-out wookie and acted like a wolverine, but something in his personality just touched me. It was funny how aggressive he was.

"He sucks," said Tracy.

"I know."

"So what's your problem?"

"He's got spunk is all. And he's sort of a clown when he isn't trying to bite."

"You're getting involved again," she said, poking me in the head. I had a habit of falling for the oddest dogs, like Johnny, Branka, Solo, or a dozen others who'd been special in some way besides their obvious attempts at murder, terrorism, or some other form of villainy. I'd convinced myself that these dogs' bad behaviors could be peeled away to reveal the fruit underneath, when, in fact, more often than I liked to admit, the layers were onion skin, and the fruit, bitter onion.

"He's funny and quick."

"Like you?"

"Point taken."

Johnny got the full attention of everyone. No biting tolerated, little independence, earned attention only. Luckily, he liked food, so the basic behaviors came quickly. But I was his primary-care person, which meant brushing, cutting nails, cleaning ears—things he deemed beneath his station.

On the second day, rather than enter into endless conflict with Johnny, I decided to pass the buck and just let Lou take over. He'd play bad cop to my good cop. I couldn't wait.

I brought Johnny into the empty classroom and unclipped his leash. Free for the first time in two days, he ran around like a ferret, sniffing and mouthing at every toy or piece of equipment. Then he stopped in his tracks and stared over at the ramped agility walkway.

Lou stared down at the little terrier, then yawned, as if to say, *Where do you find them?* Now nearly six years old, he approached these situations with the same skill set, but with more grace and authority. He'd learned over the years to read dogs well, and he knew what to expect based on size, attitude, breed, and I guess scent, too, ever an indicator of mood and intent. And with smaller, aggressive dogs, instead of bandying about, he'd taken to humbling them quickly with a theatrical display of power and sound, then hanging back and letting the runt come over and kiss up.

Johnny ran over to bark at Lou, who leaped down like a panther, then casually walked over. When Johnny made the mistake of charging, Lou roared, reared, then pounced down on the little weevil, pinning him with a front paw and grabbing his neck in his strong jaws. It was pure physics: Johnny felt the folly of his bluff, and the strength and heat of Lou coursing down on him. Lou snarled, then subtly shifted his weight in response to Johnny's struggles.

'Wait for it," I said to Lou. He glanced at me with a calm, almost complacent look, his jaws still clamped down. *Here comes checkmate, bro.* Lou played the role well and knew that the terrier's surrender was pending. When Lou amped up the pressure a bit, Johnny started to squeal like a rat. Lou held on for a few moments more, shook Johnny a bit, then let him go.

Johnny scampered over to me like a broken bully, his overlong nails clicking like hermit crabs across the floor. I picked him up by the scruff and belly, turned him onto his back, held him in my arms, and stared at him. "That's Lou. He's the enforcer. You bite me, he bites you."

Johnny looked up at me through slitted lids, his pink tongue flagging, bravado gone. I put him down, and as Lou walked over, Johnny tried to hide behind me. But there was no hiding from Lou, who walked through my legs and trotted after the little biter, who finally went belly-up on the mat. Lou sniffed and licked his privates and face, then walked over to me and sat for a cookie.

"Aroogla."

"Yes, you did great. Good job."

From that day on, Johnny never tried to bite me or Lou again, except later that week when I tried to trim his nails. Instead of fighting him, I simply brought in Lou, who, when Johnny again tried to bite me, pinned him to the floor and shook him like a maraca. *You bite him, you deal with me.*

It was quite flattering, really.

. . .

Chief came in at the same time as Johnny. A four-year-old rough collie, the spitting image of Lassie, sweet and calm, smart and loving. Looked right at you, studied you, hung out with you like a chum. A big, noble guy who liked Lou and me right off. What a dog. I could picture him reading bedtime stories to a roomful of sleepy puppies.

Chief was the first dog I thought came close to having Lou's brand of charisma. Great dogs own a presence, an indefinable magnetism—what an Ali or a Hepburn had. When they walk into a room, a countenance precedes them; you know right off that the dog is special and competent, without vice or flaw. Chief had it all in spades.

He'd come in for some touch-up training but quickly went up for adoption when his ailing, elderly owners decided that they didn't have the energy to take care of him. He boarded with us for the time being, and I made it a point to spend as much time as possible with him.

Chief mellowed people and dogs out with his nobility and goodwill; when Lou and I took him out for a romp in a field or a walk somewhere, we'd both feel calmer and more refreshed afterward, as if we'd been to a spa. I couldn't think of a reason not to adopt him as soon as possible.

Then one came up.

"Johnny's getting put down this afternoon," said Colleen.

"Why? He's way better now."

"For us, maybe. But the mom has made up her mind not to take him back. Believe me, when a dog hurts your kid, the last thing you think about is its well-being. She's had a few weeks to think about it, and she's gone sour on him."

"He could be adopted out."

"By whom? Anyone with less skill than you or I and he'll revert. You know that. Johnny needs to wear a uniform and salute the flag every day for the rest of his life, or else it's curtains. She can't— won't do it. And no one I know would, either."

"You could take him."

"I don't like him, Steve."

"But he'd work in the right home, Colleen."

"You're too soft. She's decided, Steve."

She was right. No one would adopt a dog that came with the disclaimer "may cause serious bleeding and frequent trips to the plastic surgeon." I hated what I was about to say to her.

"What if I take him for two weeks?" I said, thinking of Chief, how he was ten thousand times better than Johnny, better in every way, maybe the second-best dog I'd ever known.

"Why?"

"If he does well with me, I'll keep him; if not, I'll hand him over to the executioner."

"I thought you wanted to adopt Chief?"

"I do. But Chief will find a home fast. Johnny won't."

"Maybe that's the way it should be."

"He's not all bad. Lou keeps him in line. I love Chief, but I just don't think Johnny deserves to die."

"Should I hug you or slap you?"

"How about both?"

And so began the strange experiment named Johnny, Lou's last save at the academy. I took him home instead of Chief, wonderful Chief, and to this day I grieve over it. He found a good home a few days before Johnny's two-week stay of execution came to an end, two weeks without biting anyone, two weeks of Lou looking at me like I was nuts, wondering when the stupid squirrel-dog was going to leave.

He didn't. He stayed, and except for a brief nipping episode with Nicki's younger boy, Jake, Johnny behaved and lived out

the rest of his short life with us, never knowing the sacrifice
Lou and I had made to save his sorry little ass from the needle
that day.

I never saw Chief again.

The bitchy little trust-fund prince with a taste for little girls' faces
wondered what the hell he was doing in the middle of the dark
forest with me, Lou, and a dozen coyotes yipping up the night.

"Don't worry, Johnny, the coyotes won't get you. Lou is here,"
I said, the three of us snug in my tent on Red Top, coyotes and a
great horned owl talking in the distance, the wind rippling the
walls of the tent. A few years later, my assurance to Johnny
would prove prophetic, not for Johnny, rest his soul, but for Lou.

Lou loved Red Top. I'd let him out and he'd hurry around like
a tourist, sniffing, peeing, dirt scratching, and chortling away,
taking inventory of the place he'd visited many times now, scenting out old campfires and pulling from them charred sticks used
to spear marshmallows for roasting.

Three stray cattle wandered around close-by, munching on
graze. They always roamed around up there and I never knew
why. Lou knew they weren't fond of dogs, so he kept his distance
and listened to them moo and chew, their tagged ears flicking at
flies and their jaws working, always working. Lou liked to smell
them from a comfortable distance, wishing perhaps that Anne's
wolves would show up to help out.

Johnny didn't share Lou's enthusiasm for the outdoors. He'd
been a spoiled little city brat whose biggest outdoor challenge
had been choosing which yard shrub to pee on. Watching Lou up
there, Johnny must have realized how little he actually knew,
how intricate the world was, how overwhelming. His old life—
that sweet-smelling girl's room with dolls on the bed—that was
gone. To him it must have seemed like a dream.

His respect for Lou grew that day in the woods. You saw it in the way he followed his big brother everywhere, and how when he'd approach a challenge he felt unsure of—a leap over an agate excavation hole or a walk across a downed nursery cedar—he'd try things the old Johnny would never have dreamed of, just to stay close to Lou.

I never babied him. I let him work it out on his own, with the guidance of his new idol. Johnny, once the least-decent dog around, had through some twist of fate been matched up with the best of the best, a joyous Huck Finn of a dog with adventure in his heart.

Miracles do happen, at least for Johnny and me. Perhaps Johnny and I had more in common than I realized.

Chief would have loved Red Top. He and Lou would have had their own television show and line of dog products. Ah, Chief. What a good name for a dog.

Lou led us up the steep path to the ranger station, then hopped across the rocks to the base of the stairway. He climbed up the near-vertical steel steps like a man, then looked back down at Johnny below, afraid to give it a go.

"Rower."

"I don't think he's going for it, Lou," I said. Johnny was big enough to climb the stairs but small enough to fall through the spaces between; though he circled and whined and pawed at the first step, his heart just wasn't ready for it yet.

"Woof!"

"No, Lou, he's not ready yet."

Cradling Johnny in my left arm, I carried him up to where Lou waited beneath the trapdoor that led into the station itself. Johnny reached out to lick Lou's face while Lou pawed up at the heavy door.

"Look out," I said, heaving the hatch open, wondering how long it would take me to teach Lou to open it himself. Both front paws on the door while pushing off with his back legs . . . but how to prevent the heavy door from slamming back down onto his neck? Should he shove it open all the way or just enough to slither through? Given enough time, I could probably have taught him to play the piano.

Lou leaped in and danced around the planked floor, sniffing mouse droppings and lunch crumbs left by earlier hikers. I broke out a water bottle and poured some into a small dish I'd brought up for them. Lou slopped it down while Johnny stood by patiently.

"He'll let you drink with him, you know," I said. He waited anyway, and when Lou finished, the water was gone, so I poured out more and watched Johnny as he lapped it like a kitten.

"Man up, dude."

He eyed me, then finished lapping up the water. Lou sat in the middle of the room, gazing out at the view of Mount Baker. He'd slipped into his wild-boy character again.

"What do I get in exchange for this cookie?" I said, holding the large biscuit in my hand.

"Aroogla!" he said, snapping out of his trance.

"No, no, more than that."

He spun around twice to his right, then raised his left paw so high over his head that it looked as if he were reaching for a spare key above a doorjamb.

"Good wave," I said, snapping the biscuit and tossing him half. He caught it and settled down in a dusty corner to munch, holding the treat in his paws like a kid saying his prayers.

"Well?" I asked, looking at Johnny. "What have you got for me? No free lunches for you, dust bunny. Shake."

I'd taught him to shake the week after I'd chosen him over Chief, and he knew it well. But when he did it, he stuck his paw out away from his body in an almost Nazi-like salute. Embarrassing, but somehow fitting.

"Good shake, John," I said, tossing the half biscuit to him. It bounced off his nose and fell to his feet. He sneezed, then grabbed it and lay down near Lou to savor the prize.

That night in the tent, with the songs of the coyotes and the owl and the wind rippling the tent walls, Johnny spooned into Lou's protective warmth and wedged his ratty little wookie head beneath the bigger dog's chin. Lou looked at him, then looked over to me with resignation.

"Welcome to my world, pal."

Lou sighed as Johnny licked his ear.

With advances from three books in the bank and money from some private training on the side, I got by. I fell into a nice routine: take Lou and Johnny for a run or walk in the morning, then hit a coffee shop to write longhand for a while. Then I'd come home and work with Johnny, who processed information more slowly than Lou. He'd become trustworthy enough to leave out loose in the apartment while I was gone, provided Lou was there. Alone, he'd tear things up and scratch at the back door. Like it or not, Lou became the babysitter.

At night we'd either visit Nicki and her boys or they'd come visit us. I had the pool and Jacuzzi, so that happened a lot. Johnny tried to snap at Jake once and lived to regret a mother's wrath. Nicki had grown up with dogs on a farm and was no shrinking violet. Lou and I just watched and smiled.

"Try to bite my boy again and I will shave you down and use you for a piñata," she said, grabbing him by both cheeks and giving him a shake. Once someone called him on the biting, he'd turn into a lamb and never try it again. At least not with that person.

My nights were spent working on the computer. Whatever I'd written longhand that day went into the computer, got edited, improved. Lou would saunter over at 1:00 A.M. and stare at me, wondering when I'd be done. He wanted to crawl under the bed but wouldn't unless I lay above him. Approaching nine years old now, he began loving his sleep, that boy.

I got a call from an editor at Adams Media, referred by a friend. "I hear you write fast," she said. I could hear that I was on speakerphone, which meant they were having a meeting. Another crisis in publishing land.

"Depends on what I'm writing."

"Can you write a beginner's guide for cats?"

I'd learned a lot from Anne about cats over the years and had recently begun helping cat owners with behavioral issues. Cats were easier to care for than dogs, but harder to "fix."

"Sure," I said. I could write a beginner's guide to superstring theory if the money was right. "When would you need it?"

There was a pause. "In ninety days."

I laughed aloud, then realized that they were serious. "Is this a booklet?"

"No, I'm afraid. It's an Everything Guide; they average over a hundred thousand words."

"What?"

"The fellow we contracted to write it just informed us that he won't be delivering the script. We don't even think he's begun it."

"And you have a tight schedule on this."

"We really do need it in three months. Can you do it?"

Eighty-nine days later, I delivered to them a 129,000-word manuscript, in exchange for a five-figure payout. I spent the next month in a back brace, my wrists soaking in ice water, the computer off, no writing, no golf, no new words, just the dogs and me and Nicki and her boys. I'd become a cat expert with a bad case of tendinitis.

. . .

He'd been marked for death before his first birthday, and would have met his maker, the grand high exalted mystic canine ruler Gog, if not for the sacrifice of Chief and the charity of myself and Lou. He'd lived a charmed life, and now at four was a happy, levelheaded little guy who wouldn't hurt a fly, as long as Lou and I held the reins.

He'd even made a few bucks along the way, helping Colleen's husband, Jack, get rid of some Norway rats in the basement of the academy one cold winter. At five dollars a head, he'd done what he'd been bred to do—catch vermin and snap their necks. I'd let him loose in the basement for an hour or so, go eat lunch, then come back to find corpses strewn about the cement floor like washrags.

I'd taken Johnny to an empty parking lot beside a local tennis court one day to play fetch. More than anything, Johnny loved to fetch that fuzzy yellow ball. He'd literally fetch until he couldn't walk anymore; he'd just lie down panting and I'd bring him a dish of water and he'd plunk his head down into it without standing and lap away, then look up at me as if to say, *Must go home now.* The tennis ball broke all barriers; if a red-eyed sewer rat had tossed a ball for Johnny, he would have obliged. It was his muse.

Toward the end of the session, he started slowing down but still wanted me to toss the ball. So I gave it one last throw and he scampered after it, nails clicking on the asphalt like studded snow tires.

The ball bounded up to the top of an eight-foot-high rock retaining wall, and without hesitation Johnny leaped after it. He almost made it up there, too, that spry little guy; just a foot or two more and he would have been on top, where his beloved ball was, bright and yellow and spit-shined, bouncing around like a pinball.

He didn't make it. Though he drank like a kitten, he fell like a dog. Done in by gravity and obsession, Johnny crashed down to the asphalt in a torrent of screams. The funny little wookie whom we'd spared three years before fell hard.

The ball bounced back down and dribbled by him. He glanced at it, thinking that if he could just focus on it, get up and grab it, that it alone would heal him and the nightmare would be gone and we could go back home to Lou, we could rest and come back again tomorrow and forget it ever happened. He watched the ball roll by and he cried and crawled toward me, looked at me with confusion and dread and pain.

I ran to the car, grabbed a floor mat, and ran back. I thought he'd probably hurt his back, so I gently slid him onto the mat and carried him back to the car.

On the way to the vet, he miraculously popped up and looked around, as if nothing had happened.

"Are you okay, pal?" I asked, astonished, carefully palpating his back, legs, and neck. He grinned and looked at me, then sat up and stuck his head out the window. His wookian locks blew back and made him look like a baby werewolf.

"*Ruff!*" he said, his bark high-pitched and sudden. Then he spotted the tennis ball in the cup holder and grabbed it.

I decided to take him home and watch him for a few hours. He'd most likely just twisted something or tweaked a nerve coming down.

"You are indestructible, dude."

I put him in his crate and made him rest until dinner. Lou came over and sniffed the heck out of him, then returned to the back window to stare out. Johnny finally settled and caught a nap before dinner.

For the rest of the evening Johnny seemed fine. He ate, then ran around outside like the clown he was before finally doing his business. "You need to sleep in your crate tonight, little guy; you had a bad fall and I want you to rest."

When I woke up the next morning, Lou had already crawled out from under my bed, something he did only if he'd heard something unusual, or if he felt poorly. I walked into the living room to find him lying beside Johnny's crate.

Johnny panted and whined. When I opened the crate, he struggled to his front feet, dragged himself out, then collapsed into Lou, who licked his little friend's belly. Johnny was in deep trouble.

I hurried Lou out the back for a quick pee. One of the gardeners yelled at him. I brought him back in, eased Johnny onto a sofa cushion, and got my keys.

"Watch the house, Lou. Johnny's hurt." Lou looked up at me with his big amber eyes and a fretful look and wondered why I was carrying Johnny around on a cushion.

"He's blown at least one disk in his lower back," said the vet. "My neurologic exam shows almost no function in his back end. Look," he said, showing how Johnny could not stand, and how he could not uncurl a paw once the vet curled the top of it underneath itself.

"He's paralyzed?"

"I'm afraid so. And there's no response to pain back here. I'm pinching him as hard as I can right now, with no response. See?"

Johnny looked up at me. He panted, his little cat tongue pink, curled.

"What can we do?"

"I can order some imaging to confirm the diagnosis, but it's very expensive and, at this point, redundant. If you'd gotten him to a veterinary neurosurgeon right away, he or she might have been able to go in and removed the disk ejecta and relieved the compression of the spinal cord. But right now, I believe the cord damage may be irreversible."

"Prednisone?"

"Too late."

"Is he in pain?"

"Yes, though I've sedated him a bit. He's paralyzed, though, and certainly incontinent."

"He's only four years old."

"I know, Steve."

I paced around the room. I did not want this. I wanted to go home. I wanted to wake up. I'd saved his sorry ass.

I killed a baby jay once that'd been mauled by something. I'd been in the woods with Lou, and he'd found it in the leaves, its mouth open wide for air, for food, for mercy. It writhed in pain in my hand. I took mercy on it and ended its life. That's what help was.

"Nothing left to do," I said.

"We really should think about helping him."

"I know, Doctor."

In *Lawrence of Arabia,* Lawrence goes back to save Gasim, a Harith Bedouin who has fallen off his camel and is lost in the Nefud Desert. Everyone else has written him off as dead. "It is written," says another Harith.

"Nothing is written!" screams Lawrence, turning back and riding all night to save Gasim. And so he brings him back from the dead, showing mercy when no one else would.

The next week, Gasim murders a member of the rival Howei-tat tribe, threatening to incite a bloody feud.

"He must be killed," says Auda, the Howeitat chief, as if dis-cussing the weather.

Nodding, Lawrence grabs his pistol and empties it into the man whose life he saved days before.

"Steve?"

"Give me a moment," I said.

"Sure."

I finger-combed Johnny's wookie hair back from his eyes, stroked his muzzle, then caressed his broken body. I wanted to lay hands on him, bring him to a chiropractor, a witch doctor, a priest. He looked up at me. *Can we please go home now?*

"I'm so sorry, John. I shouldn't have thrown the ball so hard."

I shouldn't have jumped so high.

"I can't fix you. I'm sorry but I can't. I'm not so powerful now, am I? It was all an act. We saved you once, though, right, pal?"

He licked me and looked around.

"And I'm sorry I teased you all the time about Chief."

He was high from the drugs. I started crying and tried to stop, which always makes it worse. The vet came back in.

"We should help him now."

"Okay. Let's help him."

So I kissed him goodbye and thanked him and told him how good a dog he'd been, how he'd more than made up for biting the little girl so long ago and that he needn't worry about it anymore, and that Lou would miss him and that he would take good care of his tennis ball, and that, like Lou, I was glad he'd come into my life.

And then we put him down. That's what help was.

A week later, Nicki's sweet Shyanne, thirteen years old and thin as an alder, fell over and could not get up again. She needed our help, so we put her down, too.

I lay on the rug, massaging Lou's pads. He'd always liked that. Johnny's crate sat in the corner beneath a small white table, its door open, his ball and chewed-on blanket inside. I could still smell him and I know Lou could, too. I wanted Lou to die a hero's death—drag me from a burning building or fight off a pack of pit bulls or die in his sleep like a king.

"I cannot do this with you."

15

The Mystery of the Coyote in the Cold Night

I owned miniblinds, linoleum, refrigerator magnets, and giant wooden salad utensils. I was the last adult I knew to get a cell phone. I kept clothes until they turned into disembodied lint in the clothes-dryer filter, or else shrank down to finger-puppet costumes. I had one suit, purchased in 1993, and a sport jacket with shoulder pads. Add the fact that I was slightly color-blind and you begin to grasp the measure of my savoir faire.

Because I've always been style challenged, I hadn't cared in the least that my countertops and backsplashes were puke green. In fact, if opting for lime green always got me a 20-percent discount,

I'd paint the house, the car, the dog, and my face that astounding shade.

But when my rent suddenly increased by 20 percent, I rapidly developed a sophisticated sense of style and began despising those garish surfaces. Even Lou, who is essentially color-blind, made his displeasure known by refusing even to consider counter surfing anymore.

"You're over here half the time anyway," said Nicki. "Just move in."

"What about the boys?"

"It's like a trip to New York for them every time you show up."

"Yes, but then I go home."

"Where it's quiet."

"Correct."

"Can't help you there."

I'd been single with dog for a good while. I had my writing routine down and liked it. Lou did, too. He liked having me around and didn't seem to mind that his volunteer work at the academy had come to an end.

At nearly eleven, though still healthy and strong, Lou was solidly into his retirement years. He enjoyed longer sleeps, afternoon naps, and gratis attention from me. He took longer to wake up and stretched out his legs and shoulders more often. His famous ripped physique began to morph into a less-cut appearance—Lou began to look more like a middle-aged Lab, only with a deeper, wider chest and more muscular forearms. Sort of like me. He was getting gray around the muzzle, too, and began to develop that subtle thinning of the face that older dogs get. We were both aging gracefully.

Nicki had custody of her boys every other week. During that time, the small North Seattle house became a cross between a Disney film, a gym locker, and a Vegas buffet. It was lively.

"Up to you," she said, lugging a hamper of stinky boys' clothes to the laundry room. "We'd both save money and Lou would get a yard."

"Those smell like monkey crap."

"Your face smells like monkey crap."

So I moved in.

Lou settled in faster than I did. A big yard with a fenced, covered dog run, a nice little house, and every other week two all-American boys running on nitrous all day long. What more could a dog ask for?

Zac and Jake moved up to the big upstairs dormer, leaving their small bedroom for me to set up as an office. One week I'd be a mix of friend, father, and entertainer to Nicki's boys, which, to a single guy in his early forties, seemed scarier than working a pit bull with hemorrhoids. The next week, it'd be just the two of us and Lou; the house would vibrate with the energy of the kids for a day or so, then calm back down. Week to week we rode that funny little energy roller-coaster until even it became routine.

Lou took it in stride. It was good for him to have kids in his life. It kept him young. Lou would oblige Jake or Zac's attentions and perform tricks even when tired or while waiting for his beloved dinner. After living in an L.A. apartment, a rented Castle Heights house (which he'd destroyed), a Seattle apartment, a Bothell house, a stinky ghetto crib, and a lime-green lakeside condo, he'd found his last, best home.

Part of me wondered if I wasn't prematurely putting Lou out to pasture. I was reminded of a great athlete who once retired gets fat and lazy, and I didn't want that to happen to Lou. He'd been so active and helpful—I didn't want to deny him that just because he'd turned eleven.

The answer came from my dad and from Nicki.

. . .

"Stevie, honey!" He was the only guy who could pull off calling me "honey."

"Hey, Dad, how you doing?"

"I'm great, great!"

Apart from never sleeping, drinking twenty cups of coffee a day, and fighting a bad back and a sinus infection for ten years, my then seventy-six-year-old father was in better shape than any guy his age. A Depression baby, a World War II veteran, an ex-navy boxer, a bus driver, and a garbage collector, the Bronx-born widower lived alone in the New York tenement building I'd grown up in, where Sabino the landlord had refused to take a bribe in exchange for the pup I'd wanted as a kid. My dad was old school, with a love for his country that only those who had gone through hell could understand. He'd shined shoes on the street as a kid, quit school to build planes for the military, enlisted the day after Pearl Harbor, sacrificed a brother to the war, and lost his wife to illness during his forties. He kind of reminded me of Lou.

"What's new, Dad?"

"Stevie, they gave me a new bus route, and it is a *dream*." Bored by retirement, he'd gotten a part-time job as a school-bus driver in Westchester, and loved it.

"Let me tell you something, Stevie, this outfit is huge. *Huge.* Second-biggest bus company in the nation. I got a primo route, too, with good kids."

"You keep them in line?"

"You kidding? They love me. And the parents give me gifts! One of them gave me some Japanese candy the other day; still don't know what the heck it is, but Madonna it's good!"

"Why do you keep working?"

"Oh, forget it, Stevie. You quit working, you die. I gotta work, that's it."

Lou lay beside my chair, chewing on a bone. I looked down at him at the same time he looked up at me.

"Keeps you going," I said.

"Work is life, Stevie. You stop working, you're dead."

"Susan said if you wanted to bring Lou into the preschool, you could."

"He misses it, I think."

Nicki worked full-time at a corporate-gift company and part-time as an American Sign Language teacher for hearing pre-schoolers at the New Discovery School in Seattle, owned and operated by Susan Gorman, a big-time dog lover.

"What would Lou do with the kids?" I asked.

"Well, he could help teach them sign language," she said. "Lou knows all those hand signs; why don't we inspire my kids to learn ASL by showing them that if a dog can learn sign language, so can they."

"That's perfect!" I said. Lou walked over to Nicki, tail wagging. He was always drawn to optimism.

Like my tough old dad, Lou would go back to work part-time, helping kids.

For Lou, walking into New Discovery on that first day was like letting a time machine transport him back to the days at the academy, when preschool kids would come in and get wowed by young Lou and the other dogs. Now, seeing twenty-five little kids in a circle on the carpet, waiting patiently, Lou grinned and wagged his tail like a pup. I could literally feel his heart pounding with anticipation. He loved little kids *so* much. Lou was back.

After introductions, I put Lou in a sit/stay in the middle of the room, walked off to the side, and told the kids a little about Lou, who sat there stock-still, smiling, tail whomping the carpet. He was a showman, this dog.

"I have a dog!" yelled out a red-haired little freckle factory.

"I have two dogs and some fish!"

"Why is he just sitting there?"

"Because he's waiting to show you what he knows."

"He looks like a person," said a blond sprite, barely taller than Lou sitting.

Excited to have a dog in the school, the kids asked a million questions and I answered as best I could. Most seemed bewildered that a dog would simply sit in one spot and watch them. Nicki sat on the side, grinning.

"Who knows why I brought Lou in today?" I asked.

" 'Cause he's smarter than us!" said a little Hispanic girl with pigtails.

"What do you mean?"

"He knows sign language and he can sit still."

I tossed a cookie over to Lou and he caught it with a flick of his head. Some of the kids clapped. Lou looked over at me. *Let's get the show on the road, boss.*

"Okay, who wants to see him wave without me asking him to?"

"Me, me!"

I gave Lou the sign for wave right—a subtle lift of my right hand. His paw shot up above his head. The kids cheered. Then, with his right paw still up high, I signed wave left. He dropped his right and simultaneously lifted his left. More applause. I had him go back and forth like that a few times, a doggish can-can for the kids to cheer.

We went through Lou's old routine—roll left and right, spin both ways, play dead, quick down, head down, wipe his face, bark on command, go to a mark, retrieve, start and stop—all his tricks, with no verbal commands at all.

After a while, a calmness washed over the room. It had struck them that this dog *actually* knew sign language.

"Who wants to meet Lou?" I asked, clipping his leash on.

"Me, me, me!" A chorus of *me*s as they popped up from the floor.

"You stay right there and I'll walk Lou by each and every one of you. You can pet him if you want to."

Most of the kids reached out to run their tiny hands down his body. They touched the coarse black hairs along his spine, felt the softness of his ears, kissed and hugged him, stroked his flanks, took dog kisses, and laughed at getting tail-swatted in the face. Total trust for an imposing dog they'd just met. Some, afraid at first, surrendered to the courage of others and reached out to the big guy, his handsome face gleaming with affection for these little people—like puppies, some a third his age, fresh-smelling and unaware of the things he'd done. I looked to Nicki, who as usual knew just what I was thinking. We teared up a little and smiled.

Lou looked at me, beaming with happiness and pride. *Work is life. You stop working, you're dead.*

Winter in Seattle—often an oxymoron. On the East Coast, winter often meant months of subfreezing temperatures, snow up to your waist, and Thunderdome out on the icy roads. Seattle winters, though, usually involved cold rain, clouds, more rain, perpetual darkness, vitamin D deficiencies, news spots on SAD and suicide, wind, more rain, and one or two minor snowfalls, which paralyzed the entire region for days.

Not that winter. We got socked, bad. Snow and unusually cold temperatures in December, then a warming, then bitter cold again that froze the melted snow and made an ice rink out of the entire town. A second snowstorm on top of that clinched the deal.

The neighborhood went snow-quiet. No activity except for a lone snowplow, some kids with sleds, and a snowmobile jetting around. My car sat in the driveway, the snow piled atop its roof like a cold, white fez. No school or work, people huddled inside with the heat cranked up, deliriously happy ten-year-olds throwing snowballs at one another in the middle of what once was a street.

A good snow transformed a place, took it back in time, hushed it, made you long for sleigh bells and Christmas presents. That's what it was like in Seattle on the day that Lou disappeared.

Nicki's kids played in the snow. Jake had opened the side gate to let them run from the front yard to the back. The simple pleasure of seeing kids have fun in the snow would lead to one of Lou's oddest adventures.

The next morning, I let Lou out into the snowy backyard. Though still capable of jumping the fence, I knew he wouldn't; he was too homed for that. But he still loved snow, so we frolicked in it for a while; I tossed snowballs at him and he batted them back, then ran and cut around, kicking up rooster tails of powder, dropping into play posture, and biting at the snow, his tail making its own little snow angel, his eyes bright in the snowy light.

I went inside to make a cup of tea. I left him out there to do his business and enjoy himself for a bit. Sometimes a dog just needs a minute alone.

I opened the back door and called him, but he didn't come. He'd begun to show signs of a hearing deficiency, so I thought he couldn't hear me.

I went out there. The outside thermometer said eighteen degrees. I wore my bathrobe and untied sneakers.

"Lou."

No Lou. Not in the dog run, not on the side of the house, not in the neighbors' yards. When I saw the side gate open, the dread of adrenaline rushed up into my heart like bile.

I ran into the front yard. No Lou. I saw his tracks in the fresh powder—unmistakable, one nail on his back left paw crooked, front paws bigger than the backs. The tracks showed him running, not walking, out into the street and down the block, chasing after something. Then I lost them amid a rash of kids' footprints and the swath of a plow's blade. My dog was gone.

It wasn't like a decade ago when a young Lou had gone off on a peacock hunt. This was a seasoned, homed dog of exceptional intelligence and loyalty. He just didn't run off. At best he'd wander into the front yard and sit on the stoop to watch kids and traffic pass by, or slip over to neighbor Dave's house to look for his great new love, dainty little Scamp, an adorable angora mix whom Lou would pine for at the fence. This was unusual. He'd left the neighborhood. Something uncommon had lured him away.

"It's not his fault. He's just a kid," said Nicki.

"I know. I was just looking for a patsy."

"Lou just doesn't do these things."

"Something weird happened. He *ran* out of the yard. Something lured him off."

"Kids?"

"I don't think so. He loves kids, but he wouldn't go off with them. It had to be something he thought important."

"The serious Lou?"

"Yeah. Soldier Lou."

"Old soldier."

We looked for him. Everywhere. Nicki and I knocked on every door on our street, twenty blocks in one direction and five in the other. I called out his name until I was hoarse, until the mantra of his name became hypnotic.

Eighteen degrees out, hands and feet frozen. The kids and their friends canvassed the neighborhood and the parks nearby. I drove down icy abandoned streets, now untraveled white ribbons gridding the neighborhood, snowbound cars parked like fallen dominoes as far as the eye could see.

It looked like a North Dakota winter landscape. You'd have seen a big black-and-tan dog walking around out there. But my alter ego was in a place I could not see or touch. He was figuring things out, like a Martian rover forty million miles away.

I had no kids. I had a dog. The best dog. He was eleven, out in the cold, on his own. I was panicked and sick in my heart.

"Lou is a survivor," said Nicki. "He'll be all right until we find him."

She was right. With any other dog I would have held out less hope, but Lou was dog, owner, and spirit wrapped together in one package, a thinking machine with stamina and fur and a wild heart, with a will to survive as strong as any wolf's who'd gnaw off his own paw to escape and keep living. He'd stay warm long enough and work out whatever drama he'd gotten himself mixed up in, then track his way back home. He'd eat snow and garbage and squirrels if need be. I knew these things, but he was my dog and I loved him like a brother and when you love the lost it feels like falling.

We looked, came home to warm up, looked again, came home for food and tea, looked more. I felt like I was watching the Zapruder film over and over again in slow motion. I felt like Lindbergh.

Jake was beside himself. Nicki and Zac tried to buoy us up.

"It's not your fault, Jake," I said, sorry that I'd been upset before. "He never runs off. You know that. Something strange happened to make him go."

"Like what?"

"I don't know. But knowing him, it's going to make a great story."

Less than a mile from our home, the eighty-acre Hamlin Park was covered with fir, cedar, alder, and hemlock, and a dense undergrowth of blackberry, ivy, scotch broom, ferns, and holly. Hamlin Creek, a tributary of the Thornton Creek watershed, ran through it. Deer, squirrels, raccoons, possums, skunks, mice, and rats fared well, as did birds, slugs, and even small frogs and fish. I'd hiked it many a time with Lou. He loved the place because it made him remember. It was a great little park, and if I'd been a dog I'd want to go there. But dogs of another sort had already laid claim to it.

Hamlin's meager coyote population grew fat on slow rats that hid in the underbrush. The coyotes kept to themselves; most people didn't even realize that such large predators could thrive in such a small ecosystem, stuck square in the middle of a busy suburban town. But they did. Like Lou, they were survivors. Sometimes I thought that he had more in common with them than with his own kind.

The recent weather had made survival a tough task for the coyotes. Some did their best to eke out a living within the park boundaries, but others, unable to find enough food, ventured out of Hamlin. Emboldened by the abandoned streets and the carpet of snow that had turned the town into a taiga, they made their way down deserted streets in search of easy pickings—cats, small dogs, uneaten dog food, garbage, possums—whatever they could scrounge.

He'd gone missing early in the day. After midnight we decided to get some sleep, get up early, and look again, get notice out to all the shelters, vets and animal control, put up posters—the whole inventory of things one does when a dog goes missing.

I'm not sure why, but around 2:00 A.M. I decided to take one last, slow drive around the neighborhood, just in case. Just to be out there in the same place at the same time as my dog. I also knew that in the dark of night, things happened that wouldn't during the day, things we slept through each night, nature's funky graveyard shift. Standing out on my stoop in the bitter cold, I could feel it ramp up, feel the night come on. I thought he could, too.

"One more lap around the neighborhood," I said to Nicki. " "You can stay here. It's cold."

"I'm coming."

We drove slowly. I'd recently replaced the old Civic with a newer one, a wagon with all-wheel drive, and it did well enough in the ice and snow. We looked in yards and ball fields and playgrounds, checked alleys and parking lots and streets. No Lou. With every corner turned we expected to see him trundling along, nose to the ground, tail high, steering himself home. But he wasn't ever there. He was somewhere, though.

"What a douche bag," I said. "I'm so pissed. It's more his fault than Jake's. He knows better."

"Calm down. He's a dog."

"Mostly."

"Maybe somebody has him."

"No . . . he's on his own. I know him."

"Let's get some sleep. We'll look in the morning."

We rolled through an icy intersection two blocks from our house, no cars or people out, the traffic light clicking from green to yellow to red.

"Don't cry," said Nicki. "We'll find him."

"He's *Lou*. He's my best friend. I . . ."

"I know. That's why we'll find him."

Past the intersection, we drove down our block.

"When we'd get separated in the woods, he'd always find me. Always."

"He's got the schnoz."

"He'd never give up."

"I know."

The biggest coyote I'd ever seen stood there in the middle of the road, a block from our house, eyes ablaze in the headlights, fur puffed out. He stared at us, openmouthed, venting hot breath out into the cold night air.

"Big male," I said. "Fifty pounds, easy."

"He's huge."

"This is it, Nick. This is why."

"Yes. You're right."

He'd left Hamlin the night before and roamed west down the long hill, looking for something, anything, to eat. When he got to our neighborhood, he'd found Northcrest Park, close to our house, five square blocks of dense woods and cover with a trail down the middle, bordered by homes on both sides. Perfect for a hungry coyote to use as a base of operations. He could venture out, grab a cat or a schnauzer, then dash back to the park to eat in peace. It'd be all his, and if he wanted to explore a block or two farther out, the dearth of people made it easy. He hadn't planned on Lou, though.

"We have to follow him," I said. "He's connected to this. If he's killed Lou, I'll have his hide."

"There he goes."

"Northcrest. He's using Northcrest."

"Follow him."

We tracked the coyote to the north entrance of the park. He was casual about it, walking, not running, almost at ease, passing through the opened gate entrance. He might have been favoring a front leg, or else he slipped going up an icy hill; I couldn't tell.

"Take the wheel," I said, grabbing a flashlight and my Club steering-wheel lock from the backseat.

"What's that for?" she asked, sliding over.

"I can't fight a coyote with my bare hands."

"Just be careful."

"Meet me on the other side."

Northcrest's trail wound through the park for five blocks, then emptied out on the south end next to a church parking lot. Side trails branched off into the woods and dead-ended at the back fences of homes.

The coyote followed the main trail. I followed him. He knew I was there and didn't seem to care.

I kept him in sight while shining my light down side trails and into the bushes, looking for Lou, hoping he wasn't torn to shreds or bleeding to death. I feared that the coyote was returning now to feed or finish the job. Lou was old now but still seventy pounds of tough; even a coyote this big would have a hell of a fight on his hands. But he could have hurt Lou, maybe torn his hamstring.

I loved coyotes. Lou and I had listened to them so many times. We loved their music, composed a million years ago, the theme song of our time together, our spirit guide. But if this yipper had killed my sweet Lou, I'd bash his wily skull in with my antitheft device and burn his scavenging corpse.

The coyote sniffed his way down the trail, oblivious to me but now concerned about something else. He got ahead of me. He'd made for the southern entrance, so I trotted on through the woods until I got to the church parking lot. My car sat there with its lights off, waiting.

Nicki moved over to the passenger seat. I got in. "He ran through the fence and took off down the hill," she said. "He was cruising."

We took off after him.

"Open your window," I said. "I think I heard a dog bark."

"Lot of dogs on the block."

"I know his bark."

A block farther on, the coyote darted out of a driveway, then disappeared behind a parked RV. We lost sight of him.

"You didn't hear a dog barking while you were waiting for me?" I asked, watching for him, wanting something to hope for.

"No."

We pulled over and listened.

"He might be out here somewhere, ripped up, bleeding. I *know* this coyote had something to do with it."

"You can't think that coyote could beat Lou, can you?" she asked, looking at me without a shred of doubt. "Do you?"

"No, not even one that big. But two could."

"We saw one, not two. If there'd been two, they would have been together, male and female, or mother and child."

"True."

"Let's go home. We'll get a fresh start in the morning."

I drove slowly. I'd been heartened, somehow. The sight of the coyote had raised the bar and connected me to Lou in a way I hadn't ever experienced. The coyote became something to blame, too, something to focus my anger on. It made sense: only the magic of a huge coyote strolling past our home could cause this theater. But now, he too was gone.

"I am so tired," I said, drained.

"We'll sleep, then start again."

"Thanks for helping."

"Don't be ridiculous."

We pulled into our driveway.

There stood Lou, at the crossroads of heaven and hell, shoulders set, half man, half beast, trembling in the cold, determined, unyielding.

"Oh my God," said Nicki.

I walked over to him. He snarled an ancient snarl and stared at me through dark eyes, drugged by fear, ready to fight again, his blood fevered with the will to survive and defend.

He was deep into it. He was not there. For an instant, Lou did not know me. I was simply an extension of the battle he thought had ended the moment he'd found home, the moment he'd smelled the coyote surrender the street back to its rightful owner.

"Easy, pal," I said, crouching in front of him, seeing his hackles up, coat disheveled and greasy, ice in the corners of his eyes, muck and snow peppering his body. He looked like he'd fallen down the side of a mountain.

The light slowly came back into his eyes. Lou let go and it came rushing out of him like hurt from a child, so I wrapped my arms around him and felt the tension in his body go all at once and he cried like a baby and shuddered and licked my ear and molded into me, shaking uncontrollably, whining, weeping, apologizing, trying to tell me what had happened. *Happy, oh so happy.*

Nicki came over and we both hugged him, and all three of us cried there on the driveway, neither dogs nor humans but family, just family.

"He smells *awful*," said Nicki, her face a mess of tears.

"He let go his anal glands a while back, I think,' I said, cleaning off his face and checking him over. He seemed sore in spots, but I couldn't find any blood or wounds save a string of bloody saliva on his lips. "He fought the coyote all right. Nothing else would get *this* dog to let go of his anal glands. And he smells of urine, too—strong and bitter, like wolf piss."

"Oh, Lou," said Nicki, stroking his head and crying again. "You stink."

"Welcome back, pal."

"*Rower.*"

We cleaned him up, watched him, loved on him, fed him. We

savored the mystery of the coyote in the cold night, and Lou's temptation and deliverance. We wished we'd been privy to the things he'd been through. The boys laughed and cried and danced around, while, bit by bit, good old Lou came back from his visit with the dead.

The coyote searched on for something to eat—garbage, frozen cat food—anything that wouldn't fight back. He'd had his adventure, too, and must have felt it now, felt where the angry old dog had hurt him. Filled with a hunter's conceit, he'd led Lou off and almost broken our hearts, then missed his chance, but atoned for his sins by bringing Lou back home to us, and giving an old warrior back his pride.

16

Saving Flavio and Peeing on the Lottery Knight

On a summer day in 2001, he showed up inside our fenced backyard, chestnut and gold with a dark muzzle and black eyeliner, a foxy long-haired mutt, long and lanky and sweet and scared of the exploits of his own tail, scared of shadows and hands and feet and sounds and cruel memories, scared deep inside his good heart. But he'd come into *our* yard—leaped the fence to chase the scent of another, an older dog now, one who'd spent half his life saving miscreants, rabble, curs, and innocents from lethal injection. He'd retired from the life but like an old fire jumper must have missed the rush of pulling sorry asses out of the flames, and the pride of doing his job better than anyone else on earth. And so when this fence-jumping escapee from a torture chamber had the good sense to choose *our* yard, Lou's last save began.

He had the impossibly thick coat of a chow chow, the length and gait of a shepherd, and the head and heart of a retriever. If any dog could compete with Lou for looks, it was he—stunningly handsome, around two years old, with the ability to jump a six-foot fence like a rutting deer during hunting season.

I'd been buried deep in the corner of the garden, weeding out the basil patch with Nicki. Lou napped inside, the sun too warm for his taste. Then, in my peripheral vision, I saw a big dog bound over the neighbor's chain-link fence, clear it in one graceful motion, and dance into the yard. His chestnut locks burnished, his white teeth shining in the sun.

"Nick."

"Yeah?"

"Check it out."

"Whoa."

I walked over to him. Though animated and edgy, I could tell he wanted to interact, so when he pranced over to the dog run and walked in to get a drink from the bucket, I walked over and closed the gate.

"He's beautiful," said Nicki, walking over. "Let him out."

"Not yet. I want to make sure he's not insane or rabid or aggressive in any way. And it'll be easier to check his ID in there than out here."

Though half deaf by now (thank goodness I'd taught him hand signals), Lou had somehow sensed the dog's presence and was now barking and chortling away at the back door. When I opened the door, Lou walked out and made straight for the dog pen, where the gorgeous dog lapped away at the water. He woofed a bit, then sniffed at the dog through the fence, the dog sniffing back and licking Lou through the chain link.

Lou looked at me. *You're kidding, right?*

"He's lost, Lou. You'd know all about that, right?"

"Aroogla," he said, sitting in front of the pen gate, the dog inside wagging his tail and breathing hard, his mouth open wide as a baby bird's at breakfast.

"What's your guess, Lou?" I asked, slipping by him to open the gate. He tried to squeeze in with me. "Not yet. Let me check him out first." He *rowered* and pawed at the gate. "No," I said, using the hand sign this time, a short chop with my hand.

"Don't get killed," said Nicki.

"I'm more likely to get peed on than bitten, I think."

He wanted to relate but had a base fear about him. I could spot it immediately: his whole posture was one of a dog in pre-cringe. It was written all over his face: this dog grew up getting smacked and kicked so often that he expected it, identified with it.

"It's the 'where's my mallet?' syndrome," I said to Nicki, the dog letting me pet him and look at his collar.

"Huh?"

"If I hit you in the head with a mallet every twenty seconds for your whole life, then I stop hitting you with the mallet, your first reaction will be, 'Hey, where's the darned mallet?'"

"Speak for yourself."

It was true: abused dogs became so used to it that they'd seek it out, initiate it, and purposely act in a manner they knew would incite the abuser to action. You see it in omega wolves all the time. In the abused dog's mind, if negative attention is all it can get, then that's what it's going to crave.

When a dog like this is rescued by kinder folk, it still expects the harsh treatment and will find it hard to let go of that dysfunctional script. The lack of abuse confuses them, until they can be taught that life holds more than a swift kick in the ass.

He was sweet as pie, submissive, and used to being scared. When he tried to jump up on me, I stood up straight and said,

"No, off," prompting him to collapse to the ground, roll over, and release a font of pee.

"Nice," said Nicki.

"He's neutered. And there's no ID on his collar."

"Great. Another project."

I let Lou in and he immediately sniffed the dog out. Surprisingly, the dog welcomed Lou's company. Lou gruffed him back a few times and took him down by the scruff once, but beyond that, they got along fine. Even when Lou batted the dog off for being too chummy, his tail continued to wag.

"I'll leave them in here together," I said. "Lou will keep him from trying to make a break. I have a feeling he's a Steve McQueen, this one."

"What?"

"Escape artist."

"Didn't he tunnel out?"

"Technically."

"All right then."

Most of us have been there: we find a dog with no ID, tattoo, or microchip, nothing at all to help find the owner. We call shelters and vet clinics, put up flyers, walk the neighborhood with the dog, knock on doors, place ads in the paper. Sometimes we get lucky, other times not.

We spent three months searching for his owners. He wasn't chipped or tattooed and hadn't been reported missing anywhere. Flyers, ads, door-to-door walks—nothing.

"How could no one recognize him?" asked Nicki, looking at the dog we now called Flavio, named after Flavio Briatore, the managing director of Renault's F1 racing program. Our friend Jeff Daniels, a big F1 fan, came up with the name after seeing how flighty and agile Flavio was.

"Maybe they did, but just don't want him back," I said.

"That's cruel."

"Might be the nicest thing they've ever done for him."

Flavio was a mess. Terribly hand-shy, skittish, worrisome, obviously kicked. When he felt pressed or challenged in any way, he'd switch off his brain completely and either roll and pee or try to jump the fence and go. But, at the same time, he craved friendship and showed no fear aggression at all. He was a heck of a nice dog, with posttraumatic stress disorder.

Training him took patience and a reversal of standard techniques. I could use no corrections at all, not even inflection in my voice. Even extended eye contact would cause the now-famous Flavio roll-and-pee move, as if I had telekinetic control over his bladder.

Everything had to be positive and well thought out. For instance, if you wanted him to wait at the door for a moment, you had to watch your posture and eye contact; getting too close to him or using your body or a leash to block his momentum almost guaranteed pee and panic. Very wolfish.

Training had to be meted out slowly: if you gave him too much to think about, he'd slip into a nonthinking state of panic and shut down. With Flavio, it was baby steps—watching for good behaviors and rewarding them with something nonthreatening, which wasn't as easy as it sounds. Anything at any given time could be scary to Flavio: even a bowl of food placed down too abruptly or a pat on the head when he wasn't looking could set him off.

The secret salve was, of course, Lou. Flavio adored him, followed him around, feared him not at all. Lou could discipline him, manhandle him, toss him around, play rough with him, cozy up to him—nothing the old guy did scared Flavio at all. Only when Lou had to really lay down the law over food, possessions, or other perks of dominance did Flavio show any signs of dread.

Lou became the "confidence conduit." Find a scared dog's muse and you find the means to save him. That's what twelve-year-old Lou became for Flavio. Whatever his idol did must have been okay. It was the start of my "What Would Lou Do?" program.

We kept him. In our hearts, he went from being a flighty foster dog to a permanent, dysfunctional member of the house. We had to readjust our thinking, though, and get Nicki's kids to do the same if we were to avoid puddles of urine and geysers of diarrhea. Give him latitude while still building manners and trust, and create a workable routine for the scaredy-cat. And have him spend as much time with Lou as possible.

I trained him through Lou. I'd have Lou go through his basic behaviors with Flavio there, then just slowly begin teaching him the same moves. With Lou there beside him, being asked to lie down wasn't scary; it was social and safe.

When I did work with him alone, I had to constantly back off and remember what I was dealing with. Much of the training had to happen in the yard, as any perceived pressure resulted in the "dribbles." To this day, all grooming, massage, or involved handling has to be done outdoors. Flavio has the constitution of a pigeon eternally searching the skies for the inevitable falcon.

Flavio isn't stupid, but he was stymied by his fears. I learned this quickly and adjusted my expectations. To this day, he knows only enough to keep him focused and happy. His great trick was learning to let go of his fears and be a normal dog. Learning not to escape and roam the neighborhood was another trick that took several tries to master. We found that out the hard way—four times.

"Lou can pee on command, right?" said Anne.

"Yeah, or poop, for that matter."

"What's the pee command?"

"Pasta."

"What?"

"If I say 'pasta,' he will pee."

"How directed is it?"

"You mean locational?"

"Yeah."

"Depends on how close I am to him and the timing of the command. If I identify a spot, I can get him to pee on it. Why?"

"A Washington State lottery commercial is shooting in Everett soon, at a golf course. They need a dog to pee on a guy wearing a suit of armor."

"Of course."

"Can you bring him for an audition tomorrow?"

"How many other dogs can pee on command?"

"So far, just Lou."

"He's twelve, you know."

"But still healthy?"

"A little hard of hearing and some arthritis, but still peppy."

"Give it a try?"

"Sure. I'll feed him a quart of chicken broth before we show up."

"That's the spirit. Oh—why 'pasta'?"

"I was eating some leftover baked ziti the day I taught him. Just popped into my head."

"Right. See you tomorrow."

The next day, Lou and I met Anne in downtown Seattle, at a location the casting director had chosen. They needed to see him, see how he performed, and then decide if he was right. Happy to get away from the new nutcase at home, he'd drunk a big bowl of diluted chicken broth for breakfast and now had that gotta-go look in his eyes.

"Hold on, pal," I said, leashing him up and taking him out of the car.

"Steverino," said Anne, meeting me at the casting company's doorstep. "Hi, Louie boy!"

"Aroogla," he said, leaning into her.

"He looks like he's going to explode."

"If he could cross his back legs and walk, he would."

"Broth?"

"Oh yeah."

"Let's get going, then."

There's something about a fire hydrant that begs for dog pee. Once one dog uses it, every other mutt wants to do the same. It's a viral event. On the hunch that there would be a hydrant available almost anywhere downtown, I'd worked Lou beforehand, directing him to a hydrant and getting him to pee on it. Sure enough, right outside the office sat a yellow-and-green hydrant surrounded by dandelions and garbage.

"Hi, Steve," said the casting director, an impossibly thin young man with a horizontally striped blue-and-white shirt that made me dizzy. "And this is Lou?"

"In the flesh, ready to pee."

"What a handsome guy!" he said, crouching down to Lou, who waved and *rowered* at him, then turned to look at me, a look of desperation on his face. *Pee now?*

"Wait, pal."

"We'll need Lou to eventually pee on a man in a suit of armor. Think he can do that?"

"Give me a few days and I'll get him to pee in a cup," I said, watching as Lou marched in place and stared at the hydrant close-by, that lovely hydrant that smelled of forty satisfied dogs.

"Can we see him in action, then?"

"How about that hydrant?" I asked. Lou heard *hydrant* and grinned.

"Can you place him on the street corner and have him go to it?"

"Sure."

"Let's see."

I put Lou into a sit twenty feet off and asked him to wait, then walked over to the hydrant, tapped on it, and looked into Lou's eyes.

"Rower!" he pleaded, eyes big as eggs.

I spoke the words he longed to hear: "Lou—pasta!"

He trotted over to the hydrant, shot his left leg up as high as a dog could, then released a torrent of urine that ricocheted off the hydrant and onto the back fender of a Volvo parked illegally beside it.

"That's my car," muttered the director's assistant.

"Sorry," I said, Lou's stream showing no sign of ebbing. He peed for so long that he had to lower the leg, then raise it again.

"Don't be. He's hired," said the director. "I just hope the suit of armor doesn't rust."

Anne came over. "Is this an Austin Powers movie?"

"He drank a lot of broth."

"The shoot is next week, at the Legion Memorial Golf Course in Everett," she said as Lou came over, smiling from ear to ear.

"What time?"

"Seven. Bring broth."

A dog who gets the holy crap kicked out of him every day will miss the kicker. It goes deeper than logic or even the will to survive. It's a dog thing.

And so it was with Flavio.

"He's gone," I said to Nicki, grabbing my keys and rousing Lou.

"Flavio?"

"Yeah. Lifted the gate handle and jumped the back fence."

"I'll walk the block. You drive the grid?" she said.

"Yeah. Take your cell."

Lou had been the sprinter king in his youth. But Flavio could run like the wind and jump any fence. It gave him a nearly un-limited range, and me heartburn.

A week earlier, he'd gotten away from me during an off-leash training session. He'd gone west, up the hill past Northcrest Park. I'd gotten him back by using Lou as a lure. Guessing that he'd take the same route, Lou and I drove up the hill and began zigzagging down local streets, looking in yards and parks, check-ing homes I knew had yarded dogs, listening for barking. When searching for a dog, you had to think like that dog: What did he covet? What was he searching for? In Flavio's case, I guessed his ultimate goal was to find the asshole who'd owned him. I knew he (yes, it was a he) must have had other dogs, too, as Flavio adored other dogs and had a great social sense about him. That meant it was a house with an unkempt yard and barking dogs, probably left out in the yard much of the day. Flavio would be looking for his old dysfunctional pack, because he was a dog and because he hadn't yet homed to us. He was honoring the loyalty.

"Anything?" asked Nicki.

"Not yet."

"I'm checking Ridgecrest, then Northcrest."

"I'm up near the Crest Theater. Wait—there he is. Gotta go."

The Crest is a small, second-run multiplex about a half mile from our house. The neighborhood had lots of one-family homes with yards and slow local traffic. I spotted Flavio across the street in the parking lot of a bingo parlor, running like a ga-zelle.

Lou looked out the window at Flavio, who ran right by us. "Let's get him, Lou."

I drove behind him as he flew down the street, keeping pace, waiting for the chance to send Lou out to herd him back. If Lou had been five or six, I just would have let him out of the car right there and let him do the rest, but he was too old for that now.

I looked down at the speedometer. Thirty-three.

He cut hard into a yard. He acted as if he was close to home. I didn't want to have to argue and lose my temper with some troglodyte with a menagerie of scarred pit bulls and chow chows and shepherds and Rottweilers and whatever else he had chained up in his dusty yard with his metal water trough and yard tie-outs and decomposing crap all over the place and three cars up on blocks in the driveway. If Flavio found his old freak show, he wouldn't want to leave. I had to act fast.

I hung a fast right and a left to parallel Flavio's route and cut him off if he decided to go cross-country. Seeing him flash by an overgrown rhododendron, I stopped and let Lou out.

"Get Flavio, Lou! Get him!"

Lou barked out strongly, then trotted off into an adjoining yard. I lost sight of Flavio. Then Lou disappeared behind a big cedar. I waited.

Lou walked out of a yard two doors down, covered with dust and dead cedar droppings. He looked at me, then turned left. There stood Flavio, panting, on the inside of someone's fenced front yard.

"Aroogla!"

Flavio vaulted the fence, looked down the street, then looked back at Lou. I saw my chance.

"Lou! Come here!"

He walked over, an annoyed look on his face. Flavio bolted over to lick Lou's face. I held out some jerky, Lou reached for it, and as Flavio sniffed at the meat, I slipped my looped leash over his head and that was that.

"Dumbass," I said, looking him in the eye. "They hate you. We love you. Do the math."

In the next two years he'd jump ship three more times, twice while Nicki and I were away on vacation, with house sitters watching the dogs. Both times, Nicki's two boys came to the rescue, coming over from their dad's house to search for the jerk. Each time, Flavio had made for the same exact neighborhood, proving to me that he'd come from there. I'd told them where to look, and sure enough, the boys would spot him jetting past the Crest with that goofy, openmouthed grin on his face, looking for the old horror house, obeying some demented canine code. Zac, now in his late teens, actually ran him down on one occasion, tackling him and getting drenched with pee in the process. If you really want to find a lost dog, get kids to do it.

After I discovered that Flavio could lift the gate handle, I slipped a metal rod through the handle's locking hole to prevent that. Then he discovered that if he shoved his seventy-five pounds hard enough into the gate, the handle itself would slip and turn on its mounting hardware, again allowing him to get out and bolt. I finally had to set up a medieval-style, castle-door type barring device that slipped through slots mounted to the door's posts, preventing Flavio from pushing through and getting out. Once he became trustworthy enough to be in the home for extended periods of time, the dog-pen security became an issue only when he needed to be out in the pen, either when house sitters were present or if Flavio had a bout of diarrhea and needed to be al fresco.

The last time he escaped, Lou and I casually drove up to the Crest and waited. He showed up, came over, and sat with us.

"Forget about them, Flavi. They're meth heads. You live with a trainer, a family that loves you, and the best damn dog in the world."

He licked me, then did his strange little muted bark, where he'd try to vocalize but instead just snapped his jaws together a few times while making a weird, asthmatic wheezing sound. He was cute and lovable and a real birdbrain.

"Okay. Now let's go home."

Lou head butted Flavio, then jumped up into the back of the car. When he did, he winced a bit. The dog who'd once climbed trees, run Weimaraners into exhaustion, and won agility contests was having trouble getting into the car. The magnificent bastard was getting old on me.

A sunny summer morning, perfect weather. The entire golf course had been rented out for the big-budget commercial shoot, with a production crew from California set up in the parking lot. A half-dozen parked trailers, full catering, technicians, grips, camera crew, actors, miles of wiring snaked everywhere, the smell of honeysuckle, hot lights, and breakfast filling the air.

"I'll have to give him more broth," I said.

Getting the right shot was proving difficult. Lou had initially scoffed at the idea of actually peeing on a person, who, despite the heavy suit of armor, was obviously a human being. But once we'd gotten enough broth into him and after asking the actor to remain as still as possible, we started to get results.

The director was being a perfectionist, though, and kept asking for retakes. "His leg blocked the stream," or "not enough velocity," or "he looks too dejected." *Hey, pinhead, you'd be dejected, too, if I kept water-boarding you with chicken broth and asking you to pee over and over on a decent-enough guy sweating his brains out inside eighty pounds of armor.*

"Let's take a lunch break," said Anne, worried about the shot and Lou, for whom the novelty of the situation had worn off long ago.

"I'll take him for a run around the course and give him some water. The salt in the broth has got him wigged out, like a puppy drinking seawater."

"We don't want him puking on the guy."

"Actually, that would make an even better shot."

"Run him out, Steve."

I jogged him up and down the first fairway. A rabbit froze

beneath a stand of alders and watched Lou trot by. Lou hadn't even sniffed it out. He was tired, and had enough salt in him to cure a ham.

He lapped at water pooled atop a broken sprinkler head near the putting green. "I know, pal," I said, rubbing his neck and mad-dogging with him a little.

"Just when we thought we were out of Hollywood, they pull us back in!" I said. He stared at me. "Pacino, Lou . . . Pacino."

He wasn't impressed, but he licked my face anyway, his muzzle gray now and narrowing out more and more each month. His coat had dulled and roughed out a bit, too, but he was still a handsome dog.

I emptied a can of dog food into a bowl of water and gave it to him. He sloshed it up.

"He's going to have major diarrhea later," said Anne, scratching Lou's head.

"The show must go on, right, Lou?" I said.

"Aroo."

"Let's do this thing," she said.

"Come on, Lou, let's go piss on this bastard and go home."

We staged Lou twenty feet off, stage left. The actor took his position on the bench, his steel armor freshly polished and ready for another dousing.

Lou wanted to go home but he knew he had a job to do, however bizarre, so when the director said, "Action," I gave him his cue and he sauntered right up to the guy, raised his leg high, and loosed a sparkling arc of yellow right on the guy's leg, then exited stage right, just as we'd planned. It was perfect.

"Cut. Wrap!"

And so ended yet another strange chapter in Lou's life, this one an all-day pissing contest on a golf course in the warm sun, a sweaty, stinky man in a suit of armor replacing the requisite fire hydrant, all in an effort to get people to buy lottery tickets.

As had happened with the book-cover shoot with Timber the wolf, some doofus muckity-muck stuffed-shirt risk-averse boor decided that the sight of a dog pissing on a guy wasn't exactly an appropriate sight for families to watch during primetime television viewing. So they cut the scene from the commercial and replaced it with a model airplane hitting him in the head. We never got reimbursed for the gallon of chicken broth or for the carpet-cleaning machine I had to rent the next day. Lou's short career in commercials had come to a messy end, and none too soon, as far as he was concerned.

17

Even Heroes Have the Right to Bleed

We played "mad dog" in the yard. He was thirteen, deaf as a post, gray faced. He still looked good—thicker in the midsection, but otherwise fine. Arthritis in his shoulders had been addressed with a daily dose of Rimadyl, a canine antiinflammatory. Other dogs we'd known had passed on, but Lou was like Bilbo with the ring—others faded while he kept on. It was spooky.

We'd been together a long time. Long enough to forget that we were not of the same species. Enough time to ignore the unavoidable. We were alike and that was enough.

The stories, memories, and private little jokes between us. The routines that became more hallowed each time—the walks, the meals, the hikes, the games, the people, and the dogs. We were the Gemini, one immortal in the other's eyes, and the other—though equal in every way—fading.

I smacked his ass as he whirled to attack. "What's this?" I said, feeling a lump on his butt the size of an eyeball. I'd noticed a small nodule there under the skin a few weeks before but thought little of it at the time. It had grown many times larger.

"Aroo."

"Stand still, please," I said. He still wanted to play, but I needed to feel the lump. It felt like a hundred other small fatty tumors I'd felt over the years in other dogs, especially Weimaraners, boxers, and Shar-Peis.

I checked him all over. He glared at me.

"You are not getting a bath and I am not going to cut your nails."

"Rowww."

His voice had begun to sound hollow and halfhearted since deafness had come on, as if not being able to hear himself made speaking a bore. He preferred hand signals to the spoken word anyway, so we barely lost a beat.

"That's the only one. Let's call Dr. Phillips and get this looked at."

Dr. Phillips ran a one-doctor clinic close-by. I'd switched over to him after Johnny passed. He had a James Herriot way about him, just as Lou's first vet in Willits, Dr. Smith, had. A bony, gray-haired guy who never charged enough.

"Subcutaneous. It could be just a benign fatty tumor, or something worse," he said, cupping Lou's head. He knew of Lou's exploits and of my books, which by then numbered in the double digits.

"How do we diagnose?"

"We'll need to do a fine-needle aspirate of the growth, then look at the cells. I might see nothing. Or I might see evidence of a sarcoma—spindle-cell or mast-cell tumor, perhaps."

"Those are serious."

"Can be," he said, cleaning off glasses smeared by Lou's nose and tongue. He never required Lou to stand atop the slippery stainless steel table, hated by all dogs. "Depends on what stage of development it's in. Luckily, old Lou here has it in the best possible spot—his buttocks. Plenty of meat there."

"For good margins?"

"Right. If I excise it, I'll need to take out a good two or three centimeters of healthy tissue all around the tumor, for safety's sake. And I'll probably take an aspirate of the closest lymph node as well, to check for metastasis. But let's not get ahead of ourselves here. First things first."

He pulled a cookie out of a jar on the counter, the kind vets always had around, plump and crisp and impossibly healthy. "Lou—catch!" he said, flicking the treat at Lou, who snatched it out of the air like a shortstop. "Most of the cookies I toss bounce off the dogs heads, but not with old Lou here!"

He knew how many dogs Lou had helped to save.

We'd once talked about Johnny's euthanasia. "I know I'm doing a good thing when a dog or cat in great pain needs me to end the suffering. They don't have the mental strength to deal with unending pain. I lose no sleep over those," he said, sitting down and tossing his stethoscope over his shoulder. "But the young ones, the scared biters, the teenagers—putting them down breaks your heart. They were *taught* to be that way. Who does that to a dog?"

He looked at Lou and smiled. "Besides you, Steve, nobody appreciates what your dog has done more than I do. Nobody.

"He's okay with needles, if I recall," said Dr. Phillips, preparing the aspirate. A thin needle placed directly into the mass withdrew a sample of the suspect material, which would then be analyzed for signs of cancer.

"He couldn't care less. Just don't try to trim his nails. He's a bit particular about who does that."

"No problem."

The next morning, he called.

"We need to schedule surgery as soon as possible."

"What's he got?" I asked.

"Signs of a fairly aggressive spindle-cell sarcoma. You know it?"

"Spindle cells pull chromosomes apart during cell replication."

"Right. Then they die off. Except sometimes they mutate and replicate and form a tumor in the connective tissue. He's got one, and I'm not one to gamble with a dog like Lou."

"When?"

"I can clear my schedule for tomorrow morning. You were a vet tech once, right?"

"For a mobile vet a long time ago. Why?"

"Care to sit in?"

"Hell yes."

"Bring your camera. See you at nine. No food for him tonight, and nothing at all in the morning, not even water."

On the way home I bought a sirloin steak and gave it to Lou. I watched him eat it.

I'd once watched a rear-leg amputation on a big male Lab who'd been hit by a car. They fold back the many thigh muscles like a banana peel, cut the bone, then sew the muscles back over into a taut rosebud. A bloody, meaty affair. During that surgery, the vet and her tech had talked about craving pepperoni pizza. I'd wanted to barf and they knew it and laughed, but I'd held on to my lunch.

This was a simpler procedure that involved the removal of a golf ball-size mass beneath the skin on his butt, plus a good margin of healthy tissue surrounding it. In all, a plum-size hunk of Lou would have to be cut out.

I'd have no problem with this surgery. If he'd asked me, I'd have dug in there with my teeth and gnawed the damn thing out. It was Lou, and I'd be right there.

That morning, I took Lou for a walk up the hill to Northcrest Park, the same park the coyote had led me through on that cold, eerie night. Near the south end of the trail stood a small clearing surrounded by alders and pines, with a spindly scrub pine growing smack in its center. It was quiet. We'd often jog there and sit for a while, he sniffing or chewing grass and I listening to chickadees, nuthatches, or flickers busy in the trees. I'd come to call it Lou's Clearing and still do.

We walked to the clearing. I crouched there on the wet grass with Lou in front of me, spooned in like a kid, not knowing what awaited.

I touched the lump and he looked at me. *Enough already with the lump.*

"You're going to have a shaved, sore ass in a few hours, pal. And a headache and a lampshade on your head for ten days."

"*Roo.*"

I rubbed his neck and hugged him. "Piece of cake," I said. In a few hours, that piece of cake would nearly choke me.

"Scrub up," he said, getting out his shaver. "I'll give him a sedative to take the edge off, then shave the area. Will old Lou mind me giving his butt a little trim?"

"He'll behave, but he doesn't bear humiliation well. He'll pout, after."

"As would I."

I scrubbed and donned gloves and a clean surgical gown,

grabbed a mask, then rejoined Lou and Dr. Phillips. An eight-inch square had been shaved clean. Lou looked mortified. The tumor poked up out of his skin like a sci-fi incubus.

I'd never seen a patch of Lou's bare skin before; it was whiter than mine. I rubbed it, smiled, and reminded myself to tease him about it later.

Lou looked like a kid who'd peed in his pants. "He's very aware of image," I said.

"He is a public figure, after all," said Dr. Phillips. "You know, he looks a bit like Maximilian Schell."

"Yes, yes he does."

We put Lou up on the table. "On your side, Lou," I said. "No, other side."

"Raaauuw."

Punch-drunk, he obliged. *Why are you dressed like a dork . . . ?*

Dr. Phillips injected a barbiturate, and for only the second time in his life, Lou lost consciousness. He looked at me, lolled his head, licked his lips, then fell asleep. No—not asleep, *limp*. He fell limp.

I'd seen animals and people die. They just—let go. They get slack and sodden, as if the bones have left their bodies. To see Lou go limp—it was hurtful.

Dr. Phillips intubated Lou to allow for the delivery of isoflu-rane gas, an anesthetic used in veterinary procedures. Then he attached a pulse-oximeter clip sensor to Lou's tongue, hanging now from his mouth like a wind sock.

"This measures pulse and oxygen saturation in the hemoglo-bin. You'll see the numbers here on these two readouts."

"What should they read?"

"His heart rate is at ninety-eight right now, which is fine. And oxygen saturation should be as close to one hundred percent as possible. He's at ninety-six percent now, which is okay. I want you to monitor those gauges and adjust the delivery of isoflurane as I tell you, to keep his readings stable. The oxygen saturation is particularly important, as it ensures that his brain and body will remain nourished during the procedure."

"Thanks, Doctor."

"I thought you'd want to be involved. You'd have been a royal pain in the ass in the waiting room anyway."

Dr. Phillips made his incision, a more complex cut than I'd expected. Because the excised skin covering the tumor would be circular, he had to create a novel flap of skin that he could rotate down, to cover the exposed area. If memory serves, he called it a "bi-lobed flap." Above the excised circle of skin, he scalpeled out a rounded tab of about the same size. Above that, he removed a longer, thinner oblong; this would allow the tab below it to hinge down into place over the removed circle of skin. The oblong would then be sewn closed. Complicated, but cool.

"Turn the anesthesia knob a notch to the right," he said.

"Got it."

"There's the little culprit," he said, exposing the tumor, a pinkish, fatty glob with a network of capillaries around it. "Looks like it won't be too much trouble getting out. Care to snap a pic?"

"Sure," I said, almost forgetting. I took two photos, then got back to the monitor.

"Is it well defined?" I asked, hoping that the tumor hadn't spread.

"Oh yes. Nothing worming down into the musculature. I think he'll be just fine."

"Looks like bloody uni."

"Uni?"

"Sea-urchin roe."

"Ah. I prefer cooked food."

He worked fast. The tumor was out and on a specimen tray. A hunk of Lou. I thought of fava beans and a nice Chianti.

"Turn the knob down two notches."

"Right."

"Everything looks good. Pulse and oxygen saturation?"

"One hundred five and ninety-six."

"Okay. I'll start closing. We'll send that off to the lab for biopsy today. I'm sure we're fine, though. The margins look spiffy."

The pulse oximeter wailed out like a smoke detector.

"Readings?"

"Zero and zero."

We looked at each other. Lou had just died on the table.

We looked at Lou for what seemed an eternity. Then, almost imperceptibly, we saw his chest rise and fall.

"What?"

"It's the clip sensor," he said. "Must have slipped a bit on his tongue. Adjust it a bit more inboard."

I readjusted the clip onto a thicker part of Lou's tongue. My hands shook. *Come on, hairball,* I thought, ready to do CPR.

The alarm stopped screaming. "There you go," he said. "One seventeen and ninety-seven. He's fine."

"Holy crap."

"Yes indeed."

I swallowed my stomach back into place, then took a last look at Lou's living insides as Dr. Phillips sutured up the flaps.

"You okay, son?"

"Yeah. That sucked."

"Yes, sorry. Sometimes those clips slip off or move a bit."

I breathed. Lou breathed.

"You're quite the seamstress, Doc."

"Hem all my pants."

He finished the suturing, then applied a dressing to the site. "He'll need to stay here overnight for observation."

"Really?"

"I like to make sure they come out of the anesthesia well. Don't worry, my overnight tech is great. Lou will need his dressing changed twice each day for a few days. And I'm sure he'll love the cone."

"He's a real party animal, that boy."

"I'll give you some bandages, painkillers, and prednisone. I don't think he's going to need chemo or radiation, but while he's still out I'm going to aspirate the closest lymph node, just to be sure."

"You'll look at that yourself, right?"

"Yes, but the tumor has to go out to the lab. I'll get those results in a day or two."

He took out the tube and cleaned Lou up a bit around the mouth. Lou was still as limp as a rubber chicken.

"Thanks, Doc."

"Thank *you*. And sorry for the scare."

"Nothing comes easy in his world."

After I left, Lou needed a few spurts of oxygen to fully recuperate from the isoflurane, but other than that he recovered well. The biopsy on the node was clean.

Then the results on the tumor came back.

"It's good we took it out," he said. He was eating something and sounded like a kid.

"Yeah?"

"The margins were clean, but the tumor was more aggressive than I'd first thought. Good thing we took it out when we did."

"Wow."

"Yes. He continues to be a very lucky dog."

"Thanks, Dr. Phillips. And thanks for the theatrics, too."

"We staged that just to scare you off for the next time."

"Next time?"

"Kidding."

My mother had passed away of a brain aneurysm when I was fourteen. Ripped the heart out of my family. I'd seen her the day before in the hospital, doped up on morphine, barely aware of the people around her. The next day, she died.

At the wake, I walked up to the casket to pay my last respects. She lay there cool and stiff, a petite porcelain doll.

I saw her twitch. I wanted to call out for a doctor, but she was dead and I was a kid and we sat there in the funeral home in tan folding chairs for four days while people came to pay their respects. We paid homage to the good-humored little woman who'd come over from Italy when she was five, from a dirt-poor southern town destroyed by a landslide after they'd left it, the hill town of Craco, still there today, half sloughed off into the rocky valley beside it, like an ice sculpture melting in the sun.

I thought Lou had died right before my eyes. I thought he'd never move again, that he'd gone cold and hollow and taken the heart right out of me.

When I saw his chest rise and fall, I'd recalled my mirage at the funeral home. I thought I had lost Lou but I hadn't; it was only a slip of the tongue, a simple misunderstanding. He was okay.

He was a tough old bird, but I could not slow the dog years now. If I could have given him a transfusion of man years from my own veins, I would have. It would have been worth it, but I couldn't.

The next evening, we lay on the floor together. I fed him a big chunk of braised lamb. He smiled. We remembered everything.

We drove down to Bandon, Oregon, every August. We ran the dogs on the beach, built driftwood forts and fires, and stared out at skyscraper-size rocks rising out of the ocean. Gulls screamed and crapped and the wind salted your eyeglasses and face and made you tasty to the dogs. Foggy in the morning, gray whales lolling offshore, cars and faces and weathered cabins sandblasted clean by the gritty wind. Sand hitchhiked home with you, stayed on your dogs and in your car and clothes and reminded you of the sea.

The Oregon coast was a great place for dogs. They ran and

ran. They lapped at seawater and puked and dug and played tag with the waves and chased birds and got pinched by crabs and fell asleep in the wet sand and wondered what fire was. They chased after other dogs and listened to the fog horn and drank fresh water back at the cottage for so long that they had to lie down to keep drinking.

Flavio finally learned a good recall there on the beach. He was lanky and fast and three inches taller at the shoulders than Lou and longer, too, but the same weight, maybe a few pounds less. He seemed birdlike, like his bones were empty, like he could go airborne with the right wind. He did not have Lou's solidness. Lou was steel. Flavio was pumice.

Lou. A tempered bar of steel, strong, faithful, unbreakable.

That first day on the beach at Bandon, Nicki's boys played tag with the dogs. Lou drew youth from them, drew life.

"Look at him," I said to Nicki, the wind easing. "He's fourteen."

"Shyanne was a bag of bones at thirteen. He's still a stud."

"Rough around the edges, and deaf."

"Look at him."

I watched him with Zac, who at seventeen was lean and fast from years of soccer. They ran around near the surf, tagging each other, circling, rolling in the sand.

Jake lined them up on the hard pack for a race, then positioned himself about fifty yards off, close to us. Even into his early teens Lou had been faster than the boys, but they hadn't competed in a long time.

When Jake yelled, "Come here!" they both took off. For five paces it was close. Then Zac zoomed out ahead. Lou did his best but lost the race by ten yards.

He'd never lost a race before, especially not to a two-foot.

"I beat you!" Zac said, rubbing Lou's neck and slapping his butt. Lou smiled and panted and walked over. He had an odd look on his face.

"Did you see that?" I said to Nicki.

"What?"

"He bunny-hopped on a back leg."

"A limp?"

"Not exactly. Like a tendon caught. He held his back leg up in the air for a second, then came down strangely on it."

"Maybe he pulled something."

"Let's rest him up tonight."

He was fine for the rest of the trip, but I knew him in and out. I knew him like Scottie knew the *Enterprise*. He wasn't fine.

"Degenerative myelopathy?"

"An educated guess. It's a common problem with shepherds," said Dr. Phillips. "An autoimmune disorder that affects the myelin sheath surrounding the spinal cord, and eventually the nerve fibers as well. No pain, but a gradual loss of control in the back end. The neural pathways get compromised. They knuckle in their paws, get weak in the back end, have a hard time rising. They get wobbly and cross their legs while walking, tripping themselves. Eventually they become incontinent and immobile."

"Could it be anything else?"

"If it were a blown disk, we'd see pain and more immediate symptoms. Could also be spinal stenosis or a condition we call *cauda equina*—a narrowing of the spinal canal. Compresses the spinal cord, affecting mobility. When it happens in the lumbosacral area, you see symptoms like this. Of course, I could be wrong, but I don't think it's *cauda equina*. Dogs with CE typically elicit a major pain response when their tails are lifted. He shows no pain at all."

"None that I can see."

"Nor I. But he is Lou. Rottweilers are famous for sucking it up."

"He doesn't wag his tail much anymore."

"Another symptom. And look here," he said, showing me the nails on Lou's back left paw. "Wear on top of the nails. Have you heard him dragging his nails at all?"

"Now that you mention it, I have. I'd been bad about cutting his nails and thought they were just too long."

"Dogs with DM knuckle in their paws."

"Crap."

"Watch," he said, curling Lou's left rear paw in and placing it down on the floor. It took Lou a few seconds to right it. "I'll bet that's DM."

"So what do we do?"

"Before we get ahead of ourselves, I want to send you to Dr. Sanders in Lynnwood. He's the best veterinary neurologist around. Let's give him a crack at this."

"Not good, though, right?"

"No, but Lou's a tough piece of work. Sometimes DM takes a while to lay a dog low. He's no poodle, if you'll excuse the derogatory reference."

"Sanders is good?"

"The best."

Combined with his worsening shoulder arthritis, the weakness in his back end had begun to take its toll on Lou. He could still trot but couldn't cut or perform any complicated moves. And he'd begun to lose stamina as well. Superman was getting old.

Dogs don't age like people. We peak at twenty-five, then hit a slow, gradual decline into oblivion. Dogs mature fast, then plateau and stay there for a long while. Then, in the last quarter of their lives, they show steady signs of aging—arthritis, deafness, graying, slowing down.

Then they leap off the edge of the bell curve. Like it did to

Shyanne, things catch up to them all at once and beat them down fast. It was happening now to Lou.

Dr. Sanders confirmed the diagnosis of degenerative myelopathy. There wasn't a thing to do about it besides increasing his dose of Rimadyl. Surgery couldn't fix what was wrong with my tough little brother.

Lou had guts. He fought it. He kept going.

"Keep him active," Dr. Sanders had said. "Exercise within reason will maintain those nerve fibers better than just keeping him in the house."

"How long have we got?"

"Four to six months before he can't walk. In the meantime, get him out. Enjoy him."

So that's what we did. And a year later, that magnificent bastard turned fifteen and was still going.

18

The Dog Who Could Fly

Lou stared at the square loaf of lamb, beef, and kibble frosted with peanut butter, topped with fifteen candles. He stood on shaky legs, savoring it. For a moment I thought he'd blow the candles out, but he didn't, he just stared at them. I remember wondering if I could I train him to blow out candles.

We elevated his food and water bowls to make it easier for him, and installed a carpet-covered ramp leading down two steps to his eating/crate area, a small, sunken "sanctuary" room next to the kitchen, used by Nicki as an office. He'd motor up and down the ramp and check for tidbits or sneak into his crate for a midday nap.

I spoiled him. Gratis treats, food, attention, conversations about nothing—the whole thing. It wasn't going to change him or make him pushy—he'd gone beyond those facile definitions years ago.

Each morning we walked up to Lou's Clearing, then through the park and back home on surface streets—about a half mile. Climbing up the steep one-block hill to the park's entrance was a challenge for him, but we managed.

"Dr. Sanders said you need to exercise."

"Aroogla."

"Yes, yes I know, *aroogla*. Got to keep those nerve cells firing, dude."

It was hard to see him that way. Like Ali after. When people met Lou now, I wanted to add the qualifier, "You should have seen him ten years ago," but never did.

Lou discovered a shrub filled with busy chickadees on the edge of his clearing. He nosed into the bush and grinned like a grandpa watching his grandkids play tag in the yard. He seemed invisible to them, part of the landscape. I half expected one to peck at his muzzle, but it never happened.

He watched them argue for a while, then lumbered over to me, smiling his big Lou smile, walking like a tired old lion. I leaned back against the spindly scrub pine and he leaned into me hard, looked up and gave me a Mother Teresa. His weight pushed me back into the tree, bending it back. I draped an arm around him and kissed him on the nose and met his gaze, eyes even larger now that his face had shrunk with age. Renaissance eyes, sad and timeless. "Come on, Methuselah, let's finish the walk."

"You need to take him to Red Top," said Nicki.

"I know."

"Before it gets too cold," said Nicki. "And before—"

"Before he's too old to do it."

"Yeah."

So, in late September 2004, Lou and I took our last road trip together. We drove Interstate 90 over Snoqualmie Pass, through a cold mountain rain that threatened snow—hoary dark clouds swollen with ice water, cars and trucks flying across the pass without chains or studs or snow tires, driving on the raw edge of winter. Lou rode in the back of the wagon atop a layer of old blankets, peering out the rear window to watch traffic. When the rain came, the rear window fogged and he licked at its coolness, so I left the rear defroster off and watched him in the mirror, slow licks, savoring the feel of the cold window on his tongue.

The rain turned to wet snow. Lou perked up.

"Rower."

"Yep, it's snowing, Lou."

"Roo."

"No, we can't stop here. Wait until we get over the pass."

Lou enjoyed falling snow. He'd follow it down, track individual flakes, and catch them on his nose or tongue like a kid. He watched them drop now onto the wet asphalt. He looked up, down, up, down. My neat old dog watching snow fall.

Past Easton, the snow stopped. Pockets of clear skies opened ahead as we flew downhill toward eastern deserts.

I drove past Cle Elum and the cutoff for Route 97 to Red Top. I wanted to take Lou up to Vantage first, where the rusted steel ponies galloped off the hilltop and into the Columbia River below. You can see them from miles off atop the cliff near the bridge, running free, loosed upon the world. We'd been up there together many times and now we would go again, up the hill to watch the ponies run, to watch them fly.

In the parking lot, I opened the hatch and lifted him out. He could still walk just fine but couldn't jump in or out of the car anymore. It embarrassed him, so he'd try to jump out anyway until I'd stop him with a hand to his nose. Saving face still trumped pain in his Roman heart.

I didn't leash him anymore, but I brought it anyway out of respect. It was a leash I'd bought at the academy in 1991 on my first day there, when Lou was young and strong and eager; the same leash I'd trained thousands of dogs with and walked Lou on a million times. Its worn brass clip and six feet of stretched leather held the pull of many a lost soul—every inch of it a measure of their salvation. I brought it with us wherever we went now as a reminder of what we'd done, together.

We made our way up the steep trail to the hilltop, where the ponies ran. What would have taken five minutes a decade ago now took thirty. But he kept moving.

He knew where we were going and he wanted to be up on the hill to see the ponies again, see the Columbia below snaking its way east, see the cliffs and the bridge, feel the wind as it whipped through the ponies' rusty legs, moving them, ringing them like mammoth tuning forks up there on the treeless hill. He wanted to get up there and look down as he'd done fifteen years ago in Mendocino, when he'd sensed something I hadn't, something better than kin or kind. I wanted us up there beside the steel ponies because together, with this dog, things meant more.

Halfway up the rutted fire road to Red Top, Lou got diarrhea. He'd tried to warn me by chortling and staring at me in the rearview, but I just thought he was excited and happy; I hadn't picked up on his situation.

When I smelled it, I stopped the car and lifted him out. Poop smeared his butt and rear legs. He was embarrassed. It'd soaked through two of the three blankets, but it wasn't that much, and when I put him down, he immediately let go of the rest, a flood of liquid waste. He'd been having trouble keeping his balance while defecating and could no longer lift his leg to pee without falling over. So I gently held on to his collar and helped him finish up.

"Sorry, pal, my fault. Didn't catch the signs."

He shook himself off and nearly fell over, then glanced up at me with a sheepish look. He wanted to be clean, so I wet a rag and some paper towels and wiped him off as best I could.

I put the soiled blankets, rags, and towels into a plastic garbage bag. I'd toss them out up at the campsite, into the lone garbage can.

I watered him and let him rest a bit. The squall line of cumulonimbus clouds had begun to march off and the mountains were in view. The air was rain fresh and crisp. We knew the night would be cold and quiet, perfect for coyotes and owls. No matter that he could not hear them.

I wondered what he thought about deafness. Did he know he'd lost his hearing, or did he think the entire world had simply gone quiet?

We made it up to the trailhead. I hadn't gotten an overnight pass, so, after exploring the trails, we'd have to backtrack a half mile and bivouac off the main fire road, in a densely forested area I knew of, close to where the stray cattle browsed. I'd wedge my car into the pines so tightly that a ranger driving by twenty feet away wouldn't see us.

We got out of the stinky car and walked around. We had the place to ourselves. It'd warmed up into the sixties and the wind had died. Lou patrolled like he owned the place, and did his best to mark his favorite trees, using a modified puppy squat.

"They won't know the difference, pal."

"*Roo-roo.*"

"Damn straight."

At five thousand feet above sea level, a fifteen-year-old dog can't climb hills all that well. If we were to try Red Top, we'd have to do it while he still had some energy.

"Let's do it, pal."

We walked up the trail past the turn for the agate fields and up the steepening path to Red Top. I thought of Telluride, how he'd flown up the trail to Blue Lake. Now he huffed and puffed and, for the first time, lagged behind me on a wooded trail. But when we cleared the last stand of trees and the tower came into view, he perked, *rowered* up a storm, and caught up.

"There it is, Lou."

The tower stood sentinel over the Teaneway range. An army of pines standing at attention, a forest of fir and cedar and larch pointing the way.

Closed for the season, the tower's trapdoor would be padlocked. We'd settle for loafing around its foundation, still almost half a mile off.

Lou looked down at his feet, then lay down right there in the dust. I gave him a drink and he lapped at it halfheartedly between breaths. He looked at me, then up the trail at the tower, foolishly close for the young Lou, impossibly far now.

"I understand."

He'd lost muscle but still weighed close to sixty-five pounds. I picked him up in my arms and carried him the rest of the way.

He licked my glasses and looked around like a bobble head. He did not entirely dislike being carried. "You're not making this easy," I said, my face an inch from his. "You are flipping heavy," I said, putting him down before getting to the tough parts, a field of rocks and steep switchbacks. I steadied him on a flat section of rock and he stood there, panting less now, the tip of his downturned tail managing a slight wag.

"*Roo?*"

"I'm fine."

I tightened my laces, then picked him up again, crook of my left elbow beneath his chest, right arm slung under his groin from around the other side, wielding him like an M60 machine gun, one step at a time up the rocky path.

He panted. I dripped sweat onto his back. One step at a time, resting every twenty yards. "You are going to Red Top."

We were nearly there. "Didn't clean you off very well," I said, the poop stench close to my nose.

He watched me speak. Looked at my mouth, not my eyes, as if trying to read my lips. I thought that if Lou could interpret a subtle flick of a hand to mean "spin to your left 360 degrees," then why the heck wouldn't he be able to interpret an obvious facial expression? Dogs knew that human smiles meant "happy," so why not build on that?

"There wasn't enough time, Lou . . . wasn't enough time," I joked, doing my bad Brando, nearly tripping over a rodent hole. He'd watched *The Godfather* with me a hundred times. He liked watching old movies with me.

Twenty yards from the top it flattened out, so I put him down. I still had to watch him, make sure he didn't fall over the edge. I walked up to the base of the tower and sat with my back against a heavy wood stanchion. My arms and back were sore and I couldn't catch my breath. I'd just lugged a sixty-five-pound dog half a mile up a steep hill, and would probably have to do the same going back down.

He walked carefully. His back paws knuckled under a few times. You could feel his frustration, and his dedication to walking with dignity. I watched and wondered if he ever thought back to the days when he'd run those park dogs into the ground, beaten the Border collie and danced with wolves, chased down that monster and slammed him into the asphalt of the YMCA parking lot, kept him there, punished him for what he'd done. I wondered if he remembered the duel in the 7-Eleven parking lot—his teeth versus a .357.

He treaded carefully across the rocks of Red Top, stopping every few feet to look out at the mountains. Did dogs wax nostalgic? Did memories help or hurt him? Did they keep him going like I hoped they would me?

Were there other dogs like him or was he alone in the world?

I was so proud of him and terrified and happy that we were on Red Top together, and when he finally got to me he licked my face and leaned hard into me because that's what he always did when I wept.

Salli dog-sat Lou and Flavio for us in her home while we took a week off in New York, before Christmas 2004. When we got back, I drove over to pick them up.

"You didn't tell me how bad he was," she said.

"Sure I did."

"He's been incontinent half the time. And he drags his feet and falls over like a drunkard. He can't play or run or even hear me."

She broke down. Salli had known Lou during his best years and hadn't seen him for a while, and she was crushed now to see him like that, worse now than when I'd left him a week before.

"He's incontinent?"

"He peed on himself a few times in his sleep, and didn't make it out to poop yesterday."

"We have a good setup at home. He's not used to being somewhere else, around lots of young dogs. He wants to run around and school them but he can't, so he falls over trying. At home, he hangs out with me in my office or else rests in his little sanctuary."

"He's in pain, Stevie."

"No, he isn't. Sanders and Phillips made that clear. It's the opposite: the nerve pathways are dying. It doesn't hurt at all. He only has pain in his shoulders from arthritis. I have that. You have a bad hip. Should I kill you?"

"It's . . . humiliating," she said, really crying now. I hadn't realized how much he'd meant to her.

"I'm sorry. But it's not time yet."

"When will it be time?"

"He'll let me know."

He'd begun dragging his feet so often that I put booties on them to protect them. The vets said not to, that it might make foot placement harder, but he'd rubbed the skin raw and bled and now he wanted to lick at it, so I put on the boots.

"He falls over when I take him out to pee and poop in the morning," said Nicki.

"I know. I'm working on it."

I got Lou a belly sling. Bright blue, padded, fit around his midsection. Had a handle on top. Now when we walked him we could hold on to the handle and support him enough to make up for his instability.

"He looks like a suitcase," said Nicki.

"I like that. Hey, Lou, how about a new nickname?"

He plopped his face into my lap. I snuck a knee in beneath his midsection to take the weight off. The bright blue sling looked okay. "Yo, Suitcase."

"*Rrrrooo.*"

"Hey, watch your tone."

And so it began.

"We don't kill paraplegics, do we?"

"He's not human, Stevie," said Salli, the cell connection poor.

"So what?"

"He wants to run around and be a dog," she said, little dogs yapping in the background.

"If your dog got hit by a car and lost a leg, you'd put him down?"

"No."

"Why not?"

"He can still live a good life on three legs."

"What about two? If the dog has little pain and is still a great dog but can't walk that well anymore, why kill him?"

"Because he can't be a dog."

"I don't know what that means. My back kills me five days out of seven. I have to pee every twenty minutes. I have bad knees and a prostate the size of a baseball. I can't be the old Duno. Should Nicki kill me?"

"She's probably considered it."

"I know quadriplegics and people with grim pain who love their families and want to be with them. They suck it up. He wants to be with us and he's not in pain. And even if he were, who are we to say that it's not his damn right to deal with it in his own way?"

"He doesn't have the ability to choose."

"Neither does Stephen Hawking."

"Oh, Stevie."

"He's no ordinary dog. He's Lou, dammit."

I wanted to punch someone. I wasn't going to kill the greatest dog in the world just because he had a hard time walking.

Winter came and went. It was now more than a year since Dr. Sanders had given him six months. He was still moving, with a little help from the sling.

"Suitcase!"

He didn't appreciate the nickname.

"Lou, let's go for a walk."

We walked up the hill to Northcrest in the rain. Holding on

to him with the sling handle made walking much easier; he didn't drag his feet as much or cross his legs or wobble. I had to support about a fifth of his weight, but it wasn't that bad. I switched hands every fifty yards, so it wasn't that bad.

A squirrel darted across the trail. Lou barked his deaf bark and yanked at the sling. "Old tastes die hard," I said, patting his head and signing "good," the "okay" sign with my right hand.

At the edge of Lou's Clearing I signed "pasta," a fast point at the ground with a finger. He squatted and peed. Whenever he peed or pooped now, I had to support his whole back end, but he appreciated being able to get into the old position to poop without falling over.

We lay beside the spindly tree. I gave him cookies and massaged his rear end. He glanced over at the chickadee shrub.

"Under what conditions would you murder your best friend?" I asked him. "What are the parameters?"

He watched me. *"Rower."*

"You are my best friend."

He tried to guess at the things I might say, but there was no precedent, no reference point.

The endlessness of knowing him. No beginning or end. Like the little kid who asks "what came before?" or "what comes after?" or "where do dogs go?"

"You deserve to live. It should be up to you. It's not arbitrary. When you're ready you'll let me know, or you will simply go in your sleep. That's how you will go. That's how humans do it. Anyway, you should decide. If it gets too much for you, I'll make the call, but not being able to dance the tarantella is not reason enough to pull your plug."

He liked to watch me talk even if he couldn't hear me anymore. He smiled and sighed.

. . .

When we get old and frail, we lose the will to eat. It's all very sophisticated. It's all very smart and dignified and glib.

My grandfather died of leukemia and a bad heart. He came from Italy as a young man, carried his appetite with him like a family coat of arms. He worked hard and built a life.

Our Italian culture was defined by food. Food was the glue that held us together. But in his last year of life, my grandfather lost the will to eat. Meals, once like rosary beads, lost meaning. He stopped eating, praying, hoping. My grandfather, born in another century, survivor of earthquakes and landslides and Mussolini and world wars and the Depression and lonely trips across the ocean, became a wraith, then died in his bed in Queens, New York, no thoughts of tagliatelli or calzone or braccioli on his mind.

The taste for meat predates us. We were their meat before we became their masters. To a dog, food is a holy thing. Food is power, and life. I have never known a dog to fast, and if I had, I would never have trusted him.

We pray for salvation; they hunt for food. It's the same. But while we wet our death beds and pray for forgiveness, they pee in their sleep and dream of squirrels. For a dog, food lasts.

Food was now Lou's greatest passion. And why not—he was deaf and couldn't walk without someone leading him around by a sling handle. Mealtimes, especially now, were magic.

An hour before dinner, he'd get animated and chatty, chortling away in his sanctuary room beside the kitchen, where he now spent much of his day. But despite his appetite he'd been losing weight, down from a peak of seventy-five pounds to barely sixty. His rear end got bony; even his deep, wide chest and powerful shoulders had lost mass. He ate like a trooper but just couldn't process it as well.

We gave him top-notch kibble, fresh lamb, beef, chicken necks, eggs, organs—the best of the best. Because he could eat almost anything without getting sick, I'd change the menu nearly every day. He never knew what to expect, which heightened his anticipation.

Food never meant as much to Flavio. He was a "sniff first" dog; if something was unfamiliar or didn't seem quite right, he'd hem and haw, then finally settle in. By then, Lou would be done with his and looking to teach Flavio the first rule of canine eating etiquette: *Full speed ahead, dude.*

"His eyebrow hairs are growing," said Nicki.

"He looks like a wizard."

"And his coat is getting ratty," she said. "Have you bathed him lately?"

"I need to again. His sebaceous glands are not producing like before. And he can't clean himself like he used to. He always cleaned himself like a cat."

"And he farts. A lot."

"So do you."

"You should talk. You two have contests."

We wrestled a bit and then got down on the floor with Lou and managed a bit of "mad dog" with him, and that made him happy.

"See? He just farted!"

"Oh, that's vile," I said, waving the air above Lou. He grinned at us and *rowered*.

"See? He does it on purpose. He's smiling like Jake when he farts."

"Maybe I can teach him to fart on command. The lottery people might go for that."

I loved cheesy old sci-fi movies. *Attack of the 50 Foot Woman; Robot Monster; Creature from the Black Lagoon; It! The Terror from Beyond Space*—I loved how bad they were, and how they had scared the crap out of me when I was a kid.

I watched *The Brain That Wouldn't Die* with Lou one night. He lay beside me, breathing hard, watching the screen, wondering what a woman's head was doing sitting in a big steel pan.

"She lost her body, but not her evil mind!" I said, nudging him with my foot. He looked up at me and sighed.

In the movie, a renowned surgeon goes mad after his fiancée is decapitated in a car accident. He has developed a method to keep body parts alive and applies it to his fianceé's head, which for the entire film sits in an enameled pan, talking trash.

When he schemes to kill a woman and graft his beloved's head onto her sexy body, the talking head voices her objection from the pan and begins to communicate telepathically with a horrific mutant that the doctor has locked up in a nearby closet. She orders it to murder the doctor so she can die a peaceful death and escape the enameled pan.

The mutant obliges, and at the end of the film the talking head cackles and, amid searing flames, proclaims, "I told you to let me die!"

"Now that's a movie!" I said, draining my beer and getting down on the floor with him. He plopped a paw into my lap. I put my hand atop his paw. He slipped his out and plopped it back atop my hand. We played this Rottweiler game for a while, then I let him win.

"Aroogla."

"I should chop off Flavio's head and graft yours onto his body. Give you another ten years. Give us another ten years."

He looked up at me.

"Just kidding. Mostly."

I wondered if he felt like a head in a pan.

. . .

"He's not doing so well," I said.

"I see he can't stand up on his own anymore," said Dr. Phillips. I crouched beside Lou with my right knee slipped beneath his torso and a hand on the sling handle. Dr. Phillips listened to his heart and lungs.

"He's showing signs of incontinence. And he's under sixty pounds."

He palpated Lou's shoulders. Lou winced and repositioned himself.

"He's been bearing the brunt of his weight on his front legs," he said, palming Lou's head. "It's beginning to have an effect. It's hurting him."

"Should we up the Rimadyl?"

"We can, but it wouldn't be good for his liver. How is his appetite?"

"Better than ever."

"But he's still losing weight."

"Yes."

Dr. Phillips never did a hard sell. He knew me, knew Lou. He knew that Lou was a special case, like Mickey Mantle waiting for a liver transplant. He knew that accomplishment still counted for something in the end.

"I can run his blood, but just from examining him I can tell you that he's going down fast. His breathing is irregular, his coat looks terrible, and he's losing weight."

"I can't. Not right now. We're not ready."

"I understand. He's fifteen?"

"He'll be sixteen in about three weeks. At least that's the birthday we've given him—June sixth."

"D-Day."

"Yep."

"For a dog of his size and breed type to last this long . . . a miracle, really."

"His life has been a book of miracles."

"In your own time, then."

People quote Zen masters, deny the self-seeking, rise above it all, let go of the ego. I always thought that was a load of crap. The essence of Zen is to *not* talk about it. If you do, you're full of crap and you know it.

I didn't want to talk about it. That was Zen.

Lions kill because they want to eat and do not want to die. There is nothing fair or noble or high-minded about it. If I apply my ethics to the actions of a lion, then I am a fool.

You can decide to save your kid's life instead of mine. It's okay. I give you permission. Self-interest is ancient. So I honored it.

It's selfish to keep a dog around who changed your life and did so many things so well, who put his ass on the line a thousand times because it was his job, because it mattered. It's selfish. I didn't care.

My old man's back kills him every day of his life, but at eighty-five he still gets up and goes to work, because he *has* to work, and because, as he says, "What the hell else would I do?" He sucks it up and sleeps two hours a night and drinks twenty cups of coffee a day and tells the same great stories over and over because they are great stories, about his brother being killed by a tiger in World War II or his buddy stealing trees out of the median of the Robert Moses Causeway or crashing four times in military planes or fighting out of his weight class in the navy or going to school with Castro in the Bronx. He tells them, then I tell them, then everybody tells them. That's how it goes. His back is a horror film, but so what? Should his stories end when the pain gets grim, or is it his call?

Lou was a dog. He couldn't make the call. I wasn't stupid. I was selfish. And I knew he was different. Like DaVinci, like

DiMaggio. I knew there would never be another one like him. The same rules could not apply, not to him, not ever.

I was forty-eight. Lou was nearly sixteen. I'd known him for a third of my life. When he'd stopped up there on the hill that day and looked down, I'd been thirty-four, with ten different directions in my head, no bolts of lightning, no mentors, no life coaching. Lou set me straight. He gave me these words. He wrote this story.

The next few weeks were hard. Lou couldn't walk anymore without help. I didn't want that to be the reason. He was incontinent, but I didn't want that to be the reason, either.

His shoulders ached. He winced. He looked sad. He looked sorry for me.

Zac was nineteen and already living away from home. "You should spend some time with him."

"I'll come over tomorrow."

"Good."

Jake was like me. Jake sucked it up until he choked on it.

Nicki was a mom.

Our half-mile walks through the park and back around came to an end. He missed them and asked about them in the mornings.

A stunted chestnut tree along our walking route had a spindly, bare branch that jutted into the sidewalk at just the right height for Lou to walk under it without brushing his head. He had always made a game of going right under it each day. No matter if he walked on my left or right, he'd position himself to go under, like a kid playing limbo. He'd sniff at it, then walk under or sometimes lift up high enough to let the branch brush his head. He liked tradition. He missed the walks.

I walked him to the base of the hill one day. He breathed hard and looked at me. *Too tired*.

So I carried him up to the park, and together like that we went up the trail. He weighed less than when I'd carried him before, at Red Top. He felt light as air.

The June foliage lay thick along the trail. Chickadees appeared like cartoon characters. A Steller's Jay landed close-by and squawked; Lou smiled and chugged out a hello. He hadn't heard him but he'd seen him all right, his blue-black crest and azure body sleek and bold.

He perched close-by and watched us. We'd seen a hundred of them on hikes across the West, their high-handed manners proving that we were in a fine place again, like the hilly place at the beginning, before anything.

Lou watched birds. He knew how they could tell you things, and how lucky they were to be able to fly. How light and free.

We got to Lou's Clearing. I laid him down beside the tree, placed him down like a tired baby. I had the video camera with me. I wished I'd done more taping over the years. I wished I had video of Lou when he was two or three, when he could run like the wind and jump like a flea.

We talked. I took video of him. An ancient soul, struggling, wanting to stand up and walk out of the fire that burns dogs up before they are done, before they have a chance to tell us everything.

He looked me in the eye. It wasn't in him to go on his own. I could see that now. To stop eating and dreaming and loving, like my grandfather had—it made no sense to him. Lou couldn't lie down. He wouldn't. There was no quit in Lou. He'd keep going until nothing was left, until he faded away like mountains fade, until his will to live no longer had a place to call home.

I awoke each morning to find him awake, waiting for me to take him outside. More often now, I found him in a pool of urine, or worse.

He would not go in his sleep. His running dreams went on. No coyote could catch him in his running dreams. Only I could.

"I can't do it."

"He's won't go on his own," she said.

"I can't imagine him not around."

"I know."

"He's just a damn dog, for chrissakes."

"No, he isn't. You know he isn't."

"I don't know who he is. I've never known."

"He's Lou. He's your best friend and he saved your life and now you have to help him."

"He *made* my life."

"How lucky can you be?"

Each night we'd go to sleep and Lou would, too; he'd sleep heavy and hard but then wake up in the middle of the night and pine for me while dreading the disgrace of incontinence. If I got to him in time, I'd get him outside and he'd retain his dignity, but sometimes I was too slow and he'd look at me as if he'd dropped a touchdown pass to lose the game. I'd take him out and clean everything up, then spend time with him out in the yard, holding him up by the sling handle, looking at the moon, listening to the possum that lived in the neighbor's garage. Lou couldn't hear him, but he'd sniff him out and look at me and grin, probably thinking, *I should have caught that idiot years ago.* Then back in and onto the floor, he on his foam pad and I beside him, head on his chest, listening to his heart. He'd had a murmur his whole life, but it hadn't mattered, his big heart had done just fine.

His chest rose and fell. Lifted me, lowered me. Lifted, lowered. Then I'd give him a peck or a slap on the ass and go back to bed.

He had filled a space. I knew it. I'd ignored it, worked around it. It was par for the course for a long time, that space, like a limp or a stutter.

Then a dog had filled it. Not a woman or a job or a cause but a *dog*. He was what I'd wanted in that New York tenement building, what I'd thought of after watching Old Yeller or Lassie or Rin Tin Tin, what every kid should have—an absolutely faithful, dependable protector, pure of heart, unstoppable, like a superhero, like Superman. He was my rock.

Old Yeller fought off hogs and a wolf and a cow and a bear and raccoons. Travis loved him. A boy and his dog. Yeller was the best. But throughout the film you could feel it lurking, you could feel your throat ache long before the rabid wolf bit Yeller. And though you hoped that after being locked up in the corncrib for two weeks the hero would emerge healthy and healed, you knew what Disney's plan was and you hated the bastard for it, you hated what the kid had to endure there in the darkness of the corncrib when his savior snarled at him like a wild beast, when every shred of love for Travis had been erased from his rabies-riddled brain. You cried when Travis backed out of the barn, the closing door hiding his face from the camera, hiding the panic in his broken heart.

In the end, Old Yeller couldn't help himself. Only Travis could.

The next morning I made an appointment to bring Lou in that afternoon, to put him down. Nobody else could do it. Only I could. Then I broke down an hour later and canceled.

Dr. Phillips said to wait until it felt right.

"He won't quit," I said, prideful, the pride covering terror.

"He's outlived cats and Chihuahuas and every big dog and even some horses I know. But it's his time and he knows it. You know it too now, don't you, son?"

"I knew it last night."

"Good. You just let me know when. We love him too, you know. I've had to do this thousands of times, but this one is going to be . . . well, a bit like the first one, I'd say."

"Thanks, Doctor."

June 6. Lou turned sixteen. He couldn't walk, but man did he wolf down his birthday meat cake. He reveled in it, gave Flavio hell for coming too close. *Atta boy, Lou, you tell him.* Sixteen years old, there in his small sanctuary, his corncrib.

That night was a bad one. He whined and I went to him and lugged him out to pee, then lugged him back in. I lay with him as he breathed, irregular, labored, scared. I thought he would die right there, but he didn't. He fell asleep and I stayed with him. I wanted him to die right there with his head in my arms but he wouldn't, there was no quit in him. I stayed with him and watched him paw the air, chasing a squirrel, running.

Another bad night. He had trouble breathing again. His organs were failing. He looked like a kid holding his breath under water. I loved him. I'd let it go too long. I wondered how a parent could watch a child die, how a parent could go on after that—work, eat, tell jokes, make love, go to the movies. I wondered if it was anything like this.

I rescheduled for June 9.

Lou's last night on this earth. He couldn't catch a good breath. Everyone else had gone to bed. We wanted to be alone together.

I fed him cookies and he ate them between breaths. I thought of how many times we breathe in a lifetime, how forgettable, how rote. I lay there with him now, noting each breath, remembering them.

He spooned into me. My hand on his chest felt the toil inside, the grinding. Then I fell asleep and dreamed of running the trails up in the Santa Monica Mountains, Lou bounding high over the rattler into the clear sky, the smell of the ocean and manzanita and sage and dust, the scent of burning, the bitter taste of burning in my mouth as I ran down the trail and hid from Lou behind a scrub oak, laughing, knowing he'd find me, waiting for him, waiting for the sound of him sniffing up the trail. Listening, waiting in that space.

I awoke from my running dream to feel him licking my hand. Slow licks from a dry tongue, its touch like absolution.

"I fell asleep."

"Roo."

"I dreamed of the time with the snake. Remember the snake?"

"Row-row."

"I love you so much, Lou."

"Rower."

"I'm sorry I let it go too long. I thought you'd make the call."

He looked at me, his eyes bigger than ever because of his gaunt face. It was his wild stare, like trying to break through the surface facade of a 3-D painting to see the truer image hidden beneath.

I scratched his belly and counted breaths and thought of Father Flynn, one of the priests at Holy Trinity Church, where we went each Sunday morning when I was very young. My brother and I went to nine-o'clock Mass, which was just for kids back then. Pews filled with laughing and gum popping, Sister Ignacious patrolling the aisles like a Komodo dragon searching for tern eggs.

At the end of Mass, Father Flynn let us kids raise our hands and ask questions about God or the Bible or whatever else we could think of asking, just to get noticed, just to get a laugh. He was kind about it, nothing like that holy pit bull hunting the aisles looking for ears to ring.

I'd gotten my ear rung by her a few times for asking questions like "what was Jesus' shoe size?" or "was he in the carpenters' union?" I was a kidder, but the week I'd seen *Old Yeller,* I had to ask him something serious, something I wanted to know.

"Father, do dogs go to heaven?"

Sister Ignacious rushed over to ring my ear, but Father Flynn waved her off. "It's all right, Mother Superior. I think he's serious."

She sat beside me and watched me, but I was serious, I wanted to know how a dog who'd risked his life so many times, protected you, made you laugh, never let you down—why in hell wouldn't he go to heaven? I wanted to know what it would be like with just people up there, no dogs, horses, cats, trees, or eagles, no fish swimming in the ocean, no oceans or trails or wind. I wanted to know who would even want to go to heaven without those things. I didn't ask all that, but I wondered it, and he knew.

"The Bible says that only those with souls might go to heaven. Do you believe dogs have souls, Steven?"

"Sure. Don't you?"

He smiled. Sister Ignacious grabbed my ear.

"Well, my little schnauzer certainly thinks she does. And in Isaiah it says that the wolf shall dwell with the lamb, and the leopard shall lie down with the kid; and the calf and the lion and the fatling together; and a little child shall lead them. And that they shall not hurt or destroy in all my holy mountain: for the earth shall be full of the knowledge of the Lord, as the waters cover the sea. That sounds promising, I think."

"So do dogs go to heaven?"

"I can't imagine heaven without them, Steven."

June 9, Monday morning. He'd made it through the rest of the night without having an accident. *Atta boy, Lou.*

Nicki took the day off. We spent some time with Lou, took

him out into the yard, let him sniff around. He couldn't put much weight on his back legs anymore and his shoulders hurt like hell. He took a good long pee, then pooped onto the grass, a solid, single turd. He looked proud.

"Good boy. Now let's go inside. You want to eat?" I signed.

He knew that word. Like *candy* or *pizza* or *Disneyland* to a child.

His ears perked up and he licked his lips. A light came into his eyes. The sanctity of food: eat through the pain—that's dog law.

I pulled a steak out of the fridge and laid it in a hot frying pan to warm it up and get its juices flowing. Over in Lou's little sanctuary, he sat up, tried to stand but couldn't. His shoulder muscles strained. He perked his ears and licked his lips and watched me prepare his last supper.

The smell of the cooking steak filled the room. Nicki came in. "Garlic?"

"Sure, he loves garlic."

We threw a clove in and I flipped the steak, and he *rowered* and pawed at the ramp in front of him that he could no longer walk up; the sanctity of food, right to the end he wanted to eat.

A minute on each side so the meat would be warm but still bloody, still moist.

"Look," I said.

The smell of it brought him to his feet. The miracle of food, what brought people and dogs together in the dim past. Wolves crept in close to steal garbage from the camp dump while a boy staring out into the darkness from the shelter of a campfire saw eyes glowing in the night, flitting like fireflies to and fro, desperate for something, anything, willing to sign any covenant if it meant steady grub. *Will work for food, forever.*

The boy walked out into the darkness with a bit of venison in his hand and edged closer to the lights in the dark. For the wolf, the lure of the meat was stronger than fear—the lure of what could be. One thin wolf found the courage to walk closer to the smell of treasure in the boy's hand. The boy tossed the venison and the wolf summoned up his courage and ate it, and in the darkness amid distant cries of the boy's mother they saw each other clearly. They could feel the sanctity of it.

I forked the steak out of the pan, let it drip juice for a few seconds, then brought it over to him. He sat there, front legs trembling to support his still-powerful torso, licking his lips, ready for it, ready.

"Here you go, pal," I said, welling up, offering up the steak to him. Nicki watched and cried. Lou opened his mouth and gently accepted the steak into his mouth, just held it in his mouth for a second to savor the moment, the sirloin held lovingly in his jaws, dripping blood onto the floor. Then he lay down and tore it to pieces and ate it.

"Is it morbid for me to be hungry right now?" she asked.

"A little, yeah."

"He just loves it so."

He massacred the steak, then licked the floor clean. Nicki gave him the cooled pan drippings and he licked that clean, too. Lou had his priorities straight. He knew what was important.

"I feel like it's me going and not him," I said. "I feel like I'm running out of things to do or say."

"I feel like I'm falling," she said. "It's like a bad dream."

"We have to do it this time."

"I know. I can't believe it's coming to an end."

"We spent the last year holding on. Now we'll let him go."

We got down on the floor and loved on him. He licked my face; I could taste the beef and garlic. He tried to hug me like he used to with his front leg but couldn't, so I hugged him, smelled his breath, his coat, his ears. I looked into his eyes, still glazed over by the taste of meat, still distracted from the pain.

"We should go," she said.

'Wait a second."

I got out a pair of scissors and trimmed off some of his coat, some black top hairs, some tan, and some downy undercoat. He gave me a look, wondering if perhaps a dreaded nail trim was next. I put the hair into a plastic bag.

"Okay. Let's go," I said.

I laid him in the back of the car atop a blanket. He groaned from the discomfort but got jazzed at the prospect of going for a ride. "Wait," I said, running back into the house, then coming back.

"What did you forget?"

"He's walking through that door on this leash, under his own steam."

We pulled out of the driveway and out onto the street. I watched Lou crane his head up and look out the back window at the house.

Things happen to make you smile at the most dreadful of times.

I looked at him in the rearview mirror, at his fuzzy head and perked ears as he gazed down the street. I needed to drive, so I looked away. I thought a little music would help, so I turned on the radio.

"You've got to be kidding," said Nicki.

"Son of a bitch."

It came on about ten seconds into the acoustic opening everyone has tried to play sometime in their lives. I swear to God it was "Stairway to Heaven."

We looked at each other and smiled. Lou arched his head around.

"Aroo."

And so, on the way to put down my dog, we listened to the entire eight minutes of "Stairway to Heaven."

"Wow," she said.

"Only Lou."

I lifted him out of the back of the car, placed him down on the asphalt, and held on to the sling handle until he stabilized himself, until he balanced his weight on his dying frame. Then I let go of the handle and clipped my leash onto his collar.

"Let's go, boy."

We walked. His back legs were wooden stilts barely connected to Lou's grand brain. Somehow, he listened. He minded.

I grabbed the handle twice to balance him. But once we got to the door, once Nicki opened it and walked in, Lou steadied himself.

"Heel," I signed.

On my left, where he'd be always. The ceremonial leash looped down and loose. Lou stepped across, lifeless back legs deferring to his will. He stepped into the office, then wobbled and leaned into me, my free hand catching the sling handle, upholding his pride. Inside stood Dr. Phillips and his tech, treats in hand, the fat, crunchy kind Lou loved so much.

"This will relax him. Okay, Steve, you can put him up onto the table now."

"I love you, Lou."

"It's been an honor to know this dog," he said.

"You are my hero, Lou."

I wrapped my arms around him.

"Okay, Steve, I'm going to inject him now."

"I love you so much. Be a good boy. Good boy, Lou. Better? You're my hero. I love you, Lou. I love you."

The life left his body. I felt it go. The limpness, the surrender, the soul. In my arms remained the weight of the dogs he'd saved. The life he'd given to us all left him now like a bird, he flew off and left me, left his place by my side and disappeared into the trees up on the hill.

Epilogue

Dear Lou

It was hard to write about you. It brought it all back.

Living with you was like costarring in an Indiana Jones serial. I could never guess what you'd do next, but I knew it'd be something remarkable.

Sorry about almost leaving you by the side of the road that day. Big faux pas there. Like McQueen turning down the role of the Sundance Kid. I would have ended up with some bubble-headed retriever and you would have croaked or gone off with that chain-smoking trucker. You never knew how close I came to walking away, did you? Good thing Nancy was there.

You were all the things I'd wanted to be. Athlete, hero,

A-student. And you could tell good from bad. I was never that perceptive.

You taught me to stand up, be brave, never give up. You showed me how to stop, look, listen, smell. You taught me when to run and when to walk. When to abide, when to act. How to endure pain and bad times. How to find joy in work. You did these things.

I was so proud of you. So very proud.

Were there decent people in your life before me, or was it all shotguns, ganja, and squirrel meat? I'd like to think there was someone.

What did you see in me? Was I inspiring, or did you see through the charade and love me anyway?

We were blessed, my friend.

Five years later, I still wake to the sound of you stirring beneath my bed, chortling, yawning, wanting the day to begin.

I didn't take enough photos or video of you. We were too busy living to think about posterity. I wish the world could see you run the way you did when no one else could touch you. Pity the cameras weren't rolling the day you outdueled the .357 or the night you schooled the rapist.

I wish your *rower* were my ring tone.

I miss you, Lou.

When I was a boy, I lived in a one-bedroom New York tenement building with my mom and dad and brother and a sour parakeet and piles of dog books and comic books and a television and my imagination. I envisioned what kids in Wyoming had—the magic of farms, puppies, and pine, predators and prey, and nature, real nature, not just the weedy dirt lot next door that I called my playground. My ideas were big, very big.

You rekindled those ideas. You were big as a mountain. I knew how special you were and it awed me. At thirty-four I became a kid again. At thirty-four I got a dog.

Remember the humongous alley cat who'd sun herself atop the shelf outside the garage on Castle Heights? You couldn't jump that high and she knew it, so you just stared at each other every morning. She was one cool cat.

Remember the nutty guy on roller skates on the Venice boardwalk who played the rainbow-painted guitar hooked up to a Pignose amp belted to his waist, singing that creepy "Invading Aliens" song? He was nuts, but you liked how his robe smelled—saffron and bong water, maybe. He'd skate off with you by his side, your head stuck beneath his scented robe.

Remember that biker bar on the road to Big Bear? They offered to trade an old Sportster for you. The thing didn't even run.

And how about us playing fetch with a pinecone in front of Hemingway's grave?

Better to bear an unending line of sweet, tail-wagging idiots than to bury you again. Pity the dogs who follow a legend. I'm done searching for your doppelgänger.

I've had a hard time of it since you left. Some people don't get that, and it's okay. But others understand what it does to your insides to lose a great dog.

My dad used to take us fishing out on the big diesel party boats that docked in Sheepshead Bay, Brooklyn. We'd go out in search of bluefish, cod, albacore, tilefish—sometimes far out, where you couldn't see land anymore, where the ocean swells grew high as hills and the boat would fall into the troughs between them and all you could see were mountains of water on both sides, mountains of living water that lifted you, passed beneath you, moved on. You would have loved it.

Around that time, my older brother started reading a lot— *Treasure Island; War of the Worlds; Red Badge of Courage*—a lot of good books always lying around. I used to read them. In the sixth grade I read his copy of *The Old Man and the Sea* because I thought it would be a good fishing story. But it was something else and it started my head working, working. I decided to be a writer, and for thirty years after that I dreamed of writing the great American novel.

You lay there beside me many a night while I tried, Lou. Remember pleading with me to go to sleep?

But the story was right there in front of me the whole time. *You* were the Dickens ragamuffin, the rags-to-riches story. You were my great novel. When you were around, big things happened. Once you left, though, well—I sort of lost the spring in my step, if you know what I mean.

This is my try at resurrection. You pulled my ass out of the fire so many times before; now I'm calling on you to do it again. You up for it? Come on, pal. I'm ready. Come down from your hill.

Acknowledgments

Thanks so much to the professionals at St. Martin's Press, especially my editor, Daniela Rapp, a Lou lover extraordinaire, and Elizabeth Beier, a cherished friend whose influence made the book possible. They are both beautiful, talented people.

Great thanks to Folio's Jeff Kleinman, who steered me through the shoals and into port. Without his nudges, prods, and pokes, it never would have happened.

Many thanks to Jack and Colleen McDaniel at the Academy of Canine Behavior in Bothell, Washington. They took a chance on a city slicker and taught me what it really meant to be a dog trainer. And thanks to Nancy Baer, former manager at the academy, who showed me the finer points, and helped me get those first two books published. Her kindness and humor will always be treasured. And I will never forget all the talented trainers at the academy, always there when you needed a hand. Over the years they saved thousands of troubled dogs from the grim reaper; for that they should feel mighty proud.

Thanks to Nancy Banks, who convinced me on that December day in Mendocino to put the flea-bitten Lou into my car. Without her, none of the great adventures I had with Lou would have ever happened. And, thanks to Nancy's mom for teaching Lou to shake.

My friends Dean, Billy, and Jeff knew and loved Lou. Lou loved them too. Even Billy.

Dr. Myron Phillips was Lou's veterinarian for the second half of his sixteen-year life. He was old-school; a wise, patient, loving man. Thanks, Doc, for helping Lou live a long and storied life.

Thanks to the coyote who helped bring Lou back to me. I'm sorry you got your butt whipped.

Thanks to Megan and Curt Anderson, owners of Solo, one of Lou's first dog saves. Megan helps to rehabilitate injured dogs now; I'm glad Lou and I could help put you on that track. Solo was a sweet fellow; isn't it grand we saved him?

Always a friend to Lou, Anne Gordon is a crackerjack Hollywood animal trainer. I learned a lot from her, especially about cats. We even wrote a cat-trick book together. She loves animals and can make them do anything. Thanks, Anne.

It's great to have a neighbor with serious Photoshop skills. Neighbor Dave Misner is that guy. Thanks for all your help, Dave.

Thanks to my dad, Tom Duno Sr. He tried to bribe Sabino the landlord into letting us have a dog, but the old coot just wouldn't go for it.

My brother Tom left many good books and comics lying around the apartment when I was a kid. I read them all. Thanks, especially for *Old Yeller* and *Green Lantern*.

My aunt Grace would help the devil himself if he needed it,

then give him a cup of tea with honey. Thanks, Aunt Grace. How do you feel?

Nicki Mason gave Lou his last and best home. Her kids, Zac and Jake, rejuvenated the aging Lou, adding years to his life. Thanks to all three of you for loving and caring for Lou, especially in his final days; he loved you all, too, very much.

Above all, thank you, Lou. I owe you my life, and my career. You were the best friend I ever had. We will be together again.